INVESTIGATING ENGLISH DISCOURSE

In this challenging and at times controversial book Ronald Carter addresses the discourse of 'English' as a subject of teaching and learning.

Among the key topics investigated are:

- grammar in use
- correctness and standard English
- critical language awareness and literacy
- language and creativity
- the methodological integration of language and literature in the curriculum
- discourse theory and textual interpretation

Investigating English Discourse is a collection of revised, re-edited and newly written papers which contain extensive contrastive analyses of different styles of international English. These range from casual conversation to advertisements, poetry, jokes, metaphor, stories by canonical writers, public notices and children's writing. Ronald Carter highlights key issues for the study and teaching of 'English' for the year 2000 and beyond, focusing in particular on its political and ideological inflections.

Investigating English Discourse is of relevance to teachers, students and researchers in the fields of discourse analysis, English as a first, second and foreign language, language and education, and applied and literary linguistics.

Ronald Carter is Professor of Modern English Language at the University of Nottingham and was National Director of the Language in the National Curriculum (LINC) project from 1989 to 1992. He has published extensively in the fields of applied, educational and literary linguistics and has worked and given consultancies in over twenty countries worldwide. He is the editor of the *Interface* and co-editor of the *Intertext* series, both published by Routledge.

INVESTIGATING ENGLISH DISCOURSE

Language, literacy and literature

Ronald Carter

London and New York

First published 1997
by Routledge
11 New Fetter Lane, London EC4P 4EE

Simultaneously published in the USA and Canada
by Routledge
29 West 35th Street, New York, NY 10001

© 1997 Ronald Carter

Typeset in Baskerville by
Florencetype Ltd, Stoodleigh, Devon
Printed and bound in Great Britain by
Redwood Books, Trowbridge, Wiltshire

British Library Cataloguing in Publication Data
A catalogue record for this book is available from the British Library

Library of Congress Cataloguing in Publication Data
A catalogue record for this book has been requested

ISBN 0–415–14065–X (hbk)
ISBN 0–415–14066–8 (pbk)

For Jane

CONTENTS

ACKNOWLEDGEMENTS

This book has grown from contact with many places and people, sources and students and contexts and conditions in many parts of the world which are too diverse and too numerous to mention in this note. Particular thanks must however be reserved for my friends and colleagues John Richmond and John McRae from whom I have learned much in regular collaborations over many years and for Michael McCarthy who is, additionally, an almost daily source of advice, encouragement and support.

The book is dedicated to Jane Carter to whom I owe everything.

The author and publisher are grateful to the following for permission to reproduce extracts and figures from copyrighted material:

Dewan Bahasa Dan Pustraka for 'The Wall' by Abdul Ghafar Ibrahim p.225.

Edwin Sweetman, Managing Director of Subaru (UK) Ltd for the Subaru car ad on p.203.

Severn Trent Water for the publication on p.42.

Woolwich Guernsey for the ad on p.64.

The Friends of the Earth for their publication printed on p.198.

Faber and Faber for 'Metaphors' by Sylvia Plath from *Collected Poems* on p.146.

Macmillan Books (Papermac) for the first stanza from 'After a Journey' by Thomas Hardy on p.84–5.

Carcanet Press for 'Space Poem 3: Off Course' by Edwin Morgan from *Collected Poems* on p.193–4.

Reed Books Ltd for 'The Man with the Scar' by Somerset Maugham on p.188–90.

The Daily Telegraph for 'Dingo Appeal Rejected' by Dennis Warner 30 April 1983 pp.177.

INTRODUCTION

1 CLINES AND LIBERALS

Investigating English Discourse is both a book and not a book. As a book it comprises a collection of papers composed at various times during the past ten years. Most of the papers have been previously published but they have had their origins in diverse places and occasions. Some had their origin as plenary conference papers in different parts of the world; some first appeared as Festschrift contributions; others originated as chapters in books or were co-written as articles with friends and academic collaborators. And other parts of the book have been specially written or rewritten for this collection and are previously unpublished.

These diverse origins in both audience and occasion, cultural context and conditions of production, give rise, not unsurprisingly, to a range of voices not all entirely consistent with one another. In particular, there is a constant movement between more speakerly and more writerly styles which have not been brought entirely into harmony. Such a practice lays no prior claim to postmodernist relativism and heterogeneity nor to any overt admission to a deliberate dissolution of the self. Indeed, a process of careful re-editing and rewriting, together with the addition of updating 'postscripts', has sought in places to lend overall coherence and consistency to viewpoints and reading positions which have evolved over a period of time. *Investigating English Discourse* is, nonetheless, not a book which pursues a thesis in a singularly coherent voice from beginning to end.

There may, however, be a deeper underlying motivation for such diversity and for an unwillingness consistently to construct the clear assertion of a position characteristically associated with a 'book'. A defining feature of this book is the construction of continua. Clines and lines are continuously drawn between poles and positions. Nearly all the chapters of *Investigating English Discourse* attempt to describe, account for and 'read' texts and discourses along and across continua. These continua stretch, for example, between:

literary and non-literary language
process- and product-based teaching methodologies

    standard and non-standard Englishes
    high-risk and low-risk metaphors
    recognition and discourse literacy
    old-style and new-style grammar teaching
    spoken discourse and written discourse

And so on.

A respect for continua readily converts into occupation of a middle ground and into what can only be described as an old-fashioned resolution to see both sides of a coin. What emerges, if a voice emerges at all from such investigation, is a liberal voice and a set of strategies which tries to resolve oppositions, to seek solutions by negotiation and to avoid easy categorisations. If there is an 'assertion' it is that in many domains of language, literacy and literature there are grey areas but that indeterminacy is not synonymous with confusion or lack of clear-sightedness.

The liberalism inflected in the voices in this book coincides with two decades – the 1980s and the 1990s – in which liberalism has become unfashionable, mainly by being construed as a failure to see and argue clearly and to promote change by means of deliberate and uncompromising assertion, both in the area of public policy formation in education and in the institutional discourses surrounding language and language teaching and literature and literature teaching which are investigated in the two main sections of this book.

Such an explanation for the diversity of voice in this book almost amounts to an apology for it; instead, to end this part of the introduction on an uncharacteristically definite note, let me assert that many of the issues and problems explored here can only be taken forward by careful consideration of the many continua in the fields of language, literacy and literature and by an attempt to map out, however precariously, a previously heavily trodden but perhaps now not so populated middle ground.

2 PEDAGOGIES AND PRACTICES

The chapters in the book are all essentially applied linguistic in orientation, a tendency which leads to yet more concern with continua and to constant transitions between theory and practice. The dangers in occupying middle ground here are that neither linguists nor literary specialists (whose main interests are in the rigorous development of theory and theory-driven description) nor teachers (whose main interests are in applications to classroom practice) find the chapters central to their concerns. Such is the constant risk run by applied linguists seeking to find appropriate mediation of theory, committed to eclecticism of approach, concerned to find ways of investigating issues raised by pedagogy and practice and subscribing, as I do, as Widdowson (1984: 6) puts it, 'to the basic belief that effective practice depends on theory, but that the theory has to be relevant to the purposes of practice and has to yield principles which can be interpreted and tested as practical teaching techniques'.

3 TEXTS AND DISCOURSES: A NOTE ON DEFINITIONS

If one of the central structuring principles of the argumentation in this book is that of clines and continua, then the need to investigate *language as text* and *as discourse* is an equally all-pervading argument. Over the past twenty years the terms 'text' and 'discourse' have become more prominent in the study of language, literacy and literature, although they are terms that have not always been well defined. One aim in this introduction is to offer a definition of the terms in so far as they penetrate the chapters in this book.

A general looseness of definition is in part a consequence of the relative newness of the academic disciplines which form their theoretical underpinning. Written language has for at least two thousand years been dominated by the study of grammar and vocabulary, with the result that the analysis of sentences and of the structural relations between words and sentences has become a sophisticated operation, a process which has accelerated in the past fifty years and which has resulted in major and extensive grammatical studies and in the publication of comprehensive grammars and dictionaries of English. In turn, the study of the spoken language has been facilitated in this century by the development of appropriate recording technologies. The major studies have been, as in grammar and vocabulary research, confined to the more manageable and researchable units such as phonemes and speech segments, but it has been a process which has likewise accelerated in the past forty years and which has resulted in major phonetic and phonemic studies of the English language.

In this context the study of text and discourse has a much shorter history and has accelerated only in the past twenty years. It is perhaps not surprising that the field of discourse analysis and, more generally, the linguistic analysis of texts have supplied neither comparably comprehensive studies nor comparably coherent definitions of the field of enquiry. Certainly, the term 'discourse analysis' is a contested one and various groups of linguists, literary and film theoreticians, cultural historians and semioticians all argue that their work is centrally concerned with the analysis of discourse, illustrating in the process the essentially interdisciplinary character of much work in discourse analysis.

According to the subtitle of a core book in the field, linguistic discourse analysis is 'the sociolinguistic analysis of natural language' (Stubbs, 1983). The definition requires a little unpacking. It is, first of all, sociolinguistic in orientation because it is concerned with describing instances of language use in context. The context in which language use is studied should be a *real* one, according to discourse analysts. By real is meant that the examples of language studied should be genuine samples of actual data collected by or provided for the analyst rather than made up by analysts in the artificial environment of their own armchairs with normally only their own intuitions to verify whether the example is a real one or not. In this crucial respect, the data examined by discourse analysts will not be introspective; the data will be 'natural' language, i.e. naturally occurring language in a social context of actual language use.

Data collected in such contexts will not be as neat nor as manageable as introspective data. They will inevitably be messy for the analyst to describe, especially if they are spoken; and they will invariably involve *stretches of text*, for the interaction of language and social context cannot normally be adequately illustrated by samples of language which occur only within the limits of a single clause or sentence, although, as we shall see, there are exceptions in one-line texts such as newspaper headlines, titles, names of businesses, advertisements and signs such as WAY OUT.

As I have already indicated, the concern of traditional studies of grammar and phonology has been to describe systematically the operations of language below the level of the clause, and the result has been much rigorous and sophisticatedly tooled definition of the workings of individual words, morphemes and phonemes, as well as of syntactic patterns. For formalists of a transformational-generative persuasion this was also linked to a desire to *explain* the nature of a genetically endowed competence to construct what all ideal speaker/hearers know about the structure of their language. Of course, single words and sentences can also be used to perform discoursal acts, and sometimes more than one act simultaneously. For example, a single sentence, 'Isn't it time you went to bed?', spoken by a parent to a child can chain together three speech acts – a request, a command and a threat – the interpretation of which depends on more than knowledge simply of the internal interrogative form of the sentence. Similarly, interrogatives can be used, and often are in densely patterned texts such as literary texts, to assert a proposition rhetorically. However, discourse analysis is generally concerned not with isolated decontextualised sentences but with uncovering the patterns and regularities which occur between and across sentences or conversational turns as they are *used* in real contexts of language.

In the analysis of all texts of the kind discussed in this book, including texts written by and for children, poetry, advertisements, public notices and signs, jokes, novels and short stories, travel brochures, newspaper reports and casual conversations, the aim is to focus on stretches of language beyond the sentence and the individual speaking turn and to describe and interpret the ways in which language is being contextually employed. It is argued throughout that such a focus should form a basis for the pedagogic treatment of texts and serves the key purpose of posing questions about language, literacy and literature as discourse.

4 CONTEXTS AND CULTURE

The introduction of the words 'context' and 'interpretation' brings with it further issues which are investigated at several points throughout the book.

Analysing texts is not the same as interpreting texts for the simple reason that interpretation involves a human subject with a set of beliefs, values, prejudices and ideologies, all of which can influence how a particular text and the language use inscribed within it are 'read'. These influences on the interpreter are socially constituted and culturally conditioned and are therefore subject to change across time and space and, accordingly, no framework for analysis can offer a neutral, value-free description of language data for the choice of framework, its application and the analytical decisions which accompany it are also influenced by social and cultural discourses. Recognition and, where feasible, description of these 'discourses' has to be a further essential component in discourse analysis.

This last point brings us back to the title of this book. Most of the chapters are concerned as much with accounting for the discourses within which language is debated and described as they are with analysing and interpreting the language used in relation to immediate social, cultural and pedagogic contexts. So texts are central to the discussions and arguments and they are analysed as stretches of language and by means of procedures developed within the field of discourse analysis; but discourse analysis, as involving a set of practices of interpretation, involves analysis by means of discursive procedures which are ideologically formed. The following studies of language, literacy and literature and of the links between them in both theory and application benefit from being seen from within a discourse framework and it is often a discourse framework which impels upon us the need to pay due regard to clines and continua and to resist yes/no categorisations. The use of the present participle form of the verb in ***Investigating*** *English Discourse* suggests the ongoing nature of the enquiry.

Ronald Carter
Nottingham
October, 1996

Part I

LANGUAGE, DISCOURSE AND 'ENGLISH'

INTRODUCTION TO PART I

The chapters in this part of the book explore issues of language, literacy and language education, pursuing in particular a view of language as discourse and arguing that language development should be fostered by engagement with a variety of different texts functioning in a variety of different socio-cultural contexts. It is argued that popular views of language as consisting of right or wrong forms, with the sentence as the main basis for exemplification, restrict opportunities both for using language productively and for understanding how language is used.

Understanding how language works and how it is used has not been a main focus in the teaching of English in the past three or four decades but recent curricular developments in many parts of the world have brought about a renewal of attention to teaching and learning *about* language, and a recurring theme in these chapters is an emphasis on its importance both for literacy development and for producing roundly educated language users. A related argument is that such knowledge about language should embrace both detailed understanding of the differences and distinctions between spoken and written discourse and a critical awareness of the social and cultural functions of language. Throughout Part I contrasting public and professional discourses concerning key concepts such as standard English, grammar and correctness are critically investigated and their connection with different views of teaching and learning examined. Recognition of and respect for clines and continua across such discourses and in the language forms which realise them is argued to be paramount.

'English' as an academic subject is unique in the contrasting discourses of definition which surround it and in its use of the English language as a main instrument of investigation. One main argument which links several of these chapters is that encouragement by teachers and curriculum designers to greater critical awareness of the inextricable links between language and ideology can do much to develop literacy at all levels and to help position English language studies more centrally within the construction and constitution of English as a subject.

Chapter 1 considers the place of the study of the modern English language in the curriculum.

Chapter 2 examines contrasting attitudes and approaches to the teaching and study of grammar.

Chapter 3 explores the nature of political intervention in language curricula, with particular reference to a National Curriculum project in England and Wales.

Chapter 4 considers the central importance for literacy development of an understanding of the differences and distinctions between spoken and written discourse.

Chapter 5 interrogates the interrelationship of discourse, literacy and pedagogy.

'Postscripts and Prospects' reviews recent developments in the fields covered by the chapters in this section and proposes topics for further research.

1

PROPER ENGLISH: LANGUAGE, CULTURE AND CURRICULUM

Every time the question of the language surfaces, in one way or another, it means that a series of other problems are coming to the fore: the formation and enlargement of the governing class, the need to establish more intimate and secure relationships between the governing groups and the national-popular mass, in other words to reorganise the cultural hegemony.

(Gramsci, 1985: 183–4)

Let me begin by drawing your attention to some words. When and where have you heard them? When did you first hear them? How long ago?

enterprise zone/initiative	insider-dealing
fax	compassion fatigue
interface	golden hello
theme park	brat pack
street cred	loony left
wets	heritage business
handbagging	polyunsaturates
on yer bike	lean cuisine
wicked	comic relief
brill	bad
ECU	North South Divide
militant tendency	'quality time'
ozone-friendly	niche marketing
Reaganomics	'care in the community'
greenhouse effect	community service
flexible friend	community charge

These words, as I'm sure you will have inferred, are eighties words. They are eighties words because they did not appear in British English, at least with the meanings accrued during that decade, before the 1980s. They are also eighties in that they have been made to fill particular semantic spaces which had not previously been occupied or for which previously there had

5

been no semantic need. These eighties words thus reflect particular preoccupations of the decade with health foods, with the environment, with credit, with anti-egalitarianism and, above all, with accountancy and economics.

I have already noted a few words in the first years of this decade, some of them recycled from previous decades, which are strong candidates for inclusion in a lexicon of the 1990s. One term is 'ethnic cleansing' ('killing people of a different race, or creed'); others are 'friendly fire' (used to describe accidentally killing people on your own side) and 'efficiency gains', generally used to describe reductions in staffing. An 'efficiency gain' is a particularly clever nineties collocation. It accentuates the positive by a simultaneous removal of the negative associations of the seventies and 1980s word 'cuts'. Finally, the word 'community' is changing before our very eyes in the eighties and 1990s. From a basic sixties and seventies meaning which referred to an organic social group, to the eighties meaning wrested from the left wing by the right wing and established as referring to the approved practices of the state (community service; care in the community), the word now appears to be undergoing a reversal of this meaning, prompted no doubt by the cancellation of local taxes, somewhat inappropriately named the 'community' charge.

This lexical exercise has an underlying serious purpose. It is to stress two very basic points which will form the main recurring refrain for this chapter. The first is that language is subject to constant change. It is dynamic, not static. New words evolve for new contexts. Old words, no longer needed, simply die, are replaced or acquire modified meanings. My second point is that language simultaneously reflects and encodes social and cultural patterns. Words may be chosen which openly reveal shifts in the cultural order, or they may be chosen, like 'efficiency gain' or 'community charge', subtly to conceal those same changes. But the tight, indeed mutually reinforcing relationship between language and society remains.

Words always move into semantic spaces left vacant or created by shifts in ideology and in cultural practices. It can therefore be no surprise, in a society whose discourses are impregnated with the semantics of monetarist economics, that even the language of the curriculum reflects the language of the dominant culture. For example, the accountancy metaphors we now live by reveal the underlying ideology that learning has to be more measurable, that teachers, lecturers, schools and universities should compete in a market to produce an annual output, that the output satisfies (possibly at a given percentile level) externally controlled tests and that league tables of performance indicators can then be drawn up, rather in the manner of an annual balance sheet, with its clear accounts of profit and loss. I cannot help but point out the close association of 'language, culture and curriculum': the subtitle of this chapter.

During the past few years a number of linguists and English language specialists have found themselves at the centre of cultural debates about the English language, its teaching, and its formation as a subject in the new National Curriculum. It has been a fascinating if somewhat enervating exercise. The enervation comes from having been overruled in arguments for the view of language variation I have just espoused. The fascination comes from interrogating and attempting to understand better the ways in which the very terms of debate are rooted in ideologies, in the relationship between language and power and, in particular, in the different understandings of what is the proper in '*Proper* English'. This will provide the main focus. I will not be talking about the rights and wrongs of split infinitives or subject–verb agreement, but rather about the attitudes to such matters which the discourses about them reveal.

There are many keywords which are central to these debates and discourses. The following statement by the British heir to the throne, Prince Charles, much cited and commented on by press, media and government ministers, is a useful starting point. The statement was made in 1989, one week after the publication of the Cox Report (DES, 1989), the report of the government-established working party set up to devise an English curriculum within the context of National Curriculum requirements:

> We've got to produce people who can write proper English. It's a fundamental problem. All the people I have in my office, they can't speak English properly, they can't write English properly. All the letters sent from my office I have to correct myself, and that is because English is taught so bloody badly. If we want people who write good English and write plays for the future, it cannot be done with the present system and all the nonsense academics come up with. It is a fundamental problem. We must educate for character. This matters a great deal. The whole way schools are operating is not right. I do not believe English is being taught properly. You cannot educate people properly unless you do it on a basic framework and drilling system.
>
> (Prince Charles, 28 June 1989)[1]

Prince Charles makes an equation here between proper English and playwrights, which he has elaborated in subsequent pleas for the centrality of Shakespeare to the curriculum – a national poet for a national curriculum. In a subsequent speech on the degeneracy of the modern English language, particularly in relation to *The Book of Common Prayer*, he has also argued with great conviction and an almost impeccable logic that God speaks English. That should not detain us here, for even I don't regard the study of the English language as a religion, except that we should record the close connection perceived by almost all linguistic conservatives between order in language and a proper sense of spiritual and religious order.

Two especially key words used by Prince Charles in this quotation here are **proper** and **drill**. They are words which appear repeatedly in pronouncements about the English curriculum of the 1990s proposed by the Cox Committee. The attachment to drills reveals a commitment to a pedagogy in which teachers instruct pupils in the correct forms of the language, using techniques which allow pupils regular practice in these forms. The word 'drill' is especially revealing in that it derives from a militaristic context, in fact from the army parade ground, encoding an armed-services view of the individual pupil or student, who is required to march in step with a series of instructions issued by someone invested with unambiguous authority. If at first the individual cannot appropriate the required linguistic behaviour then this can be corrected by further instruction and practice. Drills thus ensure uniform linguistic behaviour according to the rules and regulations of an externally established authority to which individual differences are submitted. Marching in uniform and standardised linguistic steps with others ensures a language without differences, distinctions or variations. Language drills provide the framework within which differences are, albeit superficially, eradicated and order established.

The keyword 'proper' used by Prince Charles is also salient and seminal. The connection of the word 'English' with the word 'proper' is very common. It underlines how views of English and English teaching are encoded in terms of social propriety. There is nothing particularly unusual about this. A recent collection of articles edited by Tony Crowley (1991) and entitled *Proper English* contains numerous documents from the seventeenth century to the present day. The book ranges from Jonathan Swift's *A Proposal for Correcting, Improving and Ascertaining the English Tongue* (1712) – a key essay for understanding the social and cultural pressures of the aftermath of the English revolution of the seventeenth century – to the works of Watts and Archbishop Trench in the 1850s, who are reacting through their arguments for a national language to the social unrest caused in particular by the Chartist movement. The book also includes extracts from the Newbolt Report (1921), a government report published after the First World War with the explicit aim of promoting English as a subject of national unity and cultural harmony. The collection ends with the document *English, Our English* published in 1987 on behalf of the Centre for Policy Studies by John Marenbon which attacks much current theory and practice in the field of English teaching. Over nearly three hundred years the debates cover remarkably similar ground; the place of a standard language in relation to non-standard forms; the place of absolute rules of correctness in grammar and punctuation; the perception of a degeneracy in standards of language use. Such perceptions are most prominent when issues of nationhood and threats to national identity and to the established social order are to the fore. The quotation from Antonio Gramsci at the beginning of this chapter illustrates such points neatly.

Swift's essay is of special interest, since in it he argues for an ascertaining or standardisation of the English language which is being corrupted by the perpetual change to which it is subject. Particularly responsible for this degeneracy in language are those individuals in a period of post-Restoration moral decline such as 'university boys' and frequenters of coffee houses. In his essay Swift writes in the following terms:

My lord, I do here, in the name of all the learned and Polite Persons of the Nation, complain to Your lordship as First Minister, that our language is extremely imperfect; that its daily improvements are by no means in proportion to its daily Corruptions; that the Pretenders to polish and refine it, have chiefly multiplied Abuses and Absurdities; and that in many instances it offends against every Part of Grammar.

Swift is here addressing the Earl of Oxford, the Lord Treasurer of England, underlining yet again a connection between the linguistic currency and the general social and economic well-being of the nation.

It is no semantic accident that words such as 'standard', 'correct' and 'proper' are keywords in relation to English for, as I have already suggested, debates about the state and status of the English language are only rarely debates about language alone. English is synonymous with Englishness, that is, with an understanding of who the proper English are.

A view of one standard English with a single set of rules accords with a monolingual, monocultural version of society intent on preserving an existing order in which everyone can be drilled into knowing their place. A view which recognises Englishes as well as English and which stresses variable rules accords with a multilingual, culturally diverse view of society. Most teachers occupy a middle ground between these two positions, recognising both the importance of standard English (and teaching it accordingly as a national and international medium) and the classroom reality of the need to uphold pupils' confidence and self-esteem by working with the continua between standard language and non-standard forms. And most teachers also reject as both unremittingly naive and disempowering the extreme left-wing position that standard English is simply a class-based dialect and can be ignored in favour of local dialects.

Finally, the keyword 'standard' must be interrogated. On one level it is connected, of course, with proper and correct notions of language. There is also, however, especially in the discourses of many politicians and their media allies, a constant slippage from the word 'standard' to educational behavioural and social standards. Here is an example from a former Chairman of the British Conservative Party:

we've allowed so many standards to slip . . . teachers weren't bothering to teach kids to spell and to punctuate properly . . . if you allow standards to slip to the stage where good English is no better than bad English, where people turn up filthy . . . at school . . . all those things cause people to have no standards at all, and once you lose standards then there's no imperative to stay out of crime.

(Norman Tebbit, BBC Radio 4, 1985)

To uphold standard English is to uphold standards. The connection here between standards of English and standards of hygiene is also revealing. Standard English is a mark of purity and cleanliness, while non-standard

English is unclean. This is almost as revealing as the sequence of logical non-sequiturs which lead to Lord Tebbit's equation of illiteracy and crime. The term 'standard' itself inevitably causes problems in discussions of language. In one sense it can mean uniform, ordinary, common to all, normal. In this sense it carries the meaning of 'standard' measure, as in a standard British weight or nail or rawlplug. In a second sense 'standard' means a sign or sculptured figure or flag of a particular power, usually a political power (a king, a noble or a commander) as in a ship's standard or the Queen's standard or in the term 'standard-bearer', something around which could be grouped armies, fleets, nations. The senses also now converge in the meaning of standard as 'authoritative', so that standard English becomes the common, standard language used by those in authority. The standard becomes no longer a marker for an authority external to it, but an authority in itself. The standard language is language with a standard. The normative is reinforced as the normal. The whole process illustrates the unambiguous connection between standard language and social and political power and helps to explain the much quoted statement that any standard language is no more than a dialect with an army and a navy. In the history of the English language such a process accelerated during the eighteenth century in particular, coinciding with the growth of a centralised nation state linguistically based on the East Midlands dialect of the south-east of the country and reinforced by a central-to-region adminis-tration based in metropolitan London.

The impulse to conform to perceived standards of propriety and correct-ness is, however, for some people as important as Laura Ashley fabrics, BMW cars or clothes by Next. The phenomenon of hypercorrection neatly illustrates this point. Hypercorrection is the tendency to overcorrect low-prestige vowels with high-prestige vowels even when they are not needed. It leads to the conversion of standard English words such as 'plastic' into 'plarstic'. It leads people fearful of nuclear emissions to be convinced that not even a gas-mask but a new kind of gars-mask will be needed.

Advertisers are, as always, linguistically sensitive to such phenomena. For example, the accents used to overlay many current television and radio adver-tisements betray some fundamental British social attitudes towards accent variation. Thus, standard English accents (or Received Pronunciation) are used to sell banking and insurance policies, 'lean cuisine' ready meals, expensive liqueurs and exotic holidays; regional accents are used to market cider and beers, holidays in inclement British coastal resorts, locally bred turkeys from Norfolk and wholemeal bread which is either ''ot from t'oven' or is invariably bread 'wi' nowt teken out'. Given the connection between standard English, proper accents, purity and cleanliness it will not surprise us to learn that bleach is marketed in RP accents. Dialects may coexist with Daz, but never with Domestos. I refer you here to a book by George Thomas entitled *Linguistic Purism* (1991) in which, among other topics, the relationship between language and ethnic cleansing is explored with both sensitivity and erudition.

There are issues here once again between standard English and our national perceptions of its functions. The equation between standard English and standard English as a national language forces us to consider the semantic equation between nation and curriculum which a national curriculum compels. Here the word 'national', as the dictionary tells us, means 'common to, characteristic of, belonging to, or pertaining to a nation'. Again, however, meanings cannot be so conveniently constrained. Nation is both a polity and an administrative structure, controlled by legislation. Here a nation is a state with a government, a civil service and a national anthem. One would, therefore, expect a national curriculum to serve the interests of the state.

But within the polity there are people. These people live as members of the nation but may not have a feeling or affinity with or allegiance to the larger grouping of people within the polity. Nationality does not of itself create nationhood. A national curriculum for a pluralistic nation demands recognition of the nation as polity *and* as community. Standard English is certainly the instrumental, high-prestige and, I repeat, necessary language of the polity but to insist on its hegemony – to say that it is the *exclusive* language of the school – spoken and written, is to devalue the kinds of identity and integration connoted by the sense of nation as diverse culture and community.[2] The statement made in 1987 by the then Secretary of State for Education, Kenneth Baker, illustrates how the public pronouncements of politicians often gloss over such complexities, though whether unintentionally or not I confess I do not know:

> I see the national curriculum as a way of increasing our social coherence
> ... The cohesive role of the national curriculum will provide our society
> with a greater sense of identity.
>
> (The *Guardian*, 16 September 1987)

There is a kind of internal linguistic imperialism at work here which parallels the Victorian mission to export English as a language of civilisation and cultural unity to the colonies and beyond. Here, too, as Edward Said has demonstrated in a ground-breaking study of orientalism, a view of language is never very far away from a view of people (Said, 1976). Proper English is once again not unconnected with cultural, racial and social propriety. Nationally, in Britain at least, Proper English is a social view of who the proper English are; internationally, Proper English cannot be divorced from a view of cultural and political dominion (Phillipson, 1991).

Finally in this connection, if I may be allowed a more linguistically theoretical observation, we must recognise that the term 'standard English' is sometimes used, even by linguists, as if it were unproblematic. Certainly there is a core of grammar and vocabulary which has been largely codified in rules and which can be said to constitute standard English. But it is mainly the written language which has been codified. The spoken language has not, until the last decade, been studied systematically and we are fast learning that standard spoken English is not standard written English spoken. There is much basic descriptive work to be done on variations in standard English across the domains of spoken and written contexts which are a main source of confusion in many public pronouncements. In this regard the development of such institutions as faxes and e.mail is drawing to our attention the whole relationship of standard spoken to standard written language (see Chapter 4).

Before I move on to the substance proper of my subtitle 'language, culture and curriculum', allow me to summarise the position I hope to have established so far in respect of my main title. The most important point is that language is not a neutral entity. Those who say that language is neutral are those who have most to lose. Language always relates to specific texts and contexts and usually to a context determined by social and sociocultural factors. Second, language is also subject to change over time. An understanding of language history is essential to an understanding of language, and an understanding of language history should not, indeed cannot, be considered separately from social and cultural change. And, third, it is difficult to see language use independently from the power of those who use it or control its use or enforce its use on others. The cliché that language is power is a cliché, but the fact that it is a cliché should not obscure its truth.

What, now, are the implications of such a view of language and of the principles which inform the way in which language is seen for how we regard the proper study of modern English language in the curriculum?

The following extract is from a magazine which is specifically targeted at women readers. It is revealing to compare here the ways in which different patterns of language are associated with the two main characters:

> It had been so different three years ago, the night she'd met Stefan de Vaux. There'd been a party. Bella always threw a party when she sold a picture because poverty, she explained, was a great inspiration. She'd been wearing a brilliant blue caftan, her fair hair twisted on top of her head, the severity of it accenting her high cheekbones, the little jade Buddha gleaming on its silver chain round her neck.
>
> Claire, pale from England and the illness that had allowed her to come to Tangier to recuperate, had been passed from guest to guest – 'Ah, you're Bella's cousin' – like a plate of canapés, she thought ruefully, attractive but unexciting. Until Stefan de Vaux had taken her out onto the balcony and kissed her.
>
> 'Well?' he'd said softly, in his lightly accented voice, letting her go at last, and she had just stood there, staring at him, at his lean, outrageously handsome face, his laughing mouth, amber brown eyes. 'Angry? Pleased? Shocked?' And she'd blushed furiously, feeling all three.
>
> (*My Weekly*, 1 March 1987)

Allow me to begin the discussion of this passage by summarising briefly the meaning of 'transitive verb' in English. A transitive verb is one which requires an object for its sense to be completed. Thus 'I kicked the ball' contains a transitive verb 'kicked'. In the sentence 'An hour elapsed', 'elapsed' is an intransitive verb. We can check this because we do not normally say that 'we elapsed a nice couple of hours together'.

In the passage from *My Weekly* it is interesting to note that the transitive verbs are associated with male actions (**he kissed her**; **he (had) taken her out onto the balcony**; **he let her go**); the intransitive verbs are associated with female actions. Stefan de Vaux takes actions and takes initiatives; Claire 'just stood there' and 'blushed'. The most frequent intransitive verbs are **blush**, **smile**, **stare**, **sigh** and **moan**. (In such fiction sentences such as 'she kissed him' are almost impossible to find. 'He' always kisses 'her'.) She has things done to her and is cast in a passive and helpless role ('passed from guest to guest'). The syntactic choices here encode a conventional gender positioning of men and women, one frequently patterned in romances and stories in similar genres.

I have also been reading recently novels by Barbara Cartland. In these novels it is especially noticeable how the women are associated with the preposition **up** and the men with the preposition **down**. This is only partly because the women always appear to be very small. Some of the terms of address used of them, ostensibly as compliments or terms of endearment such as 'my sweet', 'my little love', even 'my foolish little thing', serve to represent women as a kind of diminutive confectionery. In this process of infantilisation the women are always smaller than and thus inferior to the men. He is always looking down into her eyes; she is literally and metaphorically looking up at him. His arms are over her while hers reach up around his neck. In other embraces his lips are always on hers. As Peter Thomas has put it, the endearments reflect the ideology; the prepositions reflect the propositions.[3]

The language used in these novels is also significantly more violent than I ever imagined. He 'crushes' her to him. His mouth 'possesses' her as she 'surrenders' herself, her heart 'throbbing intensely'. Notice, too, how in this passage, Claire blushes 'furiously'. It all sounds excessively painful, but this is the language of conquest and ownership and she doesn't resist the invasion, at least as long as he has a title or money or a name like Stefan de Vaux. Needless to say, all the characters in such fiction speak perfect standard English.

One cannot, of course, expect Barbara Cartland or any other writer of intentionally popular fiction to be interested in challenging existing ideologies. The strategy is to keep them in place. The strategy is not to cause discomfort. The stylistic strategy is simply to reproduce existing ideologies and gender relations as society most stereotypically construes them. This is not the case with the novelists more typically studied in university and school English departments. I will argue subsequently that in an ideal curriculum for language study, pop and art fiction should be studied together. Thus, pop lyrics should be juxtaposed with lyric poems; standard English with non-standard English representations (for example, in writers such as Dickens or Mrs Gaskell or D.H. Lawrence); transitivity in Cartland should be juxtaposed with transitivity in Conrad.

The following passage from *The Secret Agent*, by Joseph Conrad, is a remarkable one, not least because its author did not begin to learn English until he was aged twenty-four. It does it no justice to isolate just one feature of language for commentary, but my purpose is to compare one linguistic structure at work in two very different writers who have produced two very different texts:

> She started forward at once, as if she were still a loyal woman bound to that man by an unbroken contract. Her right hand skimmed lightly the end of the table, and when she passed on towards the sofa the carving knife had vanished without the slightest sound from the side of the dish. Mr Verloc heard the creaky plank in the floor, and was content. He waited. Mrs Verloc was coming. As if a homeless soul of Stevie had flown for shelter straight to the breast of his sister, guardian and protector, the resemblance of her face with that of her brother grew at every step, even to the droop of the lower lip, even to the slight divergence of the eyes. But Mr Verloc did not see that. He was lying on his back and staring upwards. He saw partly on the ceiling and partly on the wall the moving shadow of an arm with a clenched hand holding a carving knife. It flickered up and down. Its movements were leisurely. They were leisurely enough for Mr Verloc to recognise the limb and the weapon.
>
> They were leisurely enough for him to take in the full meaning of the portent, and to taste the flavour of death rising in his gorge. His wife had gone raving mad – murdering mad. They were leisurely enough for the first paralysing effect of this discovery to pass away before a resolute determination to come out victorious from the ghastly struggle with that armed lunatic. They were leisurely enough for Mr Verloc to elaborate a plan of defence, involving a dash behind the table, and the felling of the woman to the ground with a heavy wooden chair. But they were not leisurely enough to allow Mr Verloc the time to move either hand or foot. The knife was already planted in his breast. It met no resistance on its way. Hazard has such accuracies. Into that plunging blow, delivered over the side of the couch, Mrs Verloc had put all the inheritance of her immemorial and obscure descent, the simple ferocity of the age of caverns, and the unbalanced nervous fury of the age of bar-rooms. Mr Verloc, the secret agent, turning slightly on his side with the force of the blow, expired without stirring a limb, in the muttered sound of the word 'Don't' by way of protest.
>
> (Joseph Conrad, *The Secret Agent*, 1907: ch. 11)

Here transitivity patterns are once more central to the ways in which experience, action and interaction are construed. They are one key to getting Mrs Verloc's murder of her husband into better focus. They help us to understand the source of her actions, whether they are the result of unambiguous intention – she means to kill him – or whether they are the result of involuntariness and diminished responsibility (she does not know what she is doing). Such an understanding is not unconnected with the *moral* judgement we form of Mrs Verloc (in itself a moral question for the whole novel), an incrementally complex one because Verloc himself is responsible for the death of her half-witted brother, Stevie, by trying to get him to plant an anarchist bomb in Greenwich Observatory.

There are in this passage a number of key transitivity patterns. For example, in the second sentence transitivity is implicit in that Mrs Verloc clearly picks up the knife but an intransitive verb, 'vanished', is used, in 'the carving knife had vanished'. In the sentences which describe the insertion of the knife into Mr Verloc either the knife itself, or an abstract category such as chance or 'Hazard', is the subject of the sentence:

> The knife was already planted in his breast. It met no resistance on its way. Hazard has such accuracies.

The verbs have no human subject. Reference to Mrs Verloc or to any human agency is removed. Actions are intransitive and passive. It is as if things happen to Mrs Verloc or independently of her, or as if forces outside her control determine her actions. Conrad creates by such stylistic choices an impression of detachment on the part of Mrs Verloc, of someone who is not responsible for her actions. Simultaneously, however, Mrs Verloc does display some intentionality. The penultimate sentence is one example of a stylistic counter-tendency in which Mrs Verloc 'puts' (transitive verb) deep atavistic feelings into the blow which kills her husband. In a way which few popular writers could afford to countenance Conrad creates a blurring effect, a deliberate indeterminacy, which rather than simplifying Mrs Verloc's actions into one moral category or another, such as guilty or not guilty, creates a moral ambivalence which enters powerfully into the latter part of the novel.

1 LANGUAGE AND THE ENGLISH CURRICULUM

What, then, should a curriculum for modern English language study in an English department look like? What should be its principal concerns and preoccupations? What are the main methods by which the phenomenon of language should be studied? The study of the modern language is potentially diverse and all-encompassing. Anchors have to be laid down. What does the professor profess? I would propose the following:

1 *The study of language should be rooted in texts and contexts.* This means that social and political concerns will be to the fore. It means that language cannot be seen as neutral – and decontextualised. This runs counter to some dominant paradigms in the academic study of contemporary linguists. This

has to be so if our concerns are to be with social and historical realities and values. The decontextualised, narrowly objective, scientific study of language has no place in an English department. And I remain unconvinced that it has one in a linguistics department. Raymond Williams could not have put it better when he wrote in *Marxism and Literature* that: 'a definition of language is always, implicitly or explicitly, a definition of human beings in the world' (Williams, 1977: 24).

2 *The study of the modern English language must be principled and systematic.* In particular, it means drawing for purposes of description on the latest developments in the analysis of the textual and discoursal properties of language; that is, on those larger patterns which intersect most palpably with patterns in the social and cultural formation. It means subjecting different varieties of language, spoken and written, to comparative scrutiny. Comparison and contrast, between literary and non-literary, between spoken and written, between the variables of male and female, between standard and non-standard, are at the very centre of the enterprise. Such comparison is normally best undertaken in the form of projects in which language data, collected by students themselves, is investigated empirically and evaluated critically as part of a process of hypothesis exploration – scientific without being scientificist – objective but cognisant of the dangers of objectivism in research involving human subjects.

And such data may indeed sometimes be language which students themselves have produced. It is important that language study should be an active process. Investigative projects are largely active. So is an examination of creative processes of writing, of the construction by students themselves of texts for a variety of purposes and audiences. Such an emphasis on writing, on turning perception into productivity and productivity into perception through the process of writing, is an essential prerequisite for that articulate awareness of language by which an English studies graduate should be distinguished. We have all tended to neglect processes of students' own writing. In a subject such as English, where language is both the object and the medium of study, it is even more essential that students should understand the constructedness of texts from both the inside, as writers themselves, and from the outside, as textual critics. (See also Chapters 9 and 10).

3 *The study of the modern English language should be intimately connected with a study of the social and cultural change.* The 'modern' cannot exist without a sense of semantic change and of the sociocultural conditions under which linguistic discourses are constructed (Aitchison, 1991). It is important for students in a department of English studies that they understand shifts in the meaning of words. This is important for a full understanding of literature and for the discourses which the society around them constructs. In fact, as students of literature, it is especially important that the keyword 'literature' is itself examined. In a major study of language and cultural change entitled

Keywords, Raymond Williams points out, for example, how the meaning of the word 'literature' itself keeps changing (Williams, 1983). In the eighteenth century the word 'writing' in the broadest sense of the word (including diaries, travelogues, letters, journals, articles); in the nineteenth century and early twentieth century it acquired a more specialised meaning of highly creative, imaginative, and culturally valued writing (see Chapter 6 for more detailed investigation). Changes in the English curriculum in this decade and the inclusion of courses on Barbara Cartland may mean that we revert to earlier definitions. As a student of modern English language I note, however, that some eighteenth-century vestiges remain. They explain why, when we ask a travel agent for some literature on Crete or in the Prudential offices for some insurance literature, the assistants do not reach under the counter to produce a novel by Lawrence Durrell or a copy of *Double Indemnity*.

4   Implicit in my third point is that *the study of modern English language must recognise that the study of literature is central*. Such a programme of study must explore ways in which language and literature can be integrated so that they are mutually enriching. This should be done in ways which are formed by recent developments in critical and cultural theory. The work of Mikhail Bakhtin and of Michel Foucault, in which language is seen as a site of contesting social discourses, will obviously be central at the present time. In this connection I would envisage a course called, let us say, 'Introduction to the Study of Texts', which would be informed by perspectives, which were literary, linguistic and sociohistorical, presented to students in as fully integrated a manner as possible. In addition to highly valued canonical texts including, of course, dramatic texts from different historical periods, the texts would also include examples of popular fiction, insurance literature, advertisements and political speeches as well as media texts such as television soap opera and radio comedy programmes. Literary texts would thus be seen as continuous with all other kinds of texts and not as something wholly separate from them. The course would enable students increasingly to see through language. For example, when politicians, as they have been doing recently, make particular use of enthymemic structures such as a declarative clause with an object clause made from a verbal group, students should be able to recognise and describe what is going on. That is, when a politician says: 'A policy for growth is what we need and a policy for growth is what we shall get', when he or she produces the rhetorical equivalent of 'A man's gotta do what a man's gotta do', then students should be able to analyse how it is done, understand the way such a phrase is simultaneously assertive and non-committal and ultimately see through the rhetorical flourish to the underlying absence of any specific meaning at all.

They might also see through the strategy of the current leader of the British Labour Party, who is as active in divesting himself of his Scottish accent as was the former leader in divesting himself of his Welsh one.[4] The divestment of regional British accents is a simultaneous investment in the cultural values and power of a proper English one. And with the word 'investment' we end where we began, with accountancy metaphors in language, with the impact of the 1980s on national cultures and with the never-ending connections between language, culture and propriety.

The text of this chapter was first delivered as an inaugural lecture at the University of Nottingham on 3 December 1992. Some of the characteristics of the spoken discourse of its delivery have been retained in this written version; the chapter is also a modified version of a paper published in *English in Education*, 27, 3 (1993).

2

THE NEW GRAMMAR
TEACHING

1 INTRODUCTION

This chapter explores some recent developments in the study and teaching of English grammar. I argue that the entirely justifiable grounds for the rejection of old-style grammar teaching should not be allowed to prevent appraisal of new-style grammar teaching. New-style grammar is functionally oriented, related to the study of texts and responsive to social purposes. It provides a basis for developing in students of English an awareness of and knowledge about language which can be both rich and motivating as well as relevant to the main parameters of an English curriculum. The chapter makes particular reference to the National Curriculum for English for pupils aged 5–16 in schools in England and Wales but it is hoped that its arguments are also more widely generalisable.

1.1 What was grammar teaching?

The following example from an O level GCE paper (1961) demonstrates clearly what kind of grammatical knowledge was required from school children and what view of the learning process was enshrined in the English curriculum at that time:

Leaving childhood behind, I soon lost this desire to possess a goldfish. It is difficult to persuade oneself that a goldfish is happy and as soon as we have begun to doubt that some poor creature enjoys living with us we can take no pleasure in its company.

Using a new line to each, select one example from the above passage of each of the following:

(i)   an infinitive used as the direct object of a verb
(ii)   an infinitive used in apposition to a pronoun
(iii)   a gerund
(iv)   a present participle
(v)   a past participle
(vi)   an adjective used predicatively (i.e. as a complement)

19

(vii)   a possessive adjective
(viii)   a demonstrative adjective
(xi)   a reflexive pronoun
(x)   an adverb of time
(xi)   an adverb of degree
(xii)   a preposition
(xiii)   a subordinating conjunction

The main test here is of a pupil's ability to identify grammatical forms as a set of discrete items and to label them. Learning how to do this would have involved innumerable practice exercises and a commitment to memory of certain facts, including an accompanying metalanguage. It is not unlikely that this information would have been quickly forgotten after the examination, no matter how intensive the drilling exercises or transmissive the teaching strategies. Although it is argued below that such evidence should not invalidate a connection between learning about grammar and language competence, research findings based on this kind of grammar teaching generally draw bleak conclusions for the effects of such grammar study on pupils' own use of language.[1] In fact, the learning process probably did not involve, on the part of pupils, actual productive *use* of the forms they were learning to identify and label. The kinds of texts used are also, it should be noted, always remote from actual use, are not especially motivating and are normally drawn from those lesser late Victorian prose writers with the most otiose styles – a necessary strategy because it is only in such otiose formality that a wide enough range of testable forms can be found embedded.

Lest we should imagine that such exercises belong to a distant past, here is an example of an exercise from a currently bestselling series of textbooks for the junior school:

> Underline the correct alternative to complete the sentences.
>
> Haven't you (any/no) shoes my size?
> There are (any/no) shoes your size.
> There is (anything/nothing) left.
> We haven't (anything/nothing) left.
> There were (any/none) of the books I wanted.
> They didn't have (any/none) of the books I wanted.
> Isn't there (anyone/no one) here to help?
> There is (anyone/no one) here to help.

The exercises illustrate the central role of drilling 'correct' forms, of learning grammar by heart as if it were a set of unchanging facts about English. The exercises are furthermore constructed on a deficiency pedagogy. Pupils lack the necessary knowledge and the gaps should therefore be filled. It is, of course, no accident that gap-filling is one of the main teaching and testing devices associated with such exercises with the teachers fulfilling the role of a kind of linguistic dentist, polishing here and there, straightening out, removing decay, filling gaps and occasionally undertaking a necessary extraction. The deficiency view here is that pupils lack the right language and that such deficiencies or gaps have to be made good. It should be noted too, that the exercise is a test of whether pupils avoid double negatives. Double negation (e.g. we have**n't nothing** left) is a taboo grammatical construction in books of this kind, although it is a standard feature of many modern dialects of English.

The exercise here is drawn from a textbook bought in large numbers by parents wishing to help their children with English. For the majority of parents this *is* an English lesson and it is the kind of English which many parents are prepared to pay for. It is also exactly what is meant by 'grammar' when used by politicians, employers, Secretaries of State for Education and Prince Charles. For such people improving one's grammar is equivalent to a kind of linguistic etiquette. Knowing how to distinguish a count from an uncount noun or that a sentence should not be ended with a preposition is rather like knowing which spoon to choose to eat (or is it drink?) your soup *with* (with which to eat your soup). There is a clear social and institutional relevance to grammar which cannot be discounted and we will return to this later.

However, one further rather more insidious connection between social forces and old-style grammar teaching needs to be deconstructed at this stage. As we saw in the previous chapter, it comes out clearly in the equation, made regularly by some politicians and public figures, between lack of attention to grammar and a general decline in standards of behaviour and social discipline. In particular, the drilling of grammatical forms is seen to impart discipline and character. There is a clear connection made in such thinking between grammatical order and the social order where it is only one small step from splitting infinitives to splitting heads open on football terraces. (This might also give some pause to those who debate whether or not English is a 'discipline'.) It is no coincidence, of course, that in grammatical exercises the word 'drill' is a metaphoric extension from the parade-ground and from an armed-services view of the individual. In the army the individual is disciplined to assume a common and uniform identity, to move in step with a homogeneous whole, subjugating the personal to the larger requirements of the nation state, having deficiencies corrected, acquiring 'character' and backbone, being knocked into shape to speak, as it were, one language. The metaphor also serves to clarify the intimate connection found by many in authority between English and being English; between English as language and Englishness as nationality.[2]

Other main contemporary complaints about grammar teaching and English teaching (for the two are indistinguishable to many people) are based on a view of language as static, as an unchanging order. Changes in grammatical usage, therefore, come to be regarded as equivalent to a 'decay' or breakdown in our institutions. For some, and even more illogically, such changes are equivalent to slovenliness of thought. Evidence that language is a dynamic process and is, of its very nature, subject to perpetual change is inadmissible. The fact that there has been a 'complaint' tradition, which in the history of grammar study and teaching dates back to the early seventeenth century, is discounted.[3]

It does not help either clear thinking or principled discussion when the word grammar is itself misunderstood. Teachers, in particular, need to know that many people use the term 'grammar' *not* to mean the syntactic ordering of language within the clause but rather as a hold-all word for spelling, punctuation, standard accent, formal as opposed to slang expressions, as well as for grammatical features in their own right.

Many of the above views are, of course, misconceptions, but in their dismissal of such misconceptions many teachers have been drawn into what I would argue is an equally unsatisfactory counter-position, which is usually founded on the following main assumptions:

1 Teaching grammar or about grammar would necessarily involve a return to old-style grammar teaching with the imposition of rules regulating the individual's creativity with language.
2 Learning about grammar does not lead to enhanced language competence and should not therefore be undertaken.
3 Only the more academically advanced students can discuss patterns of grammar explicitly. If we do this, we foster a kind of cultural elitism.
4 Issues of language must enter our consciousness in the way that our mother tongue is first acquired, implicitly, obliquely and unconsciously.

The recommendations of the Kingman and the Cox Committees (DES, 1988, 1989) do not include a return to old-style, traditional grammar teaching as the core of English. Both reports, however, make recommendations for explicit teaching about language to occupy more space on the English curriculum. It is not suggested that such knowledge about language (henceforth KAL) should be separately tested and it is stressed that it should be integrated within existing domains such as reading, writing, speaking, listening, literary and media studies. There is also a clear recognition that there is more to language than grammar; grammar is, after all, only one level and one set of patterns in language organisation. However, grammar study *is* recommended as part of KAL. What are the implications of this? To what extent is a new grammar study emerging and how different is it from the old?

1.2 Grammar and ideology

The 'syllabus' for KAL, as specified in the Cox Report, represents a clear rejection of the old-style instrumentalist conception of grammar. KAL involves approaches to language which stress its endless variety of forms and functions and requires a methodology which is not transmissive and teacher-centred but investigative and project-based. Instead of factual information to be learned probably by rote and with a focus on linguistic form in isolation from context or from broader social functions, the Cox Report underwrites a KAL which is attentive to the ways language is used across varieties of spoken and written modes, in literary and non-literary contexts and as an expression of social attitudes especially in relation to central ideological functions such as standard English. Although claims to improve performance in the *use* of language which might result from such explicit attention to language are sensibly played down in the Cox Report, there is much of demonstrable value for pupils in being better informed about the uses of language, including their own use, and in learning not simply to look through language to the content of a message but rather to *see through* language (Carter and Nash, 1990) and to be empowered better to understand and explain the ways in which messages are mediated or shaped, very often in the interests of preserving a particular viewpoint or reinforcing existing ideologies.

An example of the differences between old-style and new-style grammar can be provided by an examination of the following headlines taken from British national newspapers in 1984 at a time when a national coal strike led to a not inconsiderable polarisation of political positions. The three headlines are taken from (1) The *Guardian* (2) The *Daily Express* and (3) The *Morning Star*.

1 NCB CHIEF FIT AFTER INCIDENT AT PIT
2 COAL SUPREMO FELLED IN PIT FURY
3 MACGREGOR SCRAPS PIT VISIT IN FACE OF ANGRY DEMO

There are several features of language which merit comment here. These include: the characteristic conventions of newspaper headlines such as omission of articles; the deletion of a main finite verb; abbreviations (**demo**) and alliterative patterning (**pit/fit**; **felled/fury**); the formality differences signalled by lexical choices e.g. **incident/demo** and by naming devices; **Coal Supremo**; **MacGregor**; **NCB chief**. And so on. Also relevant here would be features not immediately recognised when the headlines are laid out as above. These are such features as typography, and the placement of the main caption in relation to pictures as well as to other headlines. Of some significance in this connection, for example, are the styles of sub-headlines which in some newspaper styles support the main caption.

But analysis of language in and for itself does little to reveal the contrasts between these headlines in terms of ideology. The relationship here between language and ideology is not a transparent one; it is signalled with some subtlety and works to subject the reader to a particular interpretation of events. In the case of headline (3), for example, MacGregor is placed in the role of main actor in the clause and is made responsible (**scraps visit**) himself for the act of cancellation (**scraps** is a transitive verb). There is no reference to his physical position or disposition. By contrast headline (2) represents MacGregor as acted upon (**Coal Supremo felled**) and underlines the lack of 'agency' by use of a passive verb, markedly emotive lexis (**felled/fury**) and, in contrast with (3), an intransitive verb **felled**. Headline (1) seeks to be altogether more neutral by use of the word **incident** and the use of a complement structure (**NCB chief (is) fit**) avoids a passive/active distinction with its necessary assignment of agency. In other words, each headline inserts a different view of events. In (3) there is no suggestion that those taking part in the demonstration are directly responsible for action by MacGregor whereas in (2) MacGregor is the object of an action which we assume is initiated by the fury of the miners at the pit. In the opposition between Coal Supremo and miners the headline subjects the reader to a position which is limited by a preordained interpretation of events. In (1) there is no overt taking of sides, although in the case of such struggles neutrality signals greater allegiance to those social and political forces which seek to maintain the status quo. In all three headlines there is a relationship between stylistic choice, text structure and the ideological construction of a particular reading position. In each case different grammatical and other choices encode markedly different ideologies.

This kind of language study is not a mere naming of grammatical parts for their own sake (see the example on p.19). The aim is to develop tools for talking and writing about language which encourage a critical awareness and, beyond that, a powerful capacity to analyse particular linguistic forms as they are used within a broad conception of culture. There is a metalanguage but it is introduced as needed, in context. It is not taught for its own sake but to provide an economic and precise way of discussing particular functions and purposes.

2 COX, GRAMMAR AND VIEWS OF ENGLISH

The Cox Working Party Report (DES, 1989) outlines five main views of English teaching:

- a personal growth view
- an adult needs view
- a cross-curricular view
- a cultural heritage view
- a cultural analysis view

The committee points out that such views are not mutually exclusive and that such 'views' cannot be easily developed in isolation from each other. Indeed, grammar teaching and study can be shown to underlie each of these main views. The examples taken from the above headlines are a clear example of grammar being explicitly treated for purposes of cultural analysis and for developing an associated critical language awareness.

2.1 Personal growth and adult needs

One way in which personal growth and adult needs views can be developed is to compare the different grammars we hold. Such grammars are both *dialectal* grammars and *diatypic* grammars. Dialect grammars are the differential grammars we possess according to the regional and social groups into which we are born: diatypic grammars are the grammatical styles we all use along a continuum from spoken to written English. In the case of both sets of grammars, choices from the different systems depend on context, audience, purpose and, especially in the case of dialect, what view we have of ourselves, our own individual and social identities, or indeed the view we have of others, our degree of identification with the person or persons with or to whom we are talking and writing. For example, double negatives are a natural and normal part of most dialects of English except the dialect of standard English which, for arbitrary historical reasons, does not allow double or multiple negation. Teaching explicitly about such dialect grammars can be done in such a way as to show respect for personal dialects, argue against the popular media view that double negatives are illogical (in support of which there is only prejudice not evidence), yet demonstrate that for many adult writing and speaking purposes double negatives are not normally appropriate. For example, letters of application for jobs will not normally advantage the writer if double negatives are used. Such teaching of grammar is a long way from the corrective yes/no exercises of old-style grammarians tellingly illustrated by the exercise to 'correct' possible double negation in the example on p.20.

Grammatical differences between the diatypes of speech and writing can be discussed in a similarly explicit, flexible and supportive manner, and with due attention to the social functions of grammar within a broad view of language as a social semiotic (Halliday, 1978). There is space here for just two examples:

Example A

1 **The extension of fishing limits by Iceland and other countries** has meant Fleetwood's traditional grounds have been closed.
2 **Iceland and other countries** have extended their fishing limits and this has meant Fleetwood's traditional grounds have been closed.
3 **Better, more mechanised farming with increasing efficiency by farm managers** has aggravated unemployment.
4 **Farming** has improved and become more mechanised and **farm managers** have also improved their efficiency. This has . . .

Example B

1 **Paraded through the streets**, he is said to have shown defiance in the face of death.
2 **When he was paraded through the streets**, he is said to have shown defiance in the face of death.

(Examples adapted from Perera, 1984)

The examples A1 and A3 exhibit grammatical features more normally used in written texts. The particular feature in these cases is the expanded noun phrase; examples A2 and A4 are not markedly expanded and are more characteristically used in spoken texts. Similarly, example B1 is a sentence fronted by a non-finite subordinate clause, a feature more normally found in writing; the straightforward subordinate clause of time in example B2 is more likely (structurally) to be how we would say the same sentence.

Sensitive teaching will allow no absolute preferences here, for such analysis can easily result in a prescriptive stance. Instead, discussion of the respective grammars will illustrate different functional tendencies with the structures in A1, A3 and B1 being more characteristic of writing than of speech. Such teaching will also underline that, in appropriating more writerly styles, children need to be encouraged to produce certain structures more regularly than others. An 'adult needs' view of English teaching embraces such an orientation. We might also note that increasing use of expanded noun phrases is a feature of the suggested National Curriculum writing attainment target at level 4 while the use of non-finite subordinate clauses is a feature of the suggested writing attainment target at level 9. Only the most insensitive of grammar teaching and study would, however, seek an automatic or mechanical connection between individual forms and specific levels of attainment. The key words here are tendencies and orientations towards particular uses and functions of grammar.

Teaching 'explicitly' also needs glossing for it can readily suggest a transmission of facts about grammatical functions which may only be a short step from drilling knowledge of grammatical forms. Teaching explicitly about grammar here is quite obviously a matter of teacher judgement and sensitive intervention. The intention should be that such knowledge forms an incremental part of writing development and should be mainly discussed with pupils in the context of their own *use* of language. In most cases it is pedagogically and strategically preferable for the teacher to generate tasks in which competence *precedes* reflections on language and in which reflection is itself *prior* to discursive analysis of particular grammatical properties. Indeed, less formal, more individualised and expressive functions of grammar should be integrated with more formal and public uses of grammar in an essentially investigative and exploratory manner. In this way, a personal growth 'view' and an adult needs 'view' can be perceived to be neither incompatible nor mutually exclusive.

Speech and writing are also systems which are open to cultural analysis. There is a number of possible topics for investigation within this 'view' of English, such as: the social prestige of writing; the associations of the words 'literate' and 'illiterate'; differences and distinctions between societies with predominantly literate or oral cultures; the power of the spoken language in the history of language change; the effects produced on hearers by texts which are written to be spoken and those which are spoken 'unrehearsed';

the ideological factors inherent in the fact that grammars of English are currently based on written, not spoken language data – which conditions our view of what grammar is. Such exploration underlines that pedagogic and curricular approaches supporting separate 'views' of English can be usefully combined and integrated.

2.2 Cross-curricular views

The knowledge about grammar which might be fostered by a cross-curricular view of English teaching will probably include a knowledge of the grammar of texts. Such a knowledge of grammar is again functional. It takes us beyond the operation of grammar within clauses to the functions of grammar in the creation of particular types of text or **genres**. It is a knowledge of grammar that allows recognition of the typical configurations of language which societies assign to culturally significant texts, such as narrative, report, argument, instruction, explanation and so on.

Much of the recent work on the patterns of grammar within curricular genres has taken place in Australia under the influence of Michael Halliday and such work is now properly characterised as one of the most important and influential movements within language and education. Here are two texts by 11-year-old children, which have been analysed by one of Halliday's associates (see Christie, 1986). Before we examine the grammars of these texts we might ask: what are the functions of some very basic linguistic categories?

1 What is the difference between the use of singular and plural nouns in subject position?
2 What are the different functions produced by the different tenses (present v. simple past)?
3 What kinds of conjunctions characterise the two texts? What are their respective textual functions?

1 A long time ago there was a kangaroo who did not have a tail and all the animals laughed at him and that made him sad. How did he get it back? he got it back by dipping his tail into lolly-pop siarp (syrup). The animals started to like him and then thay played with him. Would you like it? I would not because it would be most annoing.

The End

2 Sharks have special sense organs that can sense things up to 1 mile away. The shark uses fins to balance itself and it has to keep swimming or else it will sink. The shark's teeth are razor sharp and although you can only see two layers of teeth there are many in the jaw. Usually smaller fish follow the sharks around in hope of gathering up scraps that the shark may leave.

First, there is a distinct difference between the nouns **sharks** and **a kangaroo**. Most obviously, 'a kangaroo' is individuated as a unique entity created for the specific purposes of this text while the pluralised 'sharks' or the reference to 'the shark' indicates a general property, somehow representative of all sharks. Second, the generality and representativeness of the shark is underlined by the present tense: e.g. **sharks have; the shark uses; the shark may leave**. The simple present tense is pervasive in this text. It functions to represent not so much presentness as permanence. Thus, it is not unlike the function of the sentence, 'Oil **floats** on water', which serves to encode a general truth rather than the particularity of a present action. In the description of the shark the present tense functions to create a state of affairs; in the 'kangaroo text' the simple past tense serves to record a particular and unique action. Third, the two texts are marked by a different use of conjunctions, which is in turn characteristic of the different text types. The first text is marked by conjunctions, such as **and** and **then** which indicate a temporal sequence; in the second text, on the other hand, the conjunctions such as **although, in (the) hope of** structure a relationship between propositions and actions which is descriptive or argumentative rather than chronological. All of the grammatical features recorded under the above headings conspire to make the first text chronological and the second non-chronological. Once again, distinctions between these genres are central to National Curriculum attainment targets and programmes of study for writing:

Level 4

(ii)   Write stories which have an opening, a setting, characters, a series of events and a resolution; produce other kinds of chronologically organised writing . . .

(iii)   Organise non-chronological writing in orderly ways.

(DES, 1990)

Although there is, of course, more to the organisation of different genres than grammar, grammar plays a central part in structuring the text, functioning in each case not as a discrete item but as an organising component. We should also note that the grammatical items discussed here are basic or core items; neither their identification nor their use in relation to the texts can be said to be in any way difficult. It is unnecessarily defensive always to claim that grammar study is difficult or elitist or only for the very brightest children.

2.3 The cultural heritage view

An inspection of grammar in relation to texts which occupy a place within the cultural heritage is on one level less problematic. It is less problematic because teachers will generally be more familiar with handling uses of language within such contexts. The tradition of practical criticism and of the close reading of texts embraces the expressive uses of grammar in poems, short stories and in extracts from longer fiction. In general, however, such treatment has not been markedly explicit or analytical in discussion of the part played by grammar in the creation of meaning. The following is a very brief example of how attention to a single basic grammatical feature can support understanding of creative uses of language:

> The car ploughed uphill through the long squalid straggle of Tevershall, the blackened brick dwellings, the black slate roofs glistening their sharp edges, the mud black with coal-dust, the pavements wet and black. It was as if dismalness had soaked through and through everything. The utter negation of natural beauty, the utter negation of the gladness of life, the utter absence of the instinct for shapely beauty which every bird and beast has, the utter death of the human intuitive faculty was appalling. The stacks of soap in the grocers' shops, the rhubarb and lemons in the greengrocers! the awful hats in the milliners! all went by ugly, ugly, ugly, followed by the plaster-and-guilt horror of the cinema with its wet picture announcements, 'A Woman's Love!, and the new big Primitive chapel, primitive enough in its stark brick and big panes of greenish and raspberry glass in the windows. The Wesleyan chapel, higher up, was of blackened brick and stood behind iron railings and blackened shrubs. The Congregational chapel, which thought itself superior, was built of rusticated sandstone and had a steeple, but not a very high one. Just beyond were the new school buildings, expensive pink brick, and gravelled playground inside iron railings, all very imposing, and mixing the suggestion of a chapel and a prison.
>
> (D.H. Lawrence, *Lady Chatterley's Lover*, 1928: ch. 11)

There are several ways in which responses to this text can be developed. It would, of course, be inappropriate in most classroom teaching sequences to put grammar under the microscope at the outset but, given an appropriate pedagogic sequence, one initial question about grammar would be to focus on the noun phrases in the first sentence and to ask what is the function of the repetition in its various forms of the word **black**.

The question prompts many different answers depending on the purpose of the lesson and the place of this text within that lesson. Observations will be likely to centre on the way in which the repetition functions to emphasise an ambience of unremitting gloom in Tevershall. But a more concentrated focus will reveal that not only is the word ***black*** repeated but it is also repeated in different grammatical categories:

- blackened brick – past participle
- black slate roofs – adjective

- black with coal-dust – post-modifier
- the pavements wet and black – complement

Black here occupies, as it were, every grammatical position available. It pervades every possible grammatical structure in the same way as it penetrates every interstice of the town of Tevershall.

The role of grammar here is to provide analytical categories not for their own sake but in support of making intuitions more precise. With a knowledge of noun-phrase organisation in English the teacher and students can, if required, penetrate further into the text and in the process make their literary insights both more accountable as well as more retrievable for others. The knowledge is also transferable to other texts and can provoke interesting discussion of why some writers (e.g. Hemingway) use only the most elemental of noun phrases with minimal adjectival pre- and post-modification. The analytical categories can, when presented sensitively, also provide a framework which is generative and creative of different meanings in different texts. Analysis of grammar is likely to fail in this context if it narrows interpretive opportunities or suggests automatic correlations between forms and meanings; instead the aim is for fuller grammatical understanding to create fuller interpretive opportunities (for further examples, see papers in Carter 1982a).

Before leaving the question of grammar study in relation to texts accepted as part of the cultural heritage, we can note that Lawrence is one of the few canonical authors to treat dialects and dialect grammars as an expressive resource in the construction of both character and context in his novels and short stories. The opposition in speech styles in a story such as 'Odour of Chrysanthemums', for example, between Elizabeth Bates, who is the main character and who uses standard English and other characters in the community, who use a local Nottinghamshire dialect, is on one level at least a social and cultural opposition. Contrasting grammars are a signal part of Lawrence's exploration of alternative worlds and styles of living; once again grammar is a central component in the expression of social meaning. Such approaches provide a basis for integrating language and literary studies – areas of the English curriculum in schools which may have been kept separate for too long.

2.4 Grammar and cultural analysis

One final example must serve now to underline the main points in this chapter so far: that grammar cannot be seen in isolation; that grammar needs to be located in use and in its creation of contextual meanings; that grammar is a social domain within which marked social and ideological patterns are created; that grammar study can play a central part within the English curriculum. The example is drawn from a recent study of *Language and Power* (Fairclough, 1989) and involves some (again) very basic grammatical analysis of the uses of language, in an interview given by the then British prime minister, Margaret Thatcher.[4]

> government should be very strong to do those things which only government can do it has to be strong to have defence because the kind of Britain I see would always defend its freedom and always be a reliable ally so you've got to be strong to your own people and other countries have got to know that you stand by your word then you turn to internal security and yes you HAVE got to be strong on law and order and do the things that only governments can do but there it's part government and part people because you CAN'T have law and order observed unless it's in partnership with people then you have to be strong to uphold the value of the currency and only governments can do that by sound finance and then you have to create the framework for a good education system and social security and at that point you have to say over to people people are inventive creative and so you expect PEOPLE to create thriving industries thriving services yes you expect people each and every one from whatever their background to have a chance to rise to whatever level their own abilities can take them yes you expect people of all sorts of background and almost whatever their income level to be able to have a chance of owning some property tremendously important the ownership of property of a house gives you some independence gives you a stake in the future.
>
> (Interview with Michael Charlton, 17 December 1985;
> Fairclough, 1989: ch. 7)

There is much that could be said concerning language and language use in this extract but of relevance to our discussion here is the deployment of two very basic categories of grammar: the use of pronouns and the use of the simple present tense. In the case of the latter feature the effects are not dissimilar from those discussed above. Here sentences such as:

a house **gives** you some independence

you **have to be** strong to uphold the value of the currency

you **expect** people to create thriving industries

frame a discourse which encodes an unchanging order within which some central 'eternal' truths prevail. The present tense serves to create a view of Britain and of people in Britain as operating according to values which are certain, non-negotiable and permanent. The use of the pronoun **you** occurs as follows:

you've got to be strong to your own people

you have to create the framework for a good education system

you have to say over to people

You operates here similarly to an indefinite pronoun. It lacks, however, the marked social connotations of **one** in the same context and serves instead to register a sense of solidarity and commonality of experience which subtly and deceptively links the speaker with 'people', allowing her to present her views and values as if they were theirs.

Discussion of this interview extract brings us back to the importance of encouraging pupils to *see through* language (see Carter and Nash, 1990). The metaphor of seeing through is important here for the aim is to take pupils beyond a stage where language is a transparent medium through which content is seen. A more lasting and generative capacity is provided if pupils recognise the ways in which grammar mediates points of view and encodes ideologies. Pupils are thus empowered to see through the ways in which language can be used to incapacitate, to distort or to hide a true state of affairs, to subtly conceal rather than to openly reveal. What can result is a critical language awareness of the relationship between language, ideology and social and cultural power – a relationship in which grammar plays a not insignificant part and for an awareness of which its study can be especially enabling.

3 KNOWLEDGE ABOUT GRAMMAR: SOME ISSUES

The new grammar teaching presents a number of pedagogic challenges for both teachers and pupils. Foremost among these is a challenge to present grammar in the classroom in ways which avoid the worst excesses of formalism without losing sight of the fact that grammar is systematically organised. A further major challenge is to find ways of teaching grammar which are sensitive to a continuum of implicit to explicit knowledge and which recognise that appropriate and strategic interventions by the teacher are crucial to the process of making implicit knowledge explicit. Additionally, there is much work to be done to explore in what ways knowledge about grammar might inform processes of language development. It is not tenable to claim that there is no connection between explicit grammar study and enhanced language performance in spite of research evidence (largely pre-1970s) disavowing such a connection, not least because such research (see note 1) investigated grammar teaching based on 'old-style' descriptive frameworks and methodologies. A new approach to grammar brings with it further questions for classroom practice and classroom-based research, about which it is essential for us to retain an open mind.

This chapter has not sought to examine pedagogies for grammar but it may be useful to posit here a number of principles which can serve to underlie hypotheses about the teaching of grammar. Such hypotheses need to be subsequently tested:

1 Competence precedes reflection   From an early age children possess considerable degrees of implicit knowledge about grammar; for example seven-year-old children are able to recognise grammatical deviation and to make grammatically correct judgements of sentences from a list (see Garton and Pratt, 1989: esp. ch. 7). Lyons (1988, 1989) demonstrates the extent of implicit grammatical knowledge which a nine-year-old child brings to a writing task. It is vital to recognise and value such knowledge and to build upon it. As argued above, the general (though not exclusive) pedagogic principle – that competence in using the language precedes effective reflection on language – should be upheld.

2 Develop existing knowledge about grammar   Research into early language development also underlines how children draw on implicit knowledge to help them in decoding word meaning, in detecting and monitoring problems of comprehension, and in structuring different types of written text (see Garton and Pratt, 1989: ch. 6). Although limited, there is evidence to support the view that reflectiveness on language occurs naturally and without prompting. Such overt awareness manifests itself in a number of ways: from a reflective and obviously pleasurable repetition of particular patterns of words and structures to explicit explanations of the 'points' of language use which are in some ways odd or playful or creative, such as jokes or puns or certain ambiguities. (See note 5 for brief discussion of the complex grammatical knowledge required to process a children's joke or an ambiguous headline.) Teachers have commented on the enhanced sense of control such conscious recognition of language use can confer. Accordingly, an important principle across primary and secondary contexts is that the process of making such knowledge explicit should not be imposed or engineered but fostered and supported as naturally as possible, as needed in specific contexts and in ways which reinforce the process as one of positive achievement with language. There can be no return to decontextualised exercises or gap-fillings or to the deficiency pedagogies in which such procedures are grounded. Much might be learned here from studies of the relationship between raised language consciousness and second language development (Bialystok, 1982; Faerch, 1985; Rutherford, 1987; Ellis, 1989).

3 Support knowledge about grammar in relation to texts   Strategies should be developed which prevent too great a degree of self-consciousness about language (which can be inhibiting) but which, in the upper-secondary years especially, also enhance understanding of the systematic nature of grammatical organisation and its uses. One primary principle which this chapter has tried to illustrate is that of, wherever possible, exploring grammar in relation to extended, preferably complete spoken or written *texts*. An examination of grammar in texts means that grammatical form is not an exclusive focus, for grammar is necessarily seen only as part of a more complex social and textual environment and as realising specific functions in a purposeful context. A study of grammar in texts is a study of grammar *in use*.

4 There is more to KAL than performance through language It is vital to continue to promote effective language use through processes which support intuitive and implicit responses to using language. We should also recognise that pupils *do* demonstrate increasing knowledge about language simply by *using* language and working with it. However, such procedures are a necessary but not sufficient condition for knowledge about language and about grammar as a component of language (see Mallett, 1988). An important principle is: however well we perform at any activity or any exercise of our human capacities we can only benefit from stepping periodically into a more reflective or analytic frame from within which our competence can be more systematically reviewed.

4 CONCLUSIONS

I have attempted to draw a line between old-style grammar teaching and a counter-position of no grammar at all. Old-style grammar teaching has been shown to be reactionary, pedagogically and methodologically arid and conceptually ill-founded. But the removal of formal grammar from the language classroom has denied children opportunities to explore a remarkable human phenomenon and to display their own considerable resources of implicit knowledge; it has also disempowered them from exercising the kind of conscious control and conscious choice over language which enables them both to *see through* language in a systematic way and to use language more discriminatingly.

The proposed changes to English in the National Curriculum involve a shift towards a more language-centred curriculum. The recommendations are bound to leave a number of questions unanswered. Some of these questions are fundamental and will, as I have indicated, require urgent exploration. But the curriculum for English nationally will undoubtedly require more explicit attention to the medium of language and to the role of grammar within that wider framework of language study. I have tried to indicate briefly how knowledge about grammar might be related to each of the five main views of English teaching developed and supported by the Cox Committee.

In this context, a return to grammar is to be welcomed. But it will need to be a new-style grammar teaching, not an old-style grammar teaching. It is unlikely that the return to grammar will restore the kinds of codes and values old-style grammar is believed by many people in authority to symbolise. But it will mean that language in the classroom is not to be encountered wholly by unconscious, implicit and indirect means.

Grammar is a fundamental human meaning-making activity which can be investigated as a fascinating phenomenon and explored from the powerful basis of considerable resources of existing knowledge possessed by the very youngest of children. In this respect, a study of grammar should always be rooted in children's positive achievements, that is, rooted in what children can already do with grammar. Knowing more about how grammar *works* is to understand more about how grammar is used and misused. Knowing more about grammar can impart greater choice and control over grammar as an expressive and interpretive medium. Knowing more about grammar, as part of KAL, is to be empowered to respond to and to use grammar as central to the creation of textual meanings.

This chapter was first published in Carter, R. (ed.) Knowledge about Language and the Curriculum: The LINC Reader (Hodder and Stoughton, Sevenoaks, 1990).

3

POLITICS AND KNOWLEDGE ABOUT LANGUAGE: THE LINC PROJECT

> Every time the question of the language surfaces, in one way or another, it means that a series of other problems are coming to the fore: the formation and enlargement of the governing class, the need to establish more intimate and secure relationships between the governing groups and the national popular mass, in other words to reorganise the cultural hegemony.
>
> (Gramsci, 1985: 183–4)

1 INTRODUCTION

The relationship between politics and knowledge about language is both comprehensive and complex. In this chapter three main perspectives are offered: a brief overview of a national language education initiative in England and Wales with a particular focus on keywords in discourses about language, English and education; the place of genre theory in relation to such an initiative; some research and development questions for teaching school students *about* language.

1.1 Examining language

Here is part of a General Secondary Education paper set for 15–16-year-old pupils in Britain in the 1940s. Questions of this kind about grammar constituted between 20 and 30 per cent of the total examination paper:

Question 1

(a) Analyse into clauses the following passage. Give the grammatical description of the clauses and show their connection with each other:

In that year (1851) when the Great Exhibition spread its hospitable glass roof high over the elms of Hyde Park, and all the world came to *admire* England's wealth, progress and enlightenment, there might *profitably* have been another 'exhibition' to show how our poor were housed and to teach the admiring visitors *some* of the dangers *that* beset the path of the vaunted new era.

(b) State the grammatical features of the words italicized in (a).

Reference is made to such an examination exercise at the very beginning of this chapter because the views of language and of language teaching enshrined within it go right to the very centre of current debates in Britain about language teaching in the context of the new National Curriculum for English in England and Wales. The debate is characterised by different political positions and, in particular, by strenuous efforts by the British government to persuade teachers to a return to the 1940s and to the kinds of practices of language teaching illustrated by this examination paper.

What are the practices which are illustrated by this example? Why do government ministers wish to see them reinstated? What do teachers think of them? What is the view taken by linguists of such practices? Answers to such questions may begin to explain why the materials for teachers produced by the Language in the National Curriculum (henceforth, LINC) project were not only refused publication by the British government, but also became the centre of contesting views about language and education.

1.2 Views of language and language teaching

The different views of language and language teaching in respect of this representative examination paper held by government, English teachers and by linguists may be broadly summarised under three headings: (1) government views; (2) teachers' views; and (3) linguists' views.

Government views

1. The examination paper illustrates a manifest concern with measurable knowledge. A body of linguistic facts can be taught, learned by pupils and then tested. Answers are either right or wrong, the body of knowledge taught is definite and measurable, and teachers can even be assessed by how well they teach it.
2. The learning which ensues is disciplined and takes places within a clear framework. It contrasts vividly with what is felt to be the vague and undirected concern with creativity and personal expression which characterises work in many English lessons at the present time.[1]
3. Such practices will help to guarantee correct grammar and standard English. They will remove sloppiness in expression and eradicate a climate in which errors are viewed only in relation to a process of language development and thus not always immediately corrected.

For further discussion see quotations from public figures, pp.7 and 9.

Teachers' views

Until recently, teachers' views have been regularly dominated by what are described as 'romantic' conceptions of English as a subject (see Christie, 1989; Carter, 1988). Romanticism in English teaching involves a classroom emphasis on language use which is person-centred, which stresses the capacity of the individual for originality and creativity, and a concern that strict rules and conventions may be inhibiting to pupils and, in the process, restrict their capacities for using the language. There is a particular stress on the primacy of speech, even in writing where individuals are encouraged by the teacher to find their own personal voice.[2] In the context of such ideologies it will be clear that many English teachers reject the view of grammar and of language study illustrated in the above examination paper. It runs very obviously counter to romantic influences on the subject. During the course of the LINC project shifts in teachers' perception of formal language study were recorded, but strong resistance remains, on the above grounds, to the decontextualised study of language, to teaching practices and pedagogies which are necessarily transmissive and narrowly knowledge-based, and which allow little or no scope for an emergence of the pupil's own 'voice'.

The views of linguists

Linguists have taken a prominent role in the shaping of the National Curriculum for English in England and Wales.[3] Most take the following main views of grammar-based teaching and testing of linguistic knowledge:

1 They point out how examination papers from the 1940s and 1950s are preoccupied with the written rather than the spoken language.
2 They point out that the analysis is invariably decontextualised since the definitions required of pupils are **formalistic**. That is, no attention is given to language use, to the functions of language or to the kinds of meanings produced by the particular forms which are isolated (Carter, 1990a). Examinations such as those above are exercises in the naming of parts.
3 They point out that such examinations are concerned with sentences rather than texts. In fact, the text here is genuinely incidental. The focus is on a bottom-up analysis of the smallest units of language with little or no interest in eliciting from pupils how such units might combine to form larger functional meanings and effects.

Accordingly, those linguists who advised the government did not recommend a return to the 1940s and to a teaching of grammatical forms by means of decontextualised drills. But they did not reject a formal study of language. Instead, they strongly advocated programmes of study for pupils in knowledge about language (KAL). It was felt that such a concentration was overdue, and had been neglected for too long, probably because of dominant romantic philosophies of English teaching which resisted most forms of explicit language analysis. However, to be successful, it was argued, and indeed eventually accepted in parliamentary statutes, that KAL needed to be based on a wider range of analysis than grammar, and needed to be clearly rooted in theories of language variation, both spoken and written. These views (of government-appointed committees) were grudgingly accepted by the government. The government was quick to recognise that knowledge about language, based on a variety of texts, includes discussion of language in context, and that discussion of context is often necessarily social. Such an orientation served only to reinforce for the government the desirability of decontextualised drills and exercises.

2 LINC: AN IN-SERVICE TEACHER EDUCATION PROJECT

Language in the National Curriculum (LINC), is designed to make the theories and descriptions of language in the new National Curriculum accessible to teachers, and to assist them with the language components of the National Curriculum for English in England and Wales. In this context it has to be remembered that, for many teachers in Britain, formal language study has not formed part of either their pre-service or in-service education. Indeed, in some teacher-training institutions there is a history of active resistance to the introduction of more linguistics-based courses in English, and for this reason English teachers and teacher-trainers did not give the publication of National Curriculum reports an unreserved welcome.[4]

Details of the remit and organisation of the LINC project are given in Appendix 1 (p.52). In basic outline the main project team was asked to produce study units for teachers which were to be used in in-service courses, in school-based follow-up and dissemination, and in self-study sessions. The resulting training package is therefore activity-based and open-ended. It contains many linguistically based tasks with accompanying commentaries so that teachers can work on the material in a range of contexts.

2.1 The LINC ban

The LINC project assumed political prominence when the government decided, in the summer of 1991, that it did not wish to publish the materials produced by the project. Neither would it allow commercial publication in spite of interest on the part of several international publishers in publishing the complete training package.[5] Although the project was allowed to continue and although the LINC training package could be made available in photocopied form for purposes of in-service training courses, such decisions amounted to an effective ban on widespread publication and dissemination of LINC materials.

Predictably, the government ban has served only to increase interest and, in particular, demand for the training package and other LINC publications. Both in this country and overseas over 20,000 samizdat versions are being used in school and training college INSET sessions, LINC/BBC TV and radio programmes (DES approved) have been widely praised and LINC publications from Hodder and Stoughton have achieved sales five times higher than planned (e.g. Carter, 1990; Bain *et al.*, 1992). Highest levels of interest overseas are in Australia, New Zealand, Canada, USA, Hong Kong and Singapore, where LINC materials are being integrated into teacher-training programmes. Particular interest has come from schools inspectors in France and Germany, who, increasingly concerned about the narrow formalism of their own language teaching, admire the balance achieved in National Curriculum English between attention both to the forms of the language and to its use.

Debates surrounding the LINC ban centre on certain keywords. They are the same keywords which recur repeatedly at times of social and cultural change when questions of language and the nature of English as a subject are always central.

It is no semantic accident that words such as **standard**, **correct**, and **proper** are among the keywords. Debates about the state and status of the English language are rarely debates about language alone. The terms of the debate are also terms for defining social behaviour. The term **English** is synonymous with Englishness, that is, with an understanding of who the proper English are. As indicated in Chapter 1, a view of one English with a single set of rules accords with a monolingual, monocultural version of society intent on preserving an existing order in which everyone knows their place. A view which recognises Englishes as well as English and which stresses variable rules accords with a multilingual, culturally diverse version of society. Both positions include politically extreme versions. These range from a view that standard English is correct English and must be uniformly enforced in all contexts of use (with dialects extirpated) and that children not drilled in the rules of standard grammar are both deviant and disempowered (strong right-wing position) to a view that standard English is a badge of upper-class power, and that to require children to learn it is a form of social enslavement (strong left-wing position I) to a view that standard English must be taught to working-class children so that they can wrest linguistic power from those more privileged than themselves (strong left-wing position II). It is striking how political positions converge in certain respects and how the pedagogical positions are often identical.

2.2 LINC and the middle ground

The overwhelming majority of teachers in the United Kingdom occupy a middle-ground position between these two extremes. They recognise and support the balanced view of language and learning provided by the Kingman and Cox Committees, in all National Curriculum documents and now in LINC courses and materials. They concede that attention to grammar and to the forms of language has been neglected and now willingly incorporate more formal knowledge about language into schemes of work which continue to stress the importance of the audiences, purposes and social contexts of language use. They are saddened that this determination to take a balanced and informed view of language learning should be constructed by some sections of the press and by some politicians as a form of left-wing extremism. They are disturbed that while research advances in medicine and other scientific domains are accepted, evidence from research into language and language development is lightly dismissed.

The LINC training materials adopt a balanced and moderate position on many of the above issues. For example, far from being opposed to grammar, in the LINC materials grammar occupies a central position. Indeed, there is more detailed description of the grammar of English there than in any mother-tongue English curriculum materials anywhere in the world, though, in keeping with all National Curriculum recommendations, there is no advocacy of a return to the decontextualised drills and exercises of the 1950s. Instead there is systematic exploration of grammatical differences between speech and writing, between standard and non-standard forms of the language, and between different varieties of English. In spite of being described in certain national newspapers as a dialect project, 97 per cent of the examples in LINC materials are of pupils speaking, reading and writing in standard English. They also demonstrate that one of the most effective ways of learning standard English is for pupils to compare and analyse differences between their own dialects and the dialect of standard English, discussing explicitly how and when different forms are appropriate. Over sixty pages are devoted to helping pupils with correct spelling and to helping their teachers understand the complexities of the English spelling system. Throughout the materials an emphasis on texts encourages teachers to focus not just on content but on the relationship between *what* is said and *how* it is said. The success of LINC's approach to the language curriculum has generated innumerable further local publications, which are eagerly sought and used.

Grammar is not neglected. Here is an example of LINC's approach to grammar taken from some local training materials. The example is based on a text in the form of a postcard delivered through the letterbox of customers of a water company.

> The following text communicates information; in this case the information concerns the interruption to water supply. Whenever instructions are given, a 'modality' enters the relationship between the writer and reader of a text. 'Modality' takes a number of different forms in English but the presence of modal verbs is particularly significant. Here are some of the main modal verbs in English:

can; could; will; would; must; should; shall; may

What is the function of modal verbs in the text that follows?

What other verb forms work, in particular, to establish a relationship between the Water Company and the customers to whom it has distributed this notice?

Notice of interruption to supply

We are sorry to inform you that necessary mains repairs in the area may cause an interruption to your water supply between the hours overleaf.

1. Every effort will be made to keep inconvenience and the duration of the shut-off to a minimum.

2. Do not draw more water than your minimum requirements.

3. If the water does go off, do not leave taps open or flooding may result when the supply is restored.

4. You may use water from the hot water system but it must be boiled before drinking.

5. Even if the domestic hot water supply runs dry there will be no risk of damage to the system, but as a precaution keep a low fire where a back boiler is installed and turn or switch off other sources of heating the water by gas, oil or electricity.

6. Central heating systems can continue to be used at moderate temperatures.

7. The main will be flushed before the supply is restored but discolouration and or chlorine may persist for a short time. Allow your cold tap to run for a few minutes to clear this water from your service pipe.

8. Do not use your washing machine or other appliances during the discolouration.

We apologise again for any inconvenience this may cause you and request your patience and co-operation. In case of any difficulty please contact the Nottingham District Office.

Please remember neighbours who may be older or disabled - they may need your help.

ST,6253

Figure 1.

Commentary

This text is in a curiously mixed mode. The Water Company has to inform its customers that repairs are unavoidable. It has to give its customers instructions which they need to follow both in their own interests and in the interests of other consumers. At the same time the company needs to reassure its customers that a more or less normal service is still available, that, in spite of the interruption to supply, the company still provides a good service and, above all, that there are no safety or health risks involved for its customers so long as they comply with the guidelines and instructions issued with the notice. It is important therefore that the company is clearly seen to be in control. This 'mixed mode' is inscribed in the different modal verbs in the texts along the following general lines:

Mode of reassurance/possibility: **may** cause an interruption; **may** persist for a short time; they **may** need your help; every effort **will** be made;

flooding **may** result; any inconvenience this **may** cause you.
Mode of control: **must** be boiled before drinking; the main **will** be flushed;
can continue to be used.

Notice that some modal verbs can signal possibility and control, depending
on the other words which surround them as well as on the context in which
they are used. For example, 'you may use water' (primarily control); 'they
may need your help' (primarily possibility).

'Control' is also established through an extensive use of imperative forms
of the verb which unambiguously inform us what to do and what not to
do. For example:

Do not leave taps open
Allow your cold tap to run
Do not use your washing machine
Please remember neighbours

Activity

Collect examples of further texts in which you would expect modal verbs
to be used quite extensively. For example,

horoscopes
weather forecasts
problem pages
school notices
recipes
legal texts

What other examples can you find? Why are modal verbs concentrated in
some texts but not others?

It is one key feature of the LINC approach to grammar that teachers and
pupils should, where possible, explore grammar in complete texts, in relation
to social and cultural contexts and with reference both to forms and functions.
For further discussion of this position in relation to both the development of
reading and writing skills see Carter and Nash (1990) and Carter (1990a)
which is an introduction to a collection of supporting articles for the LINC
Training Package. It should be recognised, however, that detailed analysis of
every grammatical component of the text is not an element of the LINC
materials. In fact, one strategic decision taken in the early stages of the project
was crucial and formative. In the time available, with curricular change encir-
cling teachers all the time and, furthermore, in the context of uncertainties
and anxieties about linguistics in relation to the English curriculum, the main
project team decided that it was preferable to take a small but discernible
step forward rather than to take a large step and lose balance completely. It

was therefore decided that the materials had to work with the grain, had to accommodate existing assumptions, and had to build on those assumptions instead of attempting radically to change them. It was important to go with the not inconsiderable – though generally unformalised – knowledge about language which teachers already possessed and with what interested them about language.

Thus the focus on grammar may be felt by some linguists to be insufficiently formalised. In the context of in-service material for teachers of English as a mother tongue it is, however, considerable and is primarily concerned with how grammar works to construct meanings in the kinds of literary texts with which many English teachers are familiar and, as in the above example, in the everyday texts we all encounter in our daily lives.

2.3 Keywords

What was effectively a ban on the publication of LINC training materials probably should have been expected. The emphasis on language variation and on language in context led to a too frequent reference to social theory and an emphasis on sociolinguistic perspectives. For governments of a particular political persuasion the word *social* is directly equitable with the word *socialist*. The training package itself was designed, it was said, in too activity-based and open a manner. The government eventually made it clear that it had preferred all along training materials which emphasised right and wrong uses of English, reinforcing such an emphasis with drills and exercises for teachers and pupils to follow, and with a printed appendix containing the correct answers to the exercises. The emphasis should be on factual knowledge which is measurable and determinable, and which can be transmitted from a position of authority rather than be discovered through activity-centred processes. As noted above (see pp. 7–8), a keyword here is the word **drill**. Finally, it was said that certain keywords do not appear in a sufficiently unambiguous way. In the training package words such as **correct**, **standard** and **proper** are always relativised to specific contexts and practices of teaching.

In respect of such keywords, linguists and teachers do, in fact, need to find a way of talking about language which better controls and engages with the existing public discourses, especially those of most sections of the press and media. In this connection, English teachers have to apply their knowledge about language to a major problem of communication. The very vocabulary currently available to talk about language variation – the essence of National Curriculum English in England and Wales – offers only apparently negative or oppositional terms which play neatly into the hands of those with the most simplistic notions of language and education. Thus, to talk about *non*-standard English can be seen as a departure from standards; to talk about the dangers of absolute rules of correctness is seen as an endorsement of incorrect English or as a failure to correct pupils' work; to suggest that proper English is relative to contexts of use is itself improper. Space does not allow further exposure of these antinomies (others are traditional v. trendy; national v. unpatriotic; basic v. progressive; simple v. complex) but it is easy to trace how the generally moderate and balanced English teacher is constructed as an offender against order, decency and common sense. Rather than talk in terms of standard and non-standard English, it would be preferable to talk in terms of descriptive language such as 'general' and 'special' English.

3 LINC AND GENRE THEORY

There are many different emphases and inflections in the LINC Training Package. There is also a focus both on continuities with existing good practice and on important recent developments in the field of language education. One of the most significant of recent developments is in the field of genre theory and in the teaching, in particular, of genres of writing. It is a controversial area of teaching and learning and LINC in-service training courses and materials engage in places directly with key aspects of genre theory, as developed in the United States, within the context of European text linguistics and of work in Australia within the context of systemic functional linguistics.[6] Here is a sample of the kind of analysis undertaken in project materials within the framework of genre theory (teachers have already undertaken analysis and classification of a range of different genres of writing):

> The following piece of writing was produced by a 10-year-old girl in a junior school in England. To which 'genre' of writing might it be assigned? Which particular features of language use support your decision? Does the writing have identifiable 'stages' of generic structure?

>> Snakes are reptiles. They belong to the lizards family. Snakes have no legs but for a long time ago they had claws to help them slither along. Snakes are not slimy, they are covered in scales. The scales are just bumps on the skin. Their skin is hard and glossy. Snakes often sunbathe on rocks. This is because snakes are cold-blooded and they need the warm sun in order to heat their body up. Most snakes lives in the country. Some snakes live in trees, some live in water, but most live on land in thick, long grass.
>>   A snake will usually eat frogs, lizards, mice and even small crocodiles.

>> (Jenny, aged 10)

> Commentary (written by a group of teachers)

> The first stage of the writing classifies the phenomenon; the second stage provides further descriptive information about the phenomenon (in this instance a snake). The genre is that of an *information report*.

This report is characterised by the following linguistic features: a timeless, simple present tense used to make generalisations and to convey general truths and facts (*live, sunbathe, have*). The iterative *will* (a snake 'will' usually eat) also serves in this instance to convey the sense of a general, repeated action. The writing is characterised by an absence of personal pronouns. In fact, nouns are more common than pronouns and many of the nouns are in a form (with an indefinite article 'a' or in the plural form 'snakes') which describes it as a general rather than an individualised or unique phenomenon. Many of the verbs used are also 'relational' (Halliday, 1985: 112ff.); for example, *is, have, belong to, consist of* support a defining style of presentation.

The vocabulary used is neutral rather than emotive or attitudinal and this corresponds to a report which is one of impersonal classification rather than personal observation. Such impersonality is reinforced by the use of the passive voice ('they *are covered* in scales').

Detailed analysis of this work must await a separate paper, but listed here are what are felt to be some main points of conclusion from LINC's work with genre theory.

3.1 Reactions to genre-based teaching

1. LINC teams have been convinced by the strength and depth of arguments for making the language structure of texts more visible on the grounds that genuine intervention by the teacher and consequent development in pupils' language use are not possible unless the relevant patterns of language are identified. Australian genre theorists have expressed reservations about romantic conceptions of English teaching which make language learning an invisible process, and which explicitly oppose attention to language on the grounds that it inhibits sensitivity to language and the personal shaping of experience through language. Such arguments are directly engaged with by LINC materials.

2. LINC teams have accepted that a primary concern with personal shaping of experience has resulted in classrooms in which there is an over-concentration on narrative to the exclusion of other genres.

3. In a related way LINC has adopted a more inclusive view of authorship, especially in the writing classroom. It accepts the view of Pam Gilbert (1990: 70) who wrote in a recent article that: 'Authorship is but one of the newest of a long line of discursive devices which serve to entrench personalist, individualist, speech-oriented theories of writing in schools.' Although such a position obscures important developmental connections between speech and writing, it establishes a basis for more impersonal writing modes, and thus a wider range of generic types of writing on which LINC has built.

4. LINC's introduction of a more genre-based approach to writing has provoked some hostility on the part of British teachers. A major concern is that such writing practices are inherently conservative and are designed to produce unreflective operatives who will be able to do no more than sustain a market economy for a conservative society. The concern of genre theorists for a wider range of writing types which are in turn closer to the requirements of the world of work is interpreted as a narrow vocationalism. What has helped to change this perception is the notion of *critical literacy*, initiated in particular by Gunter Kress and incorporated in specific materials such as the 'Language: A Resource for Meaning' project developed by Frances Christie, Joan Rothery, Mary Macken and others.[7] Here, a functional literacy is augmented by a critical literacy designed to enable learners not only to comprehend and produce society's discourses, but also to criticise and redirect them, if necessary. Inevitably, such practices link closely with the above arguments for making linguistic structure more visible. They clearly serve to differentiate such work from those ideologically conservative approaches to writing which would simply leave society's discourses intact, in so far as they were penetrated at all. As Michael Halliday has put it:

> To be literate is not only to participate in the discourse of an information society; it is also to resist it . . . it is rather perverse to think you can engage in discursive contest without engaging in the language of the discourse.[8]

Such work underlines that genre-based teaching is both revolutionary and reactionary. Teachers in Britain are more prepared to embrace genre theory if it includes more elements of critical linguistic awareness.

5. British teachers have become increasingly impressed by the precise analytical work which has enabled central, prototypical features of particular genres to be identified. It is the same explicitness of analysis which has helped both pupils and teachers to develop a critical linguistic literacy.

6. LINC teams have valued the overt, explicit and retrievable arguments advanced in particular by Martin (1989) and Kress (1989) but also by others. Taking such strong, clear argumentative lines enables others to argue with or argue against in a systematic way.

3.2 Problems and issues

Work on the LINC project has also enabled teachers to identify what seem to them to be some problems with current work in genre theory, and which may suggest directions for future research and development. These observations are listed here because of the extent of interest in this field of language education. Such is the extent of interest in Britain in genre-based work that solutions to some of these problems are already being explored in a number of action-research projects in UK schools and teacher-training colleges. The main points of concern are stated below.

1.   Existing descriptions of genre within a systemic functional tradition may have tended to neglect work in other traditions of description. For obvious reasons there has been a concentration on the realisations of schematic and generic structure in the lexico-grammar of texts. There is now a large body of work within the traditions of text-linguistics and written discourse analysis on lexical patterning, cohesion, coherence and textual macrostructure. Even work within a Hallidayan tradition on cohesion and thematic patterning has not been as extensively applied as it might have been.

2.   LINC teams keep coming across texts which do not conform to any single generic structure. They are the result of mixed genres. Examples of mixed genres are arguments which make use of narrative structures, narratives which have reporting or exposition structures embedded within them, and reports which are simultaneously impersonal and personal in form, that is, they are reports which also contain personal accounts of events and specific, person-based recommendations. LINC teams would thus want to emphasise that genres are not autonomous systems, and that accounts of genre and genre teaching may be limited in their considerable potential if they become too simplistic or narrowly monologic.

In a recent paper, Terry Threadgold (1989) put it as follows:

> Texts are not necessarily formed or produced on the basis of single generic patterns. They may also be multi-generic. These are not random differences. They are historically, socially and functionally constrained: and we will need to be able to teach the differences between and the motivations for multi-generic and single generic texts.

However, our acceptance of this does not mean that we dismiss genre theory, as John Dixon (1987), Michael Rosen (1988), Dixon and Stratta (1992), among others, have tended to do, for the fact that we mix genres must mean that generic structures exist to be mixed in the first place.

3.   Work within the framework of Australian and British genre theory on the genre of narrative tends to be a little too simplistic overall. It fails adequately to recognise that Labov's (1972) model for narrative description is a spoken model based on spoken data.[9] Because spoken narratives unfold sequentially in time, they do not normally have the characteristic embeddings, shifts in point of view, and complexities of narratorial presentation which characterise most written narratives. Within the general area of continua between spoken and written genres it is important, however, that literacy is not wholly construed as written texts.

4.   Early examples within Australian work of teachers modelling genres to a whole class were perceived by LINC to be possibly over-rigid and deter-

ministic. A common view is that there has been a tendency among some genre theorists to swing the pendulum too far in the opposite direction from romantic conceptions of learning and teaching. Research in domains of both first- and second-language teaching shows that we do learn effectively by making things our own, and by being personally involved in the processes of constructing a text. It has also been demonstrated that process-based approaches to writing, with an emphasis on ownership of the text, lead to increased motivation to use language. In a parallel way, there may be among theorists in a systemic functional tradition a tendency to overemphasise factual, impersonal genres at the expense of the personal. Accordingly, British teachers and linguists have been particularly impressed by recent work on modelling in relation to joint and individual construction which operates successfully to show writing to be both process- and product-based, and that work on genre can be integrated with more holistic approaches to language learning and development. (See again the relevance of the Australian materials cited in note 7.)

5. The identification of genres for description and teaching tends to be internal to the school. There is little attempt to identify the genres of writing commonly required in the workplace. Research directed by Margaret Berry on 'The Language of Business and Industry' which pays detailed attention to genre theory has much to offer us all. It illustrates, for example, that a report genre in a junior school is markedly different from a report genre in industrial or business work settings, as argued by Stainton (1990). It also underlines that text-intrinsic accounts of genre need to take fuller cognisance of the audience, purpose and context in which particular genres operate.

6. Encouragement to pupils to reflect on language has tended to be restricted to the patterns of language in the genre in focus. Instead, a general classroom climate needs to be established in which talking and writing about language leads to the need to analyse language. This can be stimulated and promoted in all kinds of ways. In the context of the National Curriculum in Britain there is an emphasis in LINC's work on *language awareness* – that is, general sensitivity to different styles and purposes of language use. These include differences between spoken and written language, explorations of the language of literature, the language of jokes, advertising, pop fiction, and political rhetorics, and investigations of the continua between different accents and dialects, including standard English. Such explorations, such encouragement to greater language awareness, is a necessary habit-forming prelude to looking more closely and analytically at the linguistic patterns which make up different genres. A climate of reflection is created which leads to fuller and more systematic analyses. Analysis is not always best fostered by practising analysis of and reflection on language solely within the context of individual genres. (For an outline of attainment targets for knowledge about language in the National Curriculum for England and Wales, see Appendix 1, p.54.)

Several of these observations are hardly new, and many of them have been advanced by genre theorists themselves. However, the issues mentioned above have grown out of specific contexts of applied linguistic work in relation to the National Curriculum for English in England and Wales. Teachers in Britain interested in writing development are beginning positively to embrace work on genre-theory and on genre within a functionalist perspective in particular. These observations should be viewed in a correspondingly positive light. Further detail about the whole LINC programme and the influence of Hallidayan theories of language on it is evidenced in the introductions to the Training Package itself and the accompanying Reader.[10]

4 KNOWLEDGE ABOUT LANGUAGE IN THE CLASSROOM

Once again, detailed exploration of this area must await a separate paper. It should be recognised that the primary purpose of the LINC project was to develop *teachers'* knowledge about language more systematically. The project has, however, stimulated numerous central questions about the relationship between teachers' knowledge and pupils' knowledge, and fostered, again in the context of National Curriculum requirements, high levels of interest in the teaching of knowledge about language to pupils aged between five and 16. A recent LINC-based publication (Bain *et al.*, 1992) presents over thirty classroom case studies in pupils' knowledge about language collected during the course of the project.

5 CONCLUSIONS: THE LESSONS OF LINC

A project of the scale and complexity of LINC cannot escape criticism. It is important that the lessons of both success and failure are recorded. For example, for all their successes with teachers, LINC materials need to be further adapted in three main ways. First, materials on reading should be developed to exemplify in greater detail what a mixed methods approach to reading entails. More examples and case studies would illustrate how readers use a range of different cues and clues, syntactic and semantic, phonic and visual, in the process of learning to read. More action research would illustrate when to mix methods and when to concentrate on a single teaching procedure. Future LINC materials (or their derivatives) must also enable teachers better to analyse the linguistic differences between real books and books from graded reading schemes. Second, supplements to existing units are needed on differences between spoken and written English, particularly in relation to the teaching of punctuation, which depends crucially on the relationship between grammatical structure and the rhythms and contours of speech. More examples are also needed of how standard English varies across spoken and written modes while still remaining standard English. Third, more examples are needed to show how literary texts can stimulate enhanced knowledge about language, especially the history of the language, and how greater linguistic knowledge underpins literary appreciation. LINC materials show continuities with A-level English language.[11] Although this is one of the most rapidly expanding A levels, it is vital that a balance is struck between literary and linguistic emphases.

5.1 Negative conclusions

Even if the general developments outlined above take place, they will take place against a cultural background in which both positive and negative factors are at work. The main negative factors are, first, that some teachers will continue to persist with the worst excesses of romanticism in their view of language learning and teaching. They will continue to make linguistic processes invisible and regard language only in so far as it provides a window on to content, the expression of the individual self, the world of ideas. They will continue to refuse to see forms of language as a powerful resource for creating significant domains of meaning. Second, governments may want to intervene more directly in the shaping of the English curriculum. If so, and whatever their political persuasion, governments may not want to endorse classroom language study which explores relationships between language and society, and which subjects those relationships to interrogation. They are likely to continue to be especially disturbed by classroom KAL work which encourages children to investigate such relationships independently. They may exert their powers to impose a language study which is 'neutralised' by being more decontextualised, formalist rather than functionalist in orientation, and which, above all, can be easily assessed and measured. The currently very overt demands by the British government for greater attention to phonics in the teaching of reading is but a signal of an increasing emphasis on the basics in so far as what is 'basic' often involves a decontextualised language focus.

5.2 Positive conclusions

It is a positive factor that governments are drawing attention to language, recognising it as both medium and message, mounting arguments in relation to the 'proper' study of English, attacking the positions adopted by those with a professional interest in language.

Although the battles will continue to be between those who have the power but not the knowledge, and those who have the knowledge but not the power, the very fact that governments are forced to mount explicit arguments about language is healthy both for processes of public debate and for the cause which espouses the centrality of language to the school curriculum. Increasing attention to language on the part of teachers, coupled with high degrees of enthusiasm and conviction, will lead to pupils being progressively interested in language. Increasing knowledge about language among pupils will produce within a generation a society which is likely to be less prejudiced and ignorant and more informed and articulate about matters to do with language.

Finally, a more positive view of applied linguistics emerges from projects such as the LINC project. It is a view in which teacher and linguist work more collaboratively towards common agendas. As a result, teachers become more aware of the problems of linguistic description and, in turn, linguists begin to address problems identified by teachers, rather than only those problems identified by linguists themselves – a process likely to result only in a narrowly linguistic rather than a genuinely applied linguistic agenda. Increasingly, all concerned with language have come to appreciate how notoriously fascinating, complex and ultimately *dangerous* language and language study are. In a project inspired by the work of Michael Halliday, the final word must be left to Halliday (Halliday, 1982):

> ... there is a real sense in which linguistics is threatening; it's uncomfortable, and it's subversive. It's uncomfortable because it strips us of the fortifications that protect and surround some of our deepest prejudices. As long as we keep linguistics at bay we can go on believing what we want to believe about language, both our own and everybody else's ...
>
> More than any other human phenomenon, language reflects and reveals the inequalities that are enshrined in the social process. When we study language systematically ... we see into the power structure that lies behind our everyday social relationships, the hierarchical statuses that are accorded to different groups within society ...

This chapter is a modified version of a paper of the same title in Hasan, R. and Williams, G. (eds) *Literacy in Society* (Longman, 1996). It was originally delivered as a plenary paper to the annual conference of the Australian Applied Linguistics Association, Sydney, July 1992.

APPENDIX 1

LINC is a project funded by the Department of Education and Science under an ESG (Education Support Grant). The main aim of the project is to produce materials and to conduct activities to support implementation of English in the National Curriculum in England and Wales in the light of the views of language outlined in the Kingman and Cox Reports on English language teaching and English 5–16 respectively (DES, 1988, 1989). The LINC project was designed to operate from April 1989 until March 1992.

The LINC professional development materials (LINC, 1992), were prepared in the first two years of the project (April 1989–April 1991) and were used as a basis for training of key project personnel. For the duration of the LINC programme the materials were included in LEA in-service courses and teachers were supported in considering the development needs of their own schools with regard to language in the National Curriculum. The primary aim of the materials was to form a basis for the immediate training requirements of the project; however, a further aim was to produce materials which are of use to providers of both in-service and initial teacher training over a much long period of time.

The LINC materials are characterised by the following main features:

- There are ten main units in the package; each unit is designed for approximately 1–1½ days of course time or its equivalent. The units are supported by BBC TV and Radio programmes.
- Each unit is organised around a sequence of activities to support users 'doing' things with language.
- Each unit is designed to be maximally flexible and can be supplemented or extended according to need. The loose-leaf ring binder format means that units can be easily detached and/or combined with other material.
- Units are grouped under main headings of development in children's talk, reading and writing, together with a block devoted to language and society.
- Each unit has at its centre complete texts, usually drawn from recognisable classroom contexts; the activities promote analysis of language but scrutiny of decontextualised language is normally eschewed.
- The training package draws on the many available examples of good practice in language teaching and recognises that teachers already know a lot, particularly implicitly, about language.

The foci of the project are presented diagrammatically in Figure 2.

Copies of the training materials are published in a printed desk-top version and are available from LINC project, Department of English Studies, University of Nottingham, Nottingham NG7 2RD, England.

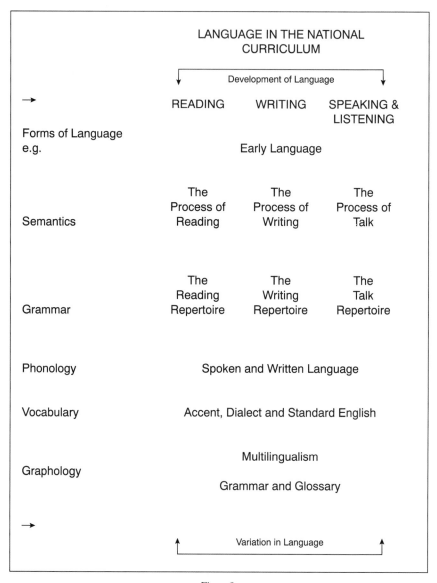

Figure 2.

4

STANDARD ENGLISHES: SPEECH AND WRITING

The victory of one reigning language (dialect) over the others, the supplanting of languages, their enslavement, the process of illuminating them with the True Word, the incorporation of barbarians and lower social strata into a unitary language of culture and truth, the canonisation of ideological systems, philology with its methods of studying and teaching dead languages, languages that were by that very fact 'unities', Indo-European linguistics with its focus of attention, directed away from language plurality to a single proto-language – all this determined the content and power of the category of 'unitary language' in linguistic and stylistic thought.

(Bakhtin, 1981)

This chapter pursues two main themes. It first explores some differences and distinctions between spoken and written English, with particular reference to grammar. It will be argued that teachers need to know more about this area of variation than they do about most aspects of language. It is an under-researched area but some recent research findings by linguists will be reported, for such a focus has important implications for literacy development. Teaching implications for developing the kind of knowledge about language which can feed into enhanced spoken and written language development will be discussed. The second theme explored is subsidiary but no less important: the need for teachers to understand better some of the discourses surrounding the English language and English language teaching – the need, for example, to know about, understand and contest the variable social discourses which underlie keywords such as proper, correct, standard, national, grammar, drill and, most prominently, the keyword English itself. In fact, it will be argued that these two themes conveniently converge in several current debates concerning the place of English in the National Curriculum. Definitions of spoken and written English are the source of much continuing confusion concerning what is correct and proper English, what is grammar and, above all, what constitutes standard English. In this respect the two main themes of the chapter come together.

But we begin with a brief historical account of the formation of standard English. Understanding something of the evolution of standard English and of processes of standardisation of English is another necessary element in understanding the nature of standard English and therefore the part it plays in educational contexts.

1 STANDARD ENGLISH: AN HISTORICAL NOTE

Written standard English began to emerge in England in the fifteenth century. Standard British English is largely based on the dialects of the eastern English Midland counties and is originally found in different versions of the Wyclif Bible as well as in several secular works. The most significant factor in its establishment, however, was the emergence of London as the political and economic centre of the country and in the long term the East Midlands forms of the language were unable wholly to withstand the influences emanating from the capital. Of particular significance was the role of the London Chancery, especially after *c.*1430 where language practices, based on both the London standard and influenced by Midlands varieties came to predominate in the language used by the Chancery scribes (previously they had used Latin and French). Chaucer's pre-eminence cannot be ignored, of course, in the prestige which attached to London English although London English was at the time of writers such as Chaucer and Gower more of a hybrid reflecting the predominantly Essex dialect of the city of London and the dialects of Middlesex, Westminster and areas to the west. The role of printing and the part of Caxton, who set up his printing presses in Westminster in 1476 and who first printed the literary works of Chaucer, was also instrumental, as was the fact that most scholars who wrote studied at the Universities of Oxford and Cambridge in the south-east of the country.

In parallel with these developments was a shift in the population of the country in the form of immigration to London from the East Midlands counties of Norfolk, Huntingdonshire, Leicestershire, Northamptonshire and Bedfordshire. Such population shifts served to reinforce the part played by East Midlands dialects in the formation of a standard written British English.

Of these formative influences in the development of a southern literary standard version of English the most significant was probably the extensive post-Caxton development of printing, a process which eventually resulted in the dissemination of a single, standardised norm across most of the country with the result that during the fifteenth century value judgements begin to be passed on other national dialect forms. In *The Arte of English Poesie* by George Puttenham (*c.*1520–90) the aspiring poet is advised to use 'the usuall speach of the Court, and that of London and the shires lying about London within lx. myles and not much above'. Such processes were subsequently further re-inforced by the codification and prescription of the standard language in the eighteenth century in representative publications such as Samuel Johnson's

Dictionary of the English Language (1755) and Lindley Murray's *English Grammar* (1794).

The following points can be made on the basis of this account, incomplete as it necessarily is. First, the process of standardisation of English is to a considerable extent an historical and geographical accident. Second, many regional dialects derive historically from early English dialects and are therefore not corruptions of the language. The dialect of standard English is not inherently superior to other dialects. Third, the role of printing was crucial in the establishment of a standard language. Fourth, the development of a standard language coincided with an elaboration of standard English, resulting in the dialect of standard English having a much more varied range of functions and uses than is usual for other dialects. Fifth, standard English is firmly equated with a written variety of the language; difficulties invariably arise as soon as attempts are made to define a working account of *spoken* standard English.

2 GRAMMAR, SPEECH AND WRITING

It is frequently the case that literacy debates, particularly as conducted in the national media of many different countries, take place in the absence of attestable evidence, thus ensuring that rising or declining standards of literacy are simply established by the clearest assertions and by the most forceful anecdotes. It is also not unusual for debates internal to the profession to be conducted without detailed scrutiny of language data. It seems appropriate therefore for the discussion in this chapter to be based on data. The first examples here are drawn from language produced by children in material collected in the course of the Language in the National Curriculum project (LINC)[1] between 1989 and 1992. At this stage it is simplest for them to be classified as examples of 'spoken' grammar.

Examples of 'spoken' grammar

1 *left-displaced subject* (with recapitulatory pronoun)
   The man with the loud voice he said.
   The women they all shouted.
2 *right-displaced subject* (with amplificatory noun-phrase tag)
   It was a really big explosion that one.
   He was an outstanding leader was Robson.
3 *repeated main verb in main clause*
   There's a few problems are likely to crop up.
4 *double relative pronoun*
   There's another person who I don't know what she's responsible for.
5 *'complete' relative clause*
   Which is why we put the Bunsen-burner on a low flame.
6 *Wh-pseudo cleft* (as 'summarizing conjunctions')

What I would do is, people should try a different policy.

7 *elliptical phrases*

Jill likes the rock group, myself the folk.

8 *fronted anticipatory phrase*

That house in Brentford Street, is that where she lives?

(LINC, 1992)

The following observations can be made:

1 The examples are attested and authentic.

2 It is not a comprehensive list by any means but it is representative of aspects of regular English usage. The examples belong more to the spoken language domain than to the domain of written language but are regularly found in pupils' writing.

3 All the examples are examples of correct standard English in so far as several of these same grammatical features are used standardly by educated users of English and are not uncommonly found in television and radio discussion programmes. With the exception of example 4 (which is more exclusively spoken), these grammatical forms could also be used unexceptionally in written contexts, albeit in contexts that are informal and in contexts in which it is wished to create a specifically spoken imprint.

4 Such grammatical structures are not normally described in the standard descriptive grammars of English; indeed, some of the definitions sound more appropriate to ice-skating rather than language study. (One can, for example, without too much difficulty imagine ice-dance champions performing a right-displaced subject with amplificatory noun-phrase tag.) The reason for this is that all the most authoritative, standard grammars are based on written examples or on examples of very formal contexts of spoken English. No recognised descriptive terms exist because the forms are not recognised as part of the standard grammar.

5 Such a situation may be illustrated further with reference to Quirk *et al.*'s *A Comprehensive Grammar of the English Language* (1985). The grammar draws its spoken data from a small corpus of words. The corpus is mostly written text and what spoken data there is is mainly based on tape-recorded formal English conversation, for example between university dons in a University of London common room in the 1960s. It may be doing such users a disservice, but it would be surprising if the English used in such contexts was anything other than a quite restricted code. It is a code in which there is minimal variation between spoken and written forms. Yet that restricted code is nevertheless used to illustrate and further reinforce definitions of what standard English grammar is. To a considerable extent standard English grammar may be best defined as the grammar of standard written English.

While it is difficult to draw precise boundaries between spoken and written standard English, it may be both unduly naive and relativistic (see below, section 2.1) to assume that all spoken forms are equally acceptable. However, the generally stigmatised uses are small and are greatly outnumbered by standard spoken English forms.

One obvious explanation for this phenomenon of *spoken standard English* is that until very recently written language was all that was available for detailed scrutiny. Even now very sophisticated technology is needed to collect spoken data properly. Written language is simply more available and collectable. This is one of the reasons why the history of linguistics has been, until the advent of discourse analysis in the late 1970s and 1980s, the history of the study of written language systems. It is one of the reasons why Dr Johnson did not record certain words in his dictionary of 1755. Johnson pronounced that words such as **sham**, **snob**, **bamboozle**, **flimsy** were ephemeral and would not last beyond a few years. They were merely spoken uses and could not be attested in written sources. They could not therefore have the standardised authority accorded to them by inclusion in a dictionary.

Another reason for this situation (and this reason cannot be easily divorced from the previous one) is that written language has more prestige. It has also been seen as something you have to learn and is indeed a mark of learning to the extent that, for many people, literacy is synonymous with the ability to read and write, while an 'illiterate' is ignorant, lacking in intelligence and may even be mentally deficient. Many of the canonical writers in the language such as Dickens, Hardy, Lawrence (and to a lesser extent Elizabeth Gaskell) have not solved the problem of the power of standard orthography for the representation of authentic spoken English. Such characters as are accorded the distinction of speaking real, informal or non-standard spoken English are inevitably therefore represented as uneducated, unintelligent, or, at best, simply idiosyncratic.

One main danger is that spoken English continues to be judged by the codified standards of written English, and that teaching pupils to speak standard English may, in fact, be to teach them to speak in formal written English. A test of spoken English may become a test of one's abilities to speak a very restricted code – a formal English used routinely by dons, civil servants and cabinet ministers. It is not very far removed from the language of formal debate. Such a view of spoken English can produce an artificial and unnatural English and can even promote a kind of *illiteracy* which is as damaging to users of English as not being able to write literate English; for to have everyone speaking and writing only one code – a standard written English code – generates an illiteracy almost as grave as would be the case if everyone were only able to use a local dialect.

To summarise, it has been argued so far:

- that there is a close relationship between standard English and the written language.

- that there are forms of spoken English which are perfectly standard and which are indeed grammatically correct. These forms do not appear in standard grammars, however, so it is easy for them to be judged as non-standard and ungrammatical.
- that there are dangers inherent in teaching children to speak using formal written English structures or indeed testing them for their ability to speak, in effect, like a book.

It is vital that teachers know more about such questions for they will then be better equipped to help pupils to learn more about one of the most central features of language and literacy. It will be argued later that such under-standings are best promoted by pedagogic processes which involve regular comparison and contrast of spoken and written texts and not by processes which focus on one to the exclusion of the other.

2.1 Language, relativism and a common core

There is also, however, a further danger. A proper view of these essential distinctions and differences between spoken and written English should not allow too great a degree of relativism to prevail. It has indeed been argued that there are dangers in allowing too writerly a view of language and grammar; but this should not obscure the fact that there is a *core* of gram-matical features which are common and central to both standard written *and* standard spoken Englishes. It is entirely appropriate that the fundamental fact of language variation is recognised but such a fact should not obscure recog-nition of this common core. For example:

1 specific forms of subject/verb agreement and subject/pronoun agreement (e.g. not 'the men goes that way' but rather 'the men go that way');
2 consistency of tenses across clause and phrase boundaries, unless specific rhetorical effects are intended (e.g. not 'the crystals, with the sharp points, dissolve in warm water' but rather 'the crystals dissolve . . .');
3 adverb forms in place of adjectives (e.g. not 'he did brilliant' or 'he played exceptional' but rather 'brilliantly', 'exceptionally');
4 double or multiple negation in structures (e.g. not 'he ain't here and he doesn't want to speak to nobody' but rather 'he isn't here and he doesn't want to speak to anybody'). Exceptions are for the expression of tenta-tiveness ('we are not uninterested . . .');
5 specific uses of pronouns and determiners (e.g. not 'she liked the present what I bought her for her birthday' but rather 'she liked the present which (or that) I bought her for her birthday');
6 discourse markers such as **you know, so, like, sort of, I mean, what's more**. However, these are a common feature of spoken English, allowing the maintenance of informal interaction and a symmetrically interpersonal communication. Although they are stigmatised by some, they cannot be

60

removed from much informal spoken discourse without making the speakers sound as if they are addressing a public meeting.

This core of features is small in range but significant in social effect and, given that written standard English is the international language of reading and writing, hugely significant in terms of educational outcomes.

With reference to both writing and speech in English it is dishonest and unduly relativistic to pretend that the alternative forms are *not* stigmatised.[2] The criticisms from media and politicians have some validity here. There is a real danger in the essentially romantic doctrine which only accepts as valid the language children produce because it is theirs and therefore part of their individual, social and cultural identity. There is an additional danger in refusing to accept another publicly voiced criticism: that there has tended to be an uncritical emphasis on what children already know and can do and on what they bring to school rather than on what they do not know, cannot do or on what the school can bring to them.

It is, in my view, necessary that teachers of English accept challenges to review practices and, if necessary, to modify them. It is not appropriate to dismiss criticism simply because it may be perceived to be 'right-wing' criticism or may emerge from a very narrow and unrepresentative pressure group which may be wishing to enforce a standard core as an unstated nationalistic aim of establishing a clearer sense of Englishness. There is some truth to the charges of unduly relativistic romanticism and to the charges that teachers are unwilling to tell and teach core facts about the language because such practices appear transmissive and authoritarian or may appear to prioritise teaching over learning. The latest versions of the National Curriculum English order (DfE/WO, 1995) may go some way to helping avoid the worst excesses of relativism by stressing some of the **core features** which are common to standard spoken and written English.

However, by being weighted towards a written model of the language, it may also insufficiently reflect the continua which exist between the written and the spoken. And such an emphasis may distort the process of students learning a standard English which is in parts invariable and in parts characterised by patterned variability. Teaching will therefore need to maximise the situation to ensure that pupils develop a rich repertoire of spoken and written functions, learn about the differences, distinctions and similarities between spoken and written language, and develop sociolinguistic knowledge about language which enables and empowers them to switch between and across modes according to context, purpose and audience for language use. The challenge, therefore, is to identify better what needs to be known about standard English, what it is and what its range is and, even more importantly, to develop a pedagogy appropriate to the teaching of standard English.

2.2 What do teachers need to know?

What do teachers need to know about language which will help them and their pupils to acquire this capacity for appropriately choosing to use core forms and appropriately choosing to use variations along continua of spoken and written discourses? What kinds of classroom practice may assist us to promote acquisition of competence in and across spoken and written English?

First, general language awareness needs to be established. Examples of such theory and practice abound in the LINC-produced volume *Looking into Language*, edited by Bain *et al.* (1992). A general language awareness involves helping pupils and students to see how written language is more permanent, more editable and more monologic whereas spoken language is more ephemeral, more dynamic and process-like and inevitably more dialogic. Second, more specific awareness can be generated by working on texts which display features of speakerly and writerly language in a wide range of contexts. The most suitable texts may be those which contain features of both spoken and written language forms. Good examples are provided by faxes, such as this example which has been slightly adapted from an authentic fax:[3]

FROM:	MIKE ROBERTSON
TO:	JEAN-PIERRE
SUBJECT:	MOTOROLA EQUIP

Hi!

We're on our way to Cantswell. One item I need your help with. We went back to Motorola and now have a tape for checking against Round Rock data. I will bring it to France with me tomorrow. Could you call/fax/E-mail Ken Barton and ask him to get us data for device D55A. It's a device fabbed on Oak Hill tell him. Either Fed Ex or datalink if possible. I'd like to do test on Wednesday if we can. Thanks a lot. Call my car if you don't understand,

Here, grammatical forms such as:

1 One item I need your help with
2 We're
3 It's a device fabbed on Oak Hill tell him
4 Either Fed Ex or datalink if possible

are speakerly in that they display contractions ('We're') and ellipsis as a result of deletion of a main finite verb (4) and (1) – where (in 1) a 'there plus verb to be' structure is ellipted (for example 'There is one item I need your help with'. (Ellipsis is much more common in speech than in writing.) Furthermore, according to written norms, the structures in (3) and (1) have an unusual placement of object (1) and a more spoken placement of the main imperative verb (3). Indeed faxes, electronic mail communications, and word-processed texts are altering before our very eyes the ways in which written language normally works. The informal nature of many such communications reinforces a notion that certain forms of the written language can be process-like and dialogic. The forms of language by which they are constructed are likely to be those which are closest to spoken discourse.

Other examples are provided by advertisements, which have the added advantage of often being interesting texts from the point of view of social and cultural practices. Figure 3 is an advertisement for an investment bank and illustrates the changing styles of advertisements by such august and even some-what staid institutions. Although the main orientation is towards formal written English, the advertisement has inscribed within it features associated with the more informal interactive styles of spoken exchange. In particular, there is not only a constant verbal play with words (for example 'Tiers of Joy'/'Tears of Joy') which is often characteristic of conversation (see Chapter 8 below) but also a constant use of personal pronouns, contractions ('you'd') and a strategic use of discourse markers such as

Not only that
In fact
Quite obviously then
Which, incidentally . . .

to allow the voice in the advertisement to appear relaxed, informal and even in places intimately reassuring.

Such texts, as Cook (1992) points out, deliberately employ this kind of inter-personal grammar because it helps to establish a dialogic and reciprocal texture which suits its overall design of interesting and involving the reader.

A further stage, designed to deepen awareness of both formal and functional distinctions between spoken and written discourse, would be to compare examples such as those constructed by Michael Halliday in his book *Spoken and Written Language* (Halliday, 1989: 81):

Written	Spoken
Every previous visit had left me with a sense of the futility of further action on my part.	Whenever I'd visited there before, I'd ended up feeling that it would be futile if I tried to do anything more.
Violence changed the face of once peaceful Swiss cities.	The cities in Switzerland had once been peaceful, but they changed when people became violent.
Improvements in technology have reduced the risks and high costs associated with simultaneous instal-lation.	Because the technology has improved it's less risky than it used to be when you install them at the same time, and it doesn't cost so much either.

Tiers of joy.

Current Interest Rates (variable) Gross p.a.	
BALANCE	RATES
£500 – £9,999	5.25%
£10,000 – £39,999	5.85%
£40,000 – £99,999	5.95%
£100,000 – £249,999	6.10%
£250,000+	6.20%

Read it and reap. Woolwich Guernsey has consistently offered excellent rates of interest in all these tiers.

Last year, in particular, our £500-£9,999 tier offered 5.75% interest, the highest rate of any offshore building society subsidiary. Which incidentally, made it the industry best buy for 1994.

And, had you invested £10,000 over the past 3 years in our £10,000-£39,999 tier, you'd now be crying with laughter, because it was also rated as industry best buy in '94.

In fact, you can now earn an impressive 5.85% in this bracket. Quite obviously then, you could do yourself a wealth of good by investing with Woolwich Guernsey. And you can rest assured your investment is secure. All deposits are 100% guaranteed by Woolwich Building Society.

Not only that, the beauty of this Woolwich Guernsey account is that it gives you instant access to your money. You're free to withdraw all or part of your investment at any time you like with no penalties at all.

To find out more, call us on 01481 715735 during weekly business hours. Alternatively fax us on 01481 715722 or clip the coupon.

Woolwich Guernsey. We wipe away the competition's tiers.

Please send me details of the Woolwich Guernsey Sterling International Gross Account.

Mr/Mrs/Miss/Ms

Address

WG40

Country

Tel/Fax No.

Return to: Woolwich Guernsey Limited, PO Box 341, La Tonnelle House, Les Banques, St Peter Port, Guernsey GY1 3UW

WOOLWICH
—— *GUERNSEY* ——

Figure 3.

Opinion in the colony greeted the promised change with enthusiasm.	The people in the colony rejoiced when it was promised that things would change in this way.

The sentences are invented examples (authentic ones would be preferable) but they can usefully exemplify particular tendencies in the construction of spoken and written grammars of English. Halliday points out that the example sentences with 'written' tendencies contain fewer clauses, have a greater lexical density and use more nouns and noun phrases including, by a process of nominalisation, nouns formed from other parts of speech (e.g. improve-**improvement**; violent-**violence**). Thus, in the first sentence the 'spoken' sentence contains four separate clauses, more grammatical words (**I**, **if**, **that**, **to**, **there**, **it**) – as opposed to the greater number of lexical words in the written equivalent but fewer nouns and noun phrases. Halliday claims that although written and spoken language are realisations of the same meaning potential (because the grammar encodes understanding of reality), they in fact offer different 'representations' of reality.

Since spoken language is more focused on the clause and on verb phrases, it represents a world of happenings, a dynamic view, a world of processes which is congruent with real experiences. Since written language is more focused on noun-phrase groups, where processes are represented as objects, it represents a world of things, a synoptic view, a world of products which conveys a metaphorical and therefore less direct representation of real experiences. Such awareness also helps explain the more abstract and reflective character of written language compared with the more immediate, real time character of spoken language.

It is worth noting in passing too that many of the kinds of texts preferred as 'canonical' in anthologies for schools are more writerly texts. Many of the texts preferred by teachers, especially teachers of more junior classes, are more speakerly in texture. This can be illustrated by popular titles such as David McKee's *Not Now, Bernard* and John Burningham's *Come Away from the Water, Shirley!* and *Get off our Train* and the very interactive styles that the authors of such books generate in order to produce more active readers.

3 FOCUS ON THE CLASSROOM

3.1 Working with standard English: a case study

The following piece of writing by a 10-year-old girl from a Sheffield junior school is representative of the kind of writing to which teachers are daily exposed. The procedures needed to support Lesley in her writing are complex and include some understanding of the particular South Yorkshire dialect which Lesley speaks, a dialect with a long history and a pattern in verb formation which differs from similar patterns in the standard dialect of British

English that Lesley is in the process of acquiring. The invariant *was* as a simple past tense verb and auxiliary verb is salient because differences in such core forms of a language are immediately perceptible; and the fact that it varies minimally from the standard (in second person 'you' and in plural – 'you', 'we', 'they') only serves to make the transition from the forms of one dialect to another more difficult, even if on the surface it may appear a relatively simple matter to 'correct'. The Yorkshire dialect forms used by Lesley are also, it should be remembered, spoken by her in a wide variety of contexts: to her mother and father, her brothers and sisters; other members of the family; with friends at school; in the community in which she lives. They will be very much part of her identity and involvement with these contexts of daily living. To change her speech forms will on one level serve to dislocate her from these relationships; to allow her to persist with these forms in most contexts of written English will on another level be to dislocate her from academic progress in her school where for purposes of public examinations in particular, the dialect required is that of standard English. Here is the writing, collected as part of the National Writing Project:

> To day at afternoon play just when we was comeing back in to school Mrs B found a pidgin in the floor next to the Haygreen Lane side. Some children had gone in but I was ther when Gary Destains said hay up thers a pidgin on floor. We all rusht up but Mrs B showted 'stop come back and let me look whats apened to it poor thing.' I just thout it was resting a bit but Dobbie said its ded. It was when Mrs B picket it up its kneck just flopped over poor thing I said to Dobbie. She lifted it up with its wings and they were like big lovley grey fans. I didn't know wings were so lovely and big with so meny fethers espeshily. When we had gon in we was just sittin in are class and telling Mrs Sandison and the others about it when Mrs B came and held it up with its lovely grey wings. I was sorry for it poor thing and Mrs Sandison was sad and we all was.

(Lesley, aged 10)

If Lesley's teacher is to correct every error in this piece of writing, it is obvious that almost every line will be covered in correction marks of one kind or another and that very few pupils are able to withstand the effects on confidence of work being returned in this form. Instead, most teachers will regard the process of correction as a developmental one and will envisage several stages of drafting in the refinement of Lesley's writing. The task for the teacher is therefore to make clear that the writing is ongoing and that a 'final' version will be produced only after three or four further drafts have been completed.

The stages of drafting can be made to correspond to stages of priority for the items for correction. Thus, errors can be prioritised and graded according to the judgement of the teacher of their learnability, their importance and their significance for the success of this piece of writing. Such a procedure allows marking of Lesley's piece of writing to be in stages so that only 'stage 1' items are indicated initially, with other specific items held back until subsequent drafts ('stage 2' and 'stage 3') are developed.

Lesley needs support from the teacher in the areas of:

grammar: in particular, the use of Yorkshire dialect forms in the past tense of the verb 'to be'; spoken grammar structures such as 'I was sorry for it poor thing' and 'It was when Mrs B picket it up its kneck just flopped over poor thing' (though different punctuation may serve to disambiguate whether 'poor thing' is in each case marked as a separate sentence).

spelling: correct forms are in brackets: comeing (coming); pidgin (pigeon); ther (there); rusht (rushed); showted (shouted); apened (happened); thout (thought); ded (dead); picket (picked); kneck (neck); lovley (lovely); meny (many); fethers (feathers); espeshily (especially); gon (gone); sittin (sitting); are (our).

punctuation and orthography: To day; quotation marks 'Hay up, there's a pigeon on (the) floor'; Dobbie said 'It's dead'; 'Poor thing,' I said to Dobbie; What's happened?

Each teacher will of course prioritise differently according to her/his perception of the needs of individual pupils but among the factors and possible stages considered will be:

Stage 1

Word and structure frequency: (these are items which include the most central and frequent words in the language, the accurate use of which must be a first priority): many; gone; coming; there; there's; what's

Intelligent errors (these are based on generalisation from known patterns or from an attempt to produce sound–letter correspondence based on existing regularities): espeshily; pidgin; kneck; lovley;

Stage 2

Overlaps from speech: whats apened (occasioned in part by the absence of an 'h' in most northern dialects of British English; I was sorry for it poor thing. (I was sorry for the poor thing?)

Apparently careless errors: lovely/lovley (?); It was. When Mrs B picked it up ... (?) These are examples that are likely to be worked out by inviting Lesley to read the passage aloud.

Stage 3

Grammar. the transition from 'we was' to 'we were' is, on account of its salience, a more delicate matter and may be best discussed as part of a lesson involving the whole class where the teacher can explain the contexts in which the different forms can be used. 'We was' is a structure which can be used in informal communications, mainly in speech, and can serve to lend authenticity to speech representation. In writing, such a form would normally be marked by use within quotation marks. 'We were' is the standard form for most contexts of written use and for formal spoken contexts such as an interview or a debate. Furthermore, there is the distinctly spoken grammar of 'what's apened to it poor thing', where the phrase 'poor thing' may act as a kind of reinforcing 'tail' to the subject 'it' and which adds an appropriately emotive contour to the overall expression. (See section 2, p.57 where similar expressions are marked as having 'right-displaced subjects'). There is no need for different grammatical structuring if the expression appears between quotation marks.

Lesley's task is to learn to build on what she has already achieved. It is a considerable feat to have introduced so much detail into the writing, to have effected comparisons as imaginative as:

She lifted it up with its wings and they were like big lovley grey fans.

and to have structured a narrative recount so vividly. In terms of styles of language use, she will need to continue to be attentive to the continuities between spoken and written forms and to learn to develop a bi-dialectal awareness of which forms serve which general and specific purposes. The process is a complex one and requires considerable patience in the light of widespread public perceptions that drills and exercises, based on decontextualised, single-sentence examples, are the most effective ways of solving the 'problem'. But the process can be approached systematically and can be enhanced by the teacher's knowledge of differences and distinctions between spoken and written discourse in English.

3.2 Speech in/and writing: a further classroom example

The pupils' work to be discussed in this section arose from classroom work in which they first studied spoken/written differences and then written reports which differ in the audiences for which they are produced. The lessons involved explicit treatment of linguistic metalanguage, and a classroom-based study of reports in different newspapers. Here are some comments about the writing task from the teacher of Claire and Sabina:[4]

As an experiment last year we studied differences between spoken and written language with all forms from the third year up . . . we're still learning the best ways of doing this but I'm convinced that a strategy of rewriting helps both with understanding and skills development of the kids. The rewriting with 3T also took the form of studying, recording, transcribing and then producing football commentaries as well as different written reports on the same match. There is more of a link than I had thought between studying something, modelling it for writing or speech purposes and getting effective language work from the kids. Sabina and Claire, who are avid Forest supporters by the way, produced several drafts of their work using a word processor (with spellcheck) before they handed it in. I discussed some things explicitly with them especially their punctuation which they had really worked at, using basic terms like stress, rhythm and conjunction in a natural way, as the need for them arose. Sabina and Claire are probably the best two at English in their class, but the quality of their work and their enjoyment of rewriting procedures surprised me.

The result is two texts in which one is distinctly more writerly and the other distinctly more speakerly. Text A, in particular, raises questions for pupils themselves about:

1 the extent to which standard orthography can properly represent the spoken language;
2 the extent to which punctuation rules follow grammatical patterns and how far such rules can represent the contours, rhythms and intonational patterns of the spoken voice;
3 the extent to which Text A is more interactive, involving and reciprocal in the relationship it creates with its readers. It does, so, of course, at the expense of standard punctuation.

MAN. UTD. V. NOTTS. FOREST

Text A

Man. Utd. O Nottingham Forest 3

Nottingham Forest are, back on the winning trail. A 3–0 victory over Manchester Utd. put a smile back on the Manager's face. Before the match Cloughie had said all the team needed was, a bit of luck. They'd worked hard all week they WERE playing like a team again. But, after they'd played a dull ten-minutes, Clough was out of the dugout. What was it now? – another defeat on his mind?; another referee against him?; another fan on the pitch? He needn't have worried. On the twelfth minute, Nigel Clough – the Manager's son – put the ball in the net and turned to the bench and waved his fist in the air – all fired up? After that, the game stepped up and two more goals for Forest. One, a snap shot from twelve yards by Crosby; the second, a one-two between Carr and Pearce blasted into the roof of Manchester's net. After the match, Clough said: 'We got it right tonight'. And disappeared. S-M-I-L-I-N-G.

(Claire and Sabina, 3T)

Text B

Manchester Utd. O Nottingham Forest 3

The flowing, fast football that Forest manager Brian Clough hoped his team would play, came back last night as his team had its first victory in seven games. Their 3–0 away defeat of Manchester Utd. was the result of a verbal lashing by Clough on the practice ground. He wanted to show the skills shown before Christmas. Their teamwork was shown by a seven-man move which covered three-quarters of the field, resulting in the first goal from Nigel Clough, ever alert, from just outside the penalty area. By contrast, Manchester Utd. were disappointing. Their football was dull on a night which saw Forest shine.

(Claire and Sabina, 3T)

Sabina and Claire show an impressive knowledge of how language varies along a continuum of written reports according to different intended readerships. Their knowledge of the different grammars of formal (closer to written) and informal (closer to spoken) is demonstrated in particular uses of language. For example:

Text A

- linkage is mainly by temporal conjunctions or adverbials (e.g. 'after that'; 'after the match')
- verbs are preferred to nouns
- adjectives are in a mainly predicative position
- clauses are mainly chained by conjunctions
- the text is lexically less dense than Text B

Text B

- linkage occurs by lexical cohesion and by formal contrastive adjuncts (e.g. 'by contrast')
- nominalisations occur (e.g. 'victory'; 'result'; 'contrast'; 'defeat')
- there is more use of adjectives in an attributive position
- clauses are in places elliptical and non-finite (e.g. 'shown before Christmas'; Nigel Clough, ever alert'; resulting in the first goal').

There are also vocabulary differences between the two texts, with Text A exhibiting appropriately informal word choices.

It is thus not always helpful to see spoken and written language in terms of polarities. The pupil's writing underlines what Deborah Tannen (1982) has termed 'the oral/literate continuum in discourse' – the overlaps and continuities that occur between speech and writing. This continuum is also sharply focused in the uses of punctuation, a point noted by Chafe (1986):

Since intonation units are identified in the first instance by prosodic criteria (pitch contours and hesitations), and since written language is notoriously impoverished so far as its representation of prosody is concerned, we might wonder how anything analogous could appear in writing. Behind that question lies another that is more interesting: Do writers (and readers) have intonation in mind at all, or is written language a kind from which all prosodic features have been removed?

It is the overlaps and continuities between speech and writing which contribute to the different uses of punctuation in the two texts. In Text B the writers show a sound knowledge of some conventional rules of punctuation. In particular, the girls use commas to considerable effect (e.g. 'Nigel Clough, ever alert') and to signal the reflective 'pause' which occurs after an adversative adjunct placed at the beginning of a clause (e.g. 'By contrast').

References to pauses indicates the close relationship between punctuation in writing and the representation of speech. In Text A Claire and Sabina have produced a report which is markedly more interactive. This is done in a number of ways including question/answer sequences, quotation and a kind of creative indirect speech which takes the reader into the mind of the main protagonist (e.g. 'What was it now?'). Claire and Sabina attempt to involve the reader by using punctuation to try to mark suspenseful pauses, to stress individual words and to dramatise events. Such involvement is achieved by commas:

Nottingham Forest are, back . . .
. . . all the team needed was, a bit . . .
But, . . .

as well as by capitals

. . . they WERE playing

and a playful invention with both grammar and punctuation:

And disappeared.

and with word shaping:

S-M-I-L-I-N-G

All these features indicate less attention to the content of the football match reports and more attention to interpersonal involvement. The girls make a fascinating effort to compensate for the contextual and prosodic impoverishment of writing and try to help the reader with the kind of temporal, spatial and logical relations which, in speaking, might be signalled more by the context, if not by prosody and gesture.

However, for the teacher there is a difficulty. Clearly some inventive uses of punctuation are more allowable than others. The play with word shape and capitalisation might be fostered; but the placing of a comma between a main finite verb and a complement (i.e. 'Nottingham Forest are, back . . .') is too close a reproduction of the stress and rhythm of speech to be tolerated by the conventions of written language and offends against a core rule of written representation which it would be unduly relativistic to deny.

Pupils/students who are able to reflect on, comment on (analyse where necessary) and produce such texts are likely to be approaching a model of literacy which is rich, sensitive to contextual variation and genuinely functional. It is rich, in my view, because it above all recognises and does not attempt to suppress the coexistence of spoken and written modes. See also Stubbs (1980, 1987); McCarthy (1991); Nunan (1994); Hammond (1990); Perera (1990) and with particular reference to grammar and standard English Woods, (1995); Wilkinson, (1995).

4 CONCLUSION

This chapter has focused on only one aspect of what we need to know in order to help our pupils learn more about language and literacy. It is hoped that the focus on spoken and written language can, however, be read as symptomatic and as illustrative of the complex relationship between knowledge about language, on the part of teachers and students, and literacy skills. As with many areas of language knowledge we need to know more and to communicate that knowledge better outside a narrow professional audience. In our teaching we need to continue to explore the central functions of spoken and written language in society, to look more closely at language itself and in particular at the tendencies to privilege written language and grammars of writing in models of literacy.

> All the scholars whose work I have cited point out that literate traditions do not replace oral. Rather when literacy is introduced, the two are superimposed upon and intertwined with each other. Similarly no individual is 'oral' and 'literate'. Rather, people use devices associated with both traditions in various settings.
>
> (Tannen, 1982: 3–4)

There is a need to continue to describe and account for the more dynamic, interpersonal and reciprocal functions of spoken language grammars. It is also necessary to continue to explore in our teaching the best ways in which to make such matters explicit for pupils and students so that they feed productively into enhanced skills in using language, the standard language in particular.

The more we reflect on spoken, written and standard language and on the discourses of society which produce language and views of language the stronger our own frameworks become for analysing, supporting and developing students' language and literacy. It requires, in spite of many publicly voiced arguments to the contrary, a constant recognition that language varies and changes, and is always, with reference to its place in education, best studied and developed in relation to real *texts* created in real human contexts by real people, not decontextualised or anaesthetised or invented single-sentence examples. As Raymond Williams put it in *Marxism and Literature* (1977: 31): 'A definition of language is always, implicitly or explicitly, a definition of human beings in society.'

Pupils' and students' understandings of such properties and functions can only be properly supported by explicit contrasts and comparisons between standard and non-standard and between spoken and written forms. It has also been argued in this chapter that there are dangers if an overwhelming emphasis on written versions of standard English prevails and if the development of knowledge about language becomes non-comparative and non-contrastive, with notions of continua regarded as peripheral rather than central. But we should not be surprised by this since a main meaning of 'standard' is uniform, and marching in uniform and standardised linguistic steps is part of a discourse of a national English-language curriculum in which there are tendencies to deny variety and difference. A single, unchangeably correct, authoritative English grammar based on the proper formalities of the written word reinforces that establishment (see Crowley, 1989: see also Chapters 1 and 3 of this volume).

Such an 'establishment' is neatly illustrated by the quotation from Michael Bakhtin, which heads this chapter, about the connection between social and cultural power and the homogenising and purifying tendencies of a centralist and standardising process in the formation of a national language. At the risk of repetitiveness, it is necessary to reassert the need for us all to interrogate such discourses and what they reveal about the continuities between spoken and written English. (For a more extended treatment of a wider range of 'keywords', see Carter, 1995.) More fundamentally still, the more teachers and students know about speech and writing as systems of language organisation and language function, the better will they be able to manipulate those systems as users of standard English.

This chapter is an extensively revised version of a paper entitled 'Standard Englishes in speech and writing' previously published in Hayhoe, M. and Parker, S. (eds) Who Owns English? (Open University Press, Milton Keynes, 1994).

5

DISCOURSE LITERACY: REWORDING TEXTS, REVISING DISCOURSE

1 INTRODUCTION

In this chapter a view and version of literacy is proposed and argued for which goes beyond most traditional accounts of literacy. The chapter asks what it means to be literate and argues that a main goal in the full development of literacy should be the achievement of discourse literacy. Discourse literacy is a competence fluently and accurately to read and write extended texts and also involves a capacity for active reconstruction and deconstruction of texts. A main related argument is that a language user who is discourse literate has a simultaneous capacity for seeing through language (Carter and Nash, 1990) in two main senses: a capacity to see through language to the ways in which we can be manipulated and in varying degrees controlled by language; and a capacity to see through language in the more active and dynamic sense of creating a vision in and with language, a capacity for constant vision and revision which empowers the user to engage with and, where necessary, to redirect society's discourses and to articulate one's personal position as a subject within those discourses.

There is thus in this chapter discussion of the nature of writing and reading as discourse practices, the role of writing and reading pedagogy in the construction of knowledge and an exploration of the 4Rs of literacy as **recognition, response, reflection** and **revision**, a developmental process of literacy acquisition which moves from a recognition of language as decontextualised form to engagement with language both as discoursally contextualised text and as a meaning-making resource for re-vision or seeing the world differently. In the course of this exploration there is a particular focus on processes of writing.

The notion of texts is interpreted broadly but I argue that a selective engagement with canonical literary texts should be basic to the development of discourse literacy. The chapter also discusses a key methodological procedure – that of rewriting texts – which lays a basis for teaching discourse literacy.

The other main argument is one in keeping with a theme of this book: that discourse analysis is interpreted in two main senses. Discourse analysis in this chapter means the analysis of stretches of language beyond the limits of the sentence and the conversational turn; and it means the analysis and interpretation of language use not just as *reference* but also as *representation*. In other words, language is seen as a means of communication in which words are used to refer to a concrete and commonsense world and it is also seen as as a mode of communication in which a speaker or writer's attitudes and stance towards that world is represented in terms of how they are positioned within a discourse community. In that process commonsense understanding may be displaced or at least relativised and questioned.

1.1 Writing, reference and representation: a case study

The above introduction is likely to appear unduly abstract without exemplification. In the following case study, which is drawn from a language research project at the University of Nottingham undertaken in connection with the National Curriculum for England and Wales, the view of language and literacy outlined above is given a more concrete illustration in the form of pieces of writing undertaken by a 15-year-old girl, Rachel. The pieces of writing which follow are two drafts produced in connection with a class project to devise an anti-smoking campaign. The writing was to form part of a class news-sheet on the dangers of smoking. Rachel undertook to write an article for the news-sheet. Draft 2 was written after Draft 1 and was produced after consultation by Rachel with her teacher who provided specific comments on the first draft and after discussion with members of the group of which Rachel was a part and who were working on other aspects of the publicity campaign.

Draft 1

There are many reasons why people should not smoke.

I think people often smoke because it makes them look cool, as in an advertisement or because they feel insecure at parties and in places like that. They don't think of other people only of themselves because they can damage their health.

Smoking can damage your health. I read in the newspaper that there are a lot of deaths in Britain (not just lung cancer) because people smoke too much. I would ban it in all public places because children get influenced. Teachers should not smoke in school. Some of our teachers do.

Research demonstrates that smoking can cut your life expectation quite dramatically. Your lungs clog up and breathing problems occur.

These are some of the reasons why people shouldn't smoke.

Draft 2

Until recently, smoking was more normal in public places. Now there is public awareness that smoking can damage your and other's health. It is dangerous and anti-social.

Research demonstrates that a number of diseases are caused by smoking. It is thought that smoking results in lung cancer but other serious illnesses including heart attacks are caused by smoking as well. Great Britain has one of the highest death rates anywhere in the world for smoking.

Advertisers must be blamed. I think people often smoke because it makes them look like actors in television or newspapers advertisements. Those people that smoke at parties because they feel nervous must also realise how much they damage others. I would also question whether people take notice of the warnings advertisers put on cigarette packets and advertisements. In colour advertisements advertisers are too clever and find ways of drawing our attention. I also feel strongly that teachers must set a good example in schools. They should not smoke in front of pupils.

These are some reasons why people shouldn't smoke.

1.2 Writing drafts: a linguistic commentary

As a genre, argumentation is a complex undertaking and an advanced literacy skill (Andrews, 1995). Argumentation is a mode of language organisation which is second only to narrative in its closeness to speech and there are innumerable arguments that are all the stronger for being rooted in personal experience and which contain a clear, personal voice; on the other hand, some examples of argument benefit from greater impersonal advocacy. Indeed, many successful arguments mix personal and impersonal modes. At all levels the writing of arguments involves the necessary shaping and reshaping of ideas in relation to different language choices and makes drafting a set of teaching and learning procedures which most classroom writers and their teachers readily regard as supportive (Harris, 1994; Abraham, 1995). Drafting is therefore bound to be central to the writing of arguments and Rachel was encouraged by her teacher to undertake such rewriting.

It is clear from the above examples that the process of drafting has helped Rachel to formulate a clearer and more cogent argument. In the progression from one draft to another the following linguistic features can be noted:

1 Draft 2 has a greater balance between personal and impersonal language use. Draft 1 contains many personal pronouns; in Draft 2 personal statements are combined with impersonal passive constructions (e.g. 'heart attacks are caused by smoking'; 'It is thought that . . .'. Other more 'impersonal' uses of language include non-animate subjects 'Research demonstrates . . .' – also in Draft 1 – and 'Great Britain has . . .'. Draft 2 also contains a greater number of grammatical metaphors (e.g. public awareness; death rates; illness) imparting a more written, more specialised, even more authoritative character to the text (Halliday, 1989, 1994).

2 Draft 2 has more packing of information in expanded noun phrases which act as subjects and objects of clauses. For example:

> Those people that smoke at parties because they feel nervous must also . . .

> . . . the warnings [that] advertisers put on cigarette packets and advertisements.

Such patterns create a more writerly presentation as a result of both greater lexical density and structural economy while at the same time conferring greater variety on the overall style. In a related way there is overall greater clausal variety in Draft 2 compared with Draft 1 which has an over-reliance on patterns of main followed by subordinate clause (e.g. 'People often smoke because . . .'). Draft 2 is not wholly writerly in character, however, since the mixing of personal and impersonal and more speakerly and writerly modes does not produce shorter, less intricate clauses across the whole text.

3 Draft 2 has an improved generic organisation and a more staged sequencing of ideas. The first paragraph contextualises the situation; the second paragraph presents a series of facts and general truths; the third paragraph presents a personal viewpoint organised almost exclusively around the theme of smoking and advertising. In fact, Draft 2 may be considered more powerful as a result of the strong personal statement being placed in a single paragraph after a more impersonal and factual case has been established. The changes do not appear to cause Rachel to lose her own personal voice.

There is of course no single correct way to present an argument, nor any set of linguistic structures which exist in a precise, one-to-one correlation with such a genre of writing. There are, however, patterns and tendencies and Rachel can continue to be supported through further drafts and further reflection on, for example: the development of conclusions; variation in the use of linking words and discourse signals; the use of narrative examples embedded within arguments; greater use of grammatical metaphor, where appropriate. And so on.

1.3 Writing drafts: rewriting, revising and reformulating knowledge

Much recent research into writing processes confirms the value inherent in drafting and redrafting texts as exemplified by Rachel through her revised choices of language. Several researchers have also, however, been at pains to stress that drafting is not simply a post-hoc editorial process, concerned only to make things clearer for the intended readership, important though that is. For Bereiter and Scardamalia (1987: 10) the writing process is one

> in which the thoughts come into existence through the composing process itself, beginning as inchoate entities and gradually, by dint of

much rethinking and restating, taking the form of fully developed thoughts.

Such a position challenges fundamentally the assumption that ideas pre-exist language, the notion that language is no more than an empty container waiting to be filled with content and meaning and the idea that writing is merely an act of transcription. Rachel's drafts in fact illustrate clearly that she is in a dialogue with her texts, working with meanings which have developed so far and making language choices as part of the formulation, refinement and extension of thought. Rachel's revisions to her text are also in one sense re-visions in that new insights and new propositional connections come into being as part of the writing process. The teacher who helped Rachel with her drafting has stimulated reflection and language awareness, which has kept Rachel at the centre of her text, responsible for a meaning-making process which involves extending organisational patterns of discourse alongside extending ideational expression.

Let us summarise here the view of literacy which has emerged from this examination of Rachel's writing. First, Rachel is in command of basic forms of **recognition literacy**, as it is termed by Hasan (1996a, 1996b). Basic skills of decoding and accurately reproducing words and sequences of words are in place and she is in control of most of the forms of language necessary for reading and writing as a mechanical process. Second, she is engaged in writing as an enunciating subject. She is not simply mechanically literate, playing a fixed stable role in an educational game of decontextualised reading and writing exercises. She is thus practising **response literacy** in so far as she exercises choice and responsibility in her use of discoursal patternings of words and she clearly responds to the content of the exercise by presenting ideas and feelings about the issue of smoking. She chooses to say one thing rather than another and in one sequence rather than another and her choices have consequences for the making and remaking of meanings. Her revisions are part of a process of seeing, understanding and presenting her ideas differently, even though Rachel's choices, like all our choices, are, given the elusive nature of intentions, probabilistic rather than deterministic. Third, she is engaged in **reflection literacy** (Hasan, 1996b) in so far as she has been encouraged to see meaning as a process which is subject to reformulation. She can stand back from herself as a writer, become conscious of alternative forms of expression and yet still not lose the sense of herself as an author or of the genre in which she is writing. She recognises that reading and writing are not necessarily monologic and isolated but are part of a dialogic interaction which is social and contextual in origin.[1]

In her increasing command of **recognition, response** and **reflection literacy**, Rachel is developing greater control over language and over language as discourse. For many researchers on literacy and for many literacy teachers Rachel will develop to fuller literacy competence by means of procedures which add in more components of recognition and reflection. There are undoubted benefits in this progression from recognition to reflection literacy and the last thirty years have witnessed major extensions to the teaching of reading and writing as a result, in particular, of increasingly refined practices of reflection.

But are other practices of literacy necessary which will make writers and readers such as Rachel even more literate citizens of societies and cultures of the twenty-first century? In the next section I argue further for the notion of **revision** or, more inclusively, **discourse literacy** as a natural and necessary further development in linguistic competence of the kind exhibited by Rachel's drafts. As a first step, however, an excursion into linguistic and discourse theory is required.

2 LANGUAGE AS FORM: LANGUAGE AS CHOICE

In the twentieth century the study and analysis of language has been dominated by paradigms in which language is treated as an abstract, decontextualised phenomenon. The major theoretical influences have been provided by De Saussure and Chomsky. A primary aim has been to account for the intuitions of the language user concerning well-formed and ill-formed structures, usually structures which do not extend beyond the level of the sentence or the individual speaking turn as an upper structural limit. Many valuable theoretical and structural insights have been generated by these paradigms and the concern with the systematic analysis of form has been reflected in elegant, formal argumentation processes developed for purposes of testing hypotheses concerning the well-formedness of particular language structures as well as in developing theories which provide explanations of particular linguistic phenomena. A fundamental aim has been to subject language to the same investigative processes as are found in the natural sciences, with a main goal of producing verifiable, cognitively oriented statements of universal applicability about the nature of language and the human mind. Here is an example of the kind of sentence subjected to rigorous analysis within this structuralist and formalist paradigm:

> The men from Glasgow went for for four Forfar men to go was impossible.

The sentence clearly pushes notions of grammatical and prosodic well-formedness to the limit. However, it is an idealised sentence made up by the analyst for purposes of laboratory inspection; such a sentence would be unlikely to be heard or to occur in actual use. Idealisation of data is certainly a necessary part of all research, including research into language, but data which are too artificially contrived are at one remove too many from the descriptive and analytical remit of discourse literacy. It may be no surprise therefore that linguistics has been felt to have little to offer to those concerned with literacy education and has been subjected to radical critique by, among others, Bourdieu (1990) for a failure to recognise the social and cultural nature of meaning-making in contexts of teaching and learning. It should be said, however, that many practitioners of formalist linguistics do not even claim to be able to make such a contribution or claim that it is appropriate to linguistic study.

As Hasan (1996b) and Kress (1995) have pointed out, the fact that there is a dominant paradigm in linguistics should not and does not preclude the existence of other paradigms in theory and practice. For example, systemic-functional models of language description such as those developed by or under the influence of Michael Halliday have a more sociolinguistic focus, accounting for contextual variation and working often from data which is naturally occurring rather than data which is invented.

> We do not experience language in isolation . . . but always in relation to a scenario, some background of persons and actions and events from which the things that are said derive their meaning.
>
> (Halliday, 1978: 84)

A systemic-functional model of language aims to account not just for forms but for choices of forms and the different meanings encoded by the choice of one form rather than another.

> Systemic theory is a theory of meaning as choice, by which language . . . is interpreted as networks of interlocking options.
>
> (Halliday, 1994: xiv)

2.1 Language as discourse

A related influence of considerable significance is that of Michel Foucault, especially his notion of discourse. Foucault's view of discourse is that it is a set of historically variable determinations (Foucault, 1972). Our knowledge and beliefs, Foucault argues, are discursively produced, that is, they are not universal and unchanging but are historically and culturally shaped. As far as interpretations of texts are concerned Foucault's position is that language does not mediate reality in any simple, commonsense or transparent way. Instead language is a site through which ideologies are produced. It is not a neutral medium (see Fowler, 1991; Simpson, 1993; Fairclough, 1992a; Fairclough, 1992a; Griffiths, 1992).

Such work parallels and reinforces a view that language users should not be idealised out of existence into some otherworldly speech community where everything is ordered, regular, non-conflictual and decontextualised. As Mary Louise Pratt has argued (1987), it is important to avoid the creation of the kinds of linguistic utopias which she feels are endemic to the dominant linguistic and even some sociolinguistic paradigms:

Social difference is seen as constituted by distance and separation rather than by ongoing contact and structured relations in a shared social space. Language is seen as a nexus of social identity, but not as a site of social struggle or a producer of social relations.

(Pratt, 1987: 56)

Foucault and Bakhtin (1981) have in their different ways demonstrated that language in context involves contestation. Our models of language, especially models for the analysis of language in literature, have to take account therefore of rules which are variable according to such factors as status, power and ideology and which recognise the fact that language involves systems which are both static (decontextualised) and dynamic (contextualised), rule-bound and rule-breaking, structured and fractured. By extension, reading and writing for a student such as Rachel should include processes which involve her in cooperating with and resisting the texts with which she engages.

3 LITERATURE AND TEXT

3.1 Language, discourse and literature

A view of discourse literacy, it is argued, should embrace a capacity for engagement with all kinds of texts, including those deemed by the dominant culture to be those texts which most clearly represent that culture. It is important therefore that the theories of reading and writing literary texts should parallel the discourse-based theories necessary for the development of discourse literacy. This chapter does not allow detailed exploration of relevant positions but, in keeping with arguments developed elsewhere (see Chapters 6 and 8), the following main perspectives on the teaching and study of literature, as part of the achievement of discourse literacy, should also be adopted:

1 Linguistic and literary-linguistic formalism has a place but only a limited place in a genuinely contextualised literary studies which sees literature as embedded within social and cultural formations. Formalisms tend to remove context. There is a correspondingly dangerous, homogenising tendency to provide decontextualised readings of texts which are read by readers who are constructed as asocial and who produce, not unsurprisingly, enduringly universal, eternal meanings for the texts they read. Language is not neutral and readings cannot be neutral and disinterested.

2 The exploration of language as variation has led to a recognition that there is a continuum between literature with a small 'l' (McRae, 1991) and literature with a capital 'L', that literariness in its variable forms can be read into a range of texts and that it is now theoretically tenable for jokes, advertising language, government warnings on cigarette packets, proverbs and political rhetorics to be analysed alongside a Shakespearean sonnet or an opening to a novel by Jane Austen, with the term 'text' serving as the

suitably inclusive category. Deviation and play with linguistic norms are not exclusively confined to what a community designates a literary text.

3 For this purpose a more socially-based linguistics of the kind developed within a functional theory of language has potential in the context of more fully integrated language and literary discourse studies. Such a linguistic paradigm stresses forms, choices and meanings, and not just forms. It also stresses that linguistics has to learn from poetry, not just poetry from linguistics. An argument close to the one advanced here is, by the way, to be found in David Birch's book *Language, Literature and Critical Practice* (Birch, 1989).

3.2 Critical language awareness: critical reflection

It will, I hope, be clear that models of language rooted in functional perspectives and in theories of language as discourse provide a basis for the development of a literacy practice which can lead to greater awareness of language and language use in relation to social and cultural contexts. Here is not the place to exemplify in detail work in critical language awareness or knowledge about language, but one next step in the development of **reflection literacy** is to foster insights into the workings of texts and into the ways in which language represents and encodes in texts different orders of reality. Language awareness has been traditionally conceived of as a reading practice and students have been encouraged to notice the part played by language in the mediation of meanings, usually meanings which are concealed between or behind the lines of a text (Carter, 1990b; Van Lier, 1995).

One brief example must suffice to summarise the nature of work in critical language awareness which has developed exponentially during the past five years in both mother-tongue and second- or foreign-language education. The example is a few representative lines taken from the presidential inaugural address given by George Bush in 1988:

> We know what works. Freedom works. We know that's right.
> Freedom's right ... We have a deficit to bring down. We have more will than wallet. But will is what we need ... We will do what we have to do. What we have always done we will continue to do.

There are number of stylistic features in this short extract which require to be seen through. Particularly striking is Bush's use of repetition. The extract shows him, or rather his speech writers, repeating individual lexical/grammatical words (*will*), key grammatical words such as pronouns (*we*) and specific syntactic structures such as verb phrases in object or complement position (e.g. *what we need*). The repetition is essentially interactive and interpersonal and the use of noun or verb phrases in subject, object or complement position is designed (especially when taken alongside the contractions and personal pronouns) to sound spoken or, at least, speakerly and to confer on Bush's rhetoric a strategic intimacy, a deliberately interpersonal sharing of thoughts, needs and decisions. The lines underscore a relationship between language and ideology in so far as the verb phrases in subject and object position enable what rhetoricians term 'enthymemia' to function. Such uses of language enable Bush to sound determinate while specifying nothing. The language operates to suggest that Bush and his administration know what they are doing at the same time as they are placing the onus on others for doing it – an essential linguistic trademark of all conservatives and republicans (see WAUDAG, 1990, for more extended analysis).

It should be noted that, as with all work in critical language awareness, the interpretation cannot be objective and decontextualised and represents my own inevitably far from neutral and disinterested position as an analyst. In the context of the main argument in this chapter, it can also be noted that critical language awareness and pedagogy are concerned primarily with reading meanings into and drawing inferences from texts. There is a danger that such practices remain as no more than a set of valuably self-reflexive but potentially inert practices which may do no more than produce readers who interpret but interpret passively, without the means for critical redirection or revision of what they see through. It is important that the skills of critical interpretation of language are built upon by pedagogies that allow a more active engagement between and integration of reflection and revision literacies. Seeing through language has to be better integrated with seeing with or by means of language; discourse analysis as text deconstruction has to be allied with discourse analysis as text construction and reconstruction.

3.3 Rewriting and pedagogy

I will conclude with some observations for the teaching of English language and literature which stem from the view of language outlined so far. One of the disappointments I have felt about developments in pedagogy in this connection is that the most exciting and relevant innovations have occurred in the teaching of English, both as a mother tongue and as a foreign language, at the pre-university level; sadly, university English departments have remained ignorant of these developments or have, possibly for reasons which may have not a little to do with academic snobbery, not responded positively to them.

The best of these pedagogic practices relate organically to a functional view of language in which students of language and literature are correspondingly viewed as language users with real choices being given to them in terms of both their own deployment of language and their responses to and inter-pretation of language. Such pedagogies make use of formal, teacher-centred lectures and seminars, but only limited use of them. The main strategies are student-centred and activity-based and are therefore concerned with real rather than imagined or idealised language contexts. As much emphasis is placed on processes of interpretation, with students directly involved in the making of those interpretations, as is placed on *ex cathedra* products of interpretation transmitted by the teacher or lecturer. To support this more process-based methodology, assessment is normally by individual project – a procedure which encourages exploratory and investigative approaches to texts, contexts and meanings. Finally, the classroom character of such practices is frequently that of work in groups and pairs, reinforcing the interactive and dialogic nature of the underlying view of language.

The pedagogic example is of a classroom procedure which is generally known as rewriting. The basic tactic with re-writing is for the teacher to transform or for the teacher to create the conditions under which students transform a text by creating alternative phrasings. The alternative phrasings can involve substituting new words, replacing or modifying grammatical structures, even constructing an alternative, contrasting genre. The main principle is that of producing a counter-text in which the rewriting is viewed or practised as writing against, with or across the grain of the original. The overall aim is to explore the play of differences in and around the text, to examine its frames of **reference** in order better to understand the frames of **preference** chosen for the text by its writer or writers.

In other words, by displacing and reconstructing the text, the theory goes, we come to know the original text better. It is a pedagogic practice rooted in the notion of linguistic choices and their consequences. It is therefore close to Halliday's view of language as social semiotic as well as close to Bakhtin's framing of the always potentially multiple voices and dialogic wordings in language and text. It is also close to the sentiments expressed in Brecht's poem 'On Judging':

> You should show what is; but also
> In showing what is you should suggest what could be
> And is not and might be successful.

> (Bertolt Brecht, *Poems 1913–1956*)

(For an extended treatment of a range of related and interrelated methodologies, see Maley, 1993.)

The process can be illustrated with reference to three main examples: a stanza from a poem by Thomas Hardy ('After a Journey'), the Bush inaugural extract and two health warnings taken from cigarette packets purchased in Britain. The last example takes us back, directly and indirectly, to the anti-smoking campaign leaflet produced by Rachel and described at the beginning of this chapter. The texts are listed below:

(1) Hereto I come to view a voiceless ghost;
> Whither, o whither will its whim now draw me?
Up the cliff, down, till I'm lonely, lost,
> And the unseen waters' ejaculations awe me.

84

Where you will next be there's no knowing,
    Facing round about me everywhere,
With your nut-coloured hair,
    And gray eyes, and rose-flush coming and going.
                    (Thomas Hardy, 'After a Journey')

(2) We know what works. Freedom works. We know that's right.
Freedom's right . . . We have a deficit to bring down. We have more
will than wallet. But will is what we need . . . We will do what we
have to do. What we have always done we will continue to do.
                    (George Bush, Presidential Inaugural, 1988)

(3) (a) H.M. Government Health Warning
SMOKING CIGARETTES CAN SERIOUSLY DAMAGE
YOUR HEALTH

(b) 5 mg TAR 0.5 mg NICOTINE
SMOKING CAUSES CANCER
Health Department's Chief Medical Officer

In the case of the poem by Hardy, substituting in key places a more markedly
written, non-dialectal style or transforming the text into formal poetic diction
throughout generates contrasts which would undoubtedly sharpen perceptions
of the functions and effects of the original lexical mixing or 'heteroglossia', to
use Bakhtin's term, in which formal words like 'ejaculation', poetic phrases
'hereto', 'whither, o whither' and colloquial structures 'there's no knowing' sit
alongside each other, encoding a kind of dissolution of the self among the
heterogeneity of words.

Rewriting the quotations from the Bush inaugural can have similar pedagogic outcomes. For example, substituting the pronoun 'you' for 'we' has an
immediately radicalising effect on the interpersonal character of the original
text. It exposes the use of 'we' to suggest an inclusive common purpose, a
subtle and possibly deliberately deceptive sense of shared values. Similarly,
reconstructing the grammar so that there are no structural repetitions, or so
that the verb phrases no longer occupy grammatically prominent subject and
complement positions, serves to deconstruct the common tactic of those in
power and authority to remove agency and responsibility for action from themselves to more impersonal forces. For example, the insertion of the verb 'to
be' and a first person pronoun forces the speaker to construct structures in
which the nature of action has to be specified.

As a final example, the grammar of the two health warnings against the
dangers of smoking can be rewritten in parallel ways. Thus, altering the modal
verb 'can' to 'may' or removing the word 'seriously' in example (a) or in
example (b) by substituting the universal present tense 'causes' – which
functions to convey an immutable truth – with a modal form such as 'can'

cause or 'may' cause or 'will' cause enables students to play with textual difference and variation in order better to understand the original textual choices.

In social and cultural terms the two texts already exist as points of historical contrast; indeed the contrasts are discoursally determined since the latter warning contains the wording now required by European law. The reader is positioned differently in relation to the authority and information structure of the message. The texts are good examples of the way in which texts change in all respects but most significantly in terms of variations in the grammar which result from changes in the discourses that produce them (space precludes comment on the visual semiotics of the use of factual information such as the data concerning nicotine content and so on). These examples are selected because they are on the edge of thematic and social sensitivities. In many contexts of teaching less controversial subject matter may be selected; newspaper headlines; reports of national sporting events; warnings on products (which encourage greater use of the product) may be preferred.

All the examples here provide opportunities in the teaching situation for students to learn actively to engage with the theories and practices of textual creation and production. Exercises in rewriting are just one example of activity-based, student-centred and process-oriented procedures which allow students to discover things for themselves, with responses to and analysis of language at the basis of the discovery. All the examples illustrate, I hope, that aspects of theory developed by Bakhtin and Foucault and others as well as theories of language choice and variation as social semiotic may be best introduced first in the context of writing workshops, in which reconstruction *precedes* deconstruction.

Such workshops do not, of course, replace lectures and seminars but pedagogically they might usefully be antecedent to them more often than tends to be the case at present. Further examples of this kind of approach to language and literary studies are provided by Nash (1986), Durant and Fabb (1990), Carter and Nash (1990), Widdowson (1992) and McRae (1991). The examples of the different wordings on cigarette packets are derived from a textbook devoted to text reconstruction activities (Pope, 1994). The books cited here all contain exercise material which, by contrast, underlines how some conventional practice in critical awareness may produce passive readers, focused only on the words on the page and not beyond. These textbooks aim instead to make readers more active, often by helping them write their way into reading more fully. Examples of rewritten texts and outlines for rewritings are provided in Appendix 1, p.88.

As a footnote to this discussion, let me say that I am not advocating the replacement of the literary canon with a new textual world of cigarette packets. For those who wish to concentrate exclusively on literary texts as traditionally constituted, one good example of what I have been saying is to take texts such as those by Yeats and Auden for example which have been rewritten *by the writers themselves* and to explore the linguistic and textual differences in the light of changes in the writers' own belief and value systems as well as in the light of changes in the social and cultural contexts in which they are differentially embedded. For Yeats, the changes resulted from quite radical changes in his view of what constituted poetic language. I do, however, believe that the teaching of literature, even as traditionally conceived, is all the richer for taking an inclusive rather than an exclusive view of texts, by setting one text against another and by seeing literary language as a continuum with a wide range of texts available for interpretation on account of patterning and play in the uses of language (see also Carter and Long, 1991; Cook, 1992; McCarthy and Carter, 1994).

3.4 Rewriting texts, reconstructing the world

Let us finally return to Rachel and to one example of the rewritings undertaken by Rachel in connection with her campaign leaflet:

(a) H.M. Government warns that your freedom may be in danger if you heed too closely medical warnings about the relationship between cancer and smoking.

(b) The Health Department's Chief Medical Officer wants you to know that smoking causes cancer but that it is also medically proven that smoking can be a cause of relaxation and pleasure to many people.

It would represent an extreme form of naive romanticism to claim that Rachel is socially empowered on account of her ability to rewrite the warnings on cigarette packets. There is a sense in which language alone cannot remake social realities. But Rachel has the advantage of having directly and actively experienced the remaking of a text which may have been thought unalterable; she has remade the text for herself and in her own voice; she has understood that meanings can be reconstructed and alternative worlds envisioned by altering the position from which things are seen; and she has challenged a position of authority by expressing in the process the feelings of many of her peer group who are regular smokers and whose views have been revealed to be different from those of the teacher with whom they were working and who controlled the nature and limits of the task of producing an anti-smoking campaign leaflet. Rachel isn't simply reproducing generic knowledge – vital though that is – (and she will need to go on learning to do it better by developing greater control over discoursal-generic patterns); she is also transforming knowledge, putting it to more active, critical and challenging use. As Michael Halliday (1996: 357) has put it: 'To be literate is not only to participate in the discourse of an information society; it is also to resist it, to defend oneself – and others – against that discourse.'

And Rachel has taken the first important steps towards becoming discourse literate. She has practised revision as a discourse process and as a process of contestation which potentially transforms the way she is positioned as a subject within discourses. By learning to be a more active, non-cooperative, resisting subject she is beginning to think more critically for herself.

4 CONCLUSION

This chapter has sought to bring together several of the main themes of the book and these can be listed here without the sense either of certainty or finality which conclusions conventionally confer.

1 Language and literature can be integrated in the English curriculum; the marriage of language and literature is more likely to be succesful if language is viewed as social discourse and if too great a degree of formalism in theory and in analytical practice is eschewed and if a more inclusive principle of text selection is adopted. In this connection it is important to recognise continuities rather than discontinuities between what a community decides is literary and non-literary. (For a historical survey see Carter and McRae, 1997.)

2 Investigating the discourses of language and literature study raises seminal questions about the nature of language and the nature of literature; the questions pertain both to theory and to classroom practice.

3 The teaching of language and literature should further develop pedagogies which relate organically to the relevant study and research paradigms. A view of language as constituted in choice and variation requires teaching which stresses choice and variation and which is process-based, activity-centred, dialogic and which, pedagogically, involves procedures such as re-writing in which textual and knowledge transformations are engaged in with the result of producing language-aware language users who not only resist what is done to them with language but who also increasingly develop a potential to become active, re-visioning readers and writers. A discourse-literate language user is able to exploit language to the full by seeing through *and* seeing with language.

This chapter has not previously been published. It is based on a plenary paper delivered at a conference on 'Language and Knowledge' at the National University of Singapore in September 1996.

APPENDIX 1: REWORDINGS, REWRITINGS, RE-VISIONS

(1) I have come to see a silent ghost
Where will its whim now lead me?
It will lead me up and down the cliff
Until I'm lonely and lost and the
Crash and roar of the sea awe me,
I do not know where I will see you next,
Facing all about me everywhere
     With your nut-coloured hair
And gray eyes and your growing blushes.

(2) We will do ... ; We will continue to do ...; What works is ...;
Freedom is ...

(3) (a) H.M. Government warns that your freedom may be in danger
if you heed too closely medical warnings about the relationship
between cancer and smoking.

    (b) The Health Department's Chief Medical Officer wants you to
know that smoking causes cancer but that it is also medically
proven that smoking can be a cause of relaxation and pleasure
to many people.

POSTSCRIPTS AND PROSPECTS

The content embraced by the chapters in Part I of the book continues to be an area of dispute and contestation between opposing interests. In Britain debate about language and descriptions of language continue; and classroom practice continues to be monitored and evaluated, although the place of English in the National Curriculum in England and Wales has been fixed until the year 2000 by a government moratorium on further changes (see Carter, 1990a; Carter and Richmond, 1996).

One result of this moratorium has been to concentrate attention on the main informing principles of English teaching: what is the curriculum? What is it for? Who is it for? What can, should, must it be and do? Whose interests, given the complex and contradictory demands explored in Part I, are likely to be best represented and why?

Fundamental research has yet to be undertaken into key questions such as the relationship between teaching knowledge *about* grammar and standard English and the extent to which enhanced performance in language use ensues from such a practice. Major longitudinal studies are needed to explore such a relationship. However, descriptive linguistic studies have clarified our understanding of the nature of spoken English grammar and its relationship to spoken standard English – a relationship which figures centrally in the latest parliamentary order governing the teaching of English in England and Wales (DfE/WO, 1995) and which has repercussions for oracy development and for language study in relation to standard English in many different parts of the world. And underlying many recent developments and debates is an increasing recognition of the centrality of a view of *language as discourse*.

In this postscript and account of prospects the relevance of two main meanings of language as discourse are to the fore: discourse as a social construction of reality in which there is a clear relationship between political power, ideology and consequent constraints both on language use and on how language use is interpreted; and discourse as a level of language description which facilitates an analysis of the language of complete texts. The following topics are therefore considered:

90

1 STANDARD ENGLISH: SPOKEN AND WRITTEN DISCOURSE

Descriptive research into spoken English discourse has begun to feed further into discussions concerning the nature of standard English and to refine understanding of differences and distinctions between spoken and written English and, in particular, spoken and written standard English. In Chapter 4 a range of different grammatical features, based on LINC data, were described. Research undertaken as part of the CANCODE project at the University of Nottingham has enabled further data to be explored: this confirms the existence of forms of English which belong standardly to standard spoken English but which are not normally found in written discourse and so are not normally codified in descriptions of standard English grammar.

CANCODE stands for Cambridge Nottingham Corpus of Discourse in English. At the time of writing, the project (which is supported and © by Cambridge University Press) has assembled almost five million words of spoken English from a variety of different speech situations with speakers drawn from different parts of Great Britain and with due attention given in corpus construction to representative sociolinguistic profiles such as gender, age, class and social context.

The following list of forms gives some idea of the data collected and the extent to which its 'non-standardness' needs to be questioned, for the forms are used routinely across the country and in a range of speech contexts. By definition, therefore, such forms should be admitted into our routine descriptions of standard English. It is all too easy to dismiss such findings as nonstandard dialectal variants but such data cannot be dialectal if they are not regionally or socially restricted. For further discussion of the main research findings to date see Carter and McCarthy (1995, 1997) and McCarthy and Carter (1995). The forms listed here are only a small sample from a much larger corpus but they illustrate nonetheless the extent to which standard English, as a description based mainly on written data and on formal contexts of spoken usage, may need to be redefined and reaccented.

1. *Ellipsis* in its various forms is pervasive in spoken discourse. Ellipsis involves a deletion of core grammatical forms such as articles, subject pronouns, generic 'you', main and auxiliary verbs:

91

Sounds terrible, doesn't it
Better go up and put a skirt on
Don't need to go through Skipton now
No decent vegetables in the shop this week

2. *Tails* are common markers of interpersonal affect, stressing a proposition and/or signalling to a listener that it is significant. Tails (in bold) in any form are extremely rare in written English:

I'm going to vote for Jeff **I am**
It's a very nice wine **that**
She'll be the best person for that job **will Jenny**

3. *Heads* also signal a marked degree of affect and create a similar effect to tails, although they function more to orientate a listener to what will follow and to establish shared frames of reference. Heads (in bold) are common in spoken but are very rare in written discourse:

Carol, this friend of mine, she'll be able to find a flat for you
The man over there in the green uniform, he's got the documentation you need

4. *Word order* is differently inflected in speech and writing, particularly in reported speech structures: for example, wh-clefts are more widespread in spoken English in use:

What fascinates me with that is the way it's rolled
That's what she said was the biggest shock

In this connection it is interesting to note how frequent are the references to spoken standard English in the latest documents guiding the teaching of English for the National Curriculum in England and Wales. For example:

In order to participate confidently in public, cultural and working life, pupils need to be able to speak . . . standard English fluently and accurately. (DfE/WO, 1995: 2)

Pupils' . . . use of standard English should be developed by involvement in activities that . . . demand the grammatical constructions of spoken standard English. (DfE/WO, 1995: 12)

Pupils should be taught to be fluent, accurate users of (spoken) standard English grammar. (DfE/WO, 1995: 18)

A number of issues surround the teaching of standard English in schools and they can be formulated as three main questions. The questions are posed with particular reference to schools and to the language situation of Great Britain but related questions can be posed in relation to most educational contexts in which there are socially significant continua between standard and non-standard discourse:

How far should standard English be taught in schools?

How far should spoken standard English be differentiated from written standard English and what are the consequences of any differentiation for teaching and learning?

What kinds of language study are most likely to foster competence in and critical awareness of the uses of standard English?

Curriculum documents are right to stress the importance of standard written English. It consists of a set of forms which are used with only minimal variation in written English and in a range of formal spoken contexts of use around the world. Such forms constitute the basis for the teaching of English internationally. Because of its provenance in writing, the dialect of standard English has a wider vocabulary range than many non-standard English dialects, thus affording more choice in the expression of verbal meanings. Standard English should therefore be taught and, where appropriate, taught explicitly, for not to learn to write standard English is to be seriously disadvantaged and disempowered.

As we saw in Chapter 4 (p.56), historically and socially, standard English in Britain is a dialect but it is a dialect which has invested in it considerable power and prestige. Standard English is a social dialect in that it is spoken by a restricted social group, by most calculations between 12 and 15 per cent of the population, most of whom occupy positions at the top of the socioeconomic scale. Standard English has a limited number of native speakers. And this leads directly into the second main question above.

The issue here is that to become a *speaker* of standard English is to become a speaker of a clearly marked, socially symbolic dialect; and a long tradition of sociolinguistic research suggests that whatever the teacher may do in the classroom and whatever the overall implications for assessment, children will not learn a dialect associated with a group with which they do not wish to be associated. By contrast, it is clear too that the minority of pupils who are already speakers of standard English as a social dialect are unfairly advantaged. Standard English can, of course, be spoken with any regional accent.

The shift from non-standard to standard spoken dialect can also become one which implies a devaluation of one dialect (and the identity derived from its use) in favour of another; and teachers know at first hand the consequences that there can be for some students, particularly those at an early age, in any attempt to replace the language of home and local community, for the complex dynamic of identity, values and self-confidence can be at the same time affected by any such replacement. The pedagogic reality for many has been well described by Perera:

> Pupils who speak non-standard English do so not because they are unintelligent or because they have not been well-taught, but because it is the variety of English used all the time by their family and friends.

Any assessment of spoken English, therefore, which gives undue weight to Standard English, is measuring not the school's effectiveness, not the pupil's ability, but their social background.

(1993: 10)

The achievement of competence in standard English, it is strongly argued by many teachers, is best brought about on the basis of pupils' understanding of and respect for their existing language competences and on the basis of teachers' respect for and interest in those varieties. Such is the centrality of standard English to the latest British National Curriculum documents that it is presented as if there neither were nor should be contaminating connections with other varieties of the language. It is presented as a curiously pure and disinfected domain of language study and it is presented insistently; political emblem overrides classroom realities and the discourses of 'verbal hygiene' (Cameron, 1995) prevail.

The situation is complicated further when the precise nature of spoken standard English remains to be more fully clarified and defined and when there is an absence of evidence from spoken data in our standard grammars and reference authorities. It is unduly ironic in this context that there should be so much emphasis on spoken standard English in National Curriculum and that pupils should be assessed on their ability to speak it, when so little appears to be known about what exactly it is. There is little doubt, however, that much is to be gained from a recognition that standard spoken and standard written English are in important respects different.

Professional discussions of grammar among English teachers have advanced considerably during the last ten years. The majority of English teachers now accept the need for grammar to be treated more extensively in the classroom, though few teachers believe in a return to formal decontextualised grammar teaching of the kind practised in the classrooms of the 1950s. Several teachers have energetically embraced the principles of 'new' grammar teaching of the kind outlined in Chapter 2. Considerable reservations are therefore expressed concerning the revised curriculum orders (DfE/WO, 1995) in which only standard English grammar is emphasised, the fact that standard English grammar forms a major component of language study and the fact that the main focus is on decontextualised grammatical structures rather than on grammar in texts and in contexts of use.

Many teachers argue that the study of grammar is best undertaken with reference to varieties of English, spoken and written, and with reference to texts and contexts which most children encounter or use in their daily lives. Indeed, they argue that standard English grammar is best taught and more likely to be successfully acquired by developing conscious awareness of non-standard grammars, not by denying that such grammars exist nor, by implication, by devaluing the large majority of those who employ them.

(For extensive methodological exemplification see Bain *et al.*, 1992; Woods, 1995; Wilkinson, 1995.)

2 VERBAL HYGIENE: PRESCRIPTION AND VALUES

> the discourse of 'standards' is not only *available* to those who dissent from conservative views about language, it is probably the only discourse in which dissent can gain a hearing.
>
> (Cameron, 1995: 115)

An important recent publication which enriches much of the foregoing discussion is Deborah Cameron's *Verbal Hygiene* (1995). Cameron ranges widely over examples in which people attempt to control and regulate how language is used: for example, in arguments concerning 'politically correct' language, the policing by editors of particular matters of style and, in Chapter 3, the teaching of English grammar in schools.

Cameron's position in 'the great grammar debate' is not one of conventional opposition to 'ill-informed' public discourse or opposition to insistent political intervention. Instead, she links the discourses of hygiene to deeply felt *values* concerning language and what it represents for ordinary people. She recognises the success of much right-wing discourse in locating the grammar debate in relation to notions of social order and discipline, playing on the fears of many ordinary people that opposition to grammar in any form by teachers is also opposition to social and moral norms. Reservations on the part of teachers and linguists about the reinstatement of traditional grammar are directly equated in such discourses with a removal of opportunities for full literacy for all children. Indeed, their concern to teach about and show respect for non-standard language variety is seen as 'unhealthy'. In these respects Cameron's chapter links squarely with similar observations made in Chapters 1 and 3 above.

Cameron underlines how perceptions of *norms* in language and strong feelings about the need for incorrect usage to be corrected link with notions of purity and wholesomeness; as she puts it: 'Verbal hygiene and social and moral hygiene are interconnected.' Cameron's central argument is that popular understandings of language are normative, involve values, and that linguists' concern with description rather than prescription is felt to be at best over-fastidious. Those professionally concerned with language are therefore publicly perceived as abdicating responsibility for making authoritative, prescriptive statements (see Wales, 1995 for parallel arguments).

In the recent debates on the place of grammar teaching in schools Cameron argues that teachers and linguists have failed fully to understand and to engage with these very basic concerns and in particular have not understood that the prevalent discourse is a discourse of *standards* (moral, social and linguistic). She believes that the only point of entry to debate is to place teachers' understandings within such a context of standards:

> The way to intervene in public debates like the one about English grammar is not to deny the importance of standards and values but to focus critically on the particular standards and values being invoked and to propose alternatives – just as the way to change unjust laws is not to abolish all laws but to make more enlightened ones. There is nothing wrong in wanting to set standards of excellence in the use of language. Rather what is wrong is the narrow definition of excellence as mere superficial correctness.
>
> (1995: 115)

In the light of Cameron's arguments one example of the way in which debate can be stimulated with a view to altering the focus of current National Curriculum documents is for arguments to be mounted for the improvements in standards which can result from increased attention to discourse grammar and to viewing language as discourse. While not denying the importance of spelling, punctuation and certain core grammatical rules, quality in writing and in formal contexts of speaking can be demonstrated to belong much more within the rhetorical domains of cohesion and of signalling, structuring and sequencing of information between and across clauses as well as in the ability to manipulate grammatical resources at the level of complete texts and different genres. It can be relatively easily demonstrated that an exclusive attention to decontextualised sentence grammar does not deliver competence in the construction of argument or reporting or narrative patterning (see Chapters 3 and 5). An increase in standards can only be achieved by modifying National Curriculum statements so that the discoursal dimension of attention to language is more clearly prioritised.

3 ENGLISH AND OTHER LANGUAGES

The pedagogic principles and issues of identity which affect the use of non-standard spoken varieties of English are also relevant, perhaps in some cases even more acutely, in the case of speakers of languages other than English. In the curriculum imperatives to produce a conformity to standard English there is an additional underlying pressure to generate centripetal linguistic forces in which a unitary language system and its study encode political and cultural dominion.

The establishment of a National Curriculum in England and Wales might have been expected, as in a number of other countries such as Australia, to have given rise to explicit policies concerning the place of and the study of other languages than English in the schools of the nation. However, the National Curriculum in its most recent manifestation (DfE/WO, 1995;

Carter and Richmond, 1996) makes explicit legal provision only for the maintenance of the Welsh language, and that maintenance applies only in relation to the territorial national boundaries of Wales, a 'provision' which ironically removes any entitlement to Welsh on the part of pupils living outside the boundaries of Wales.

The link between language and geographical territory is a conveniently pragmatic one given the multi-ethnic and multilingual character of modern Britain, for it disallows any public support for the maintenance of languages which do not conform to this notion of a territorial unit. Punjabi cannot therefore be maintained as part of the National Curriculum because the territory of the Punjab is outside England. The equation of a national language, a nation and a national curriculum is smooth, neat and on the surface nationally unifying. Seen from the position of a native speaker of a language other than English who belongs to a community whose first language is not English, the definition serves simply to assimilate such a speaker into the mainstream of English by a process of exclusion which is linguistic *and* cultural. Once again there is an unstated discoursal connection between proper, standard English and a question of who the 'proper', 'standard' English are.

The situation described here is inscribed into the silences between the lines of the parliamentary statutes governing English in the National Curriculum. And the politically motivated enforcement of this linguistic hegemony should not in any way obscure the desire of speakers of other languages to acquire standard English as a highly significant component in their linguistic repertoire.

The main issues here have been temporarily foreclosed by the government's moratorium on further changes to the curriculum until the year 2000 but debate will continue to surround the main issues: in particular, the opportunities to see other languages as a national social and economic resource; and the opportunities for enhanced knowledge about language and cultural difference which can be both drawn directly from the linguistic realities of a multilingual society and built formally into curricular realities.

4 APPROPRIACY AND ASSIMILATIONISM: A NOTE

Terms such as *appropriate* and *competence* are widely used in work in language and education and are part of established applied linguistic orthodoxy; there have been several occasions in this book when the words 'competence' and 'appropriacy' or 'appropriateness' have been used. A number of recent studies (Fairclough, 1992c; Peirce, 1989) have argued that such terms encode sociolinguistic notions which are valuable in recognising variations in language use and in resisting uniform and absolute determinations of correctness; however, these same studies also argue that appropriateness models are in themselves ideologies. They project fictional representations of sociolinguistic realities which furthermore correspond to the partisan interests of dominant sections of society. Such models and practices serve only to impose order on processes of language development and to cooperate with the dominant academic and sociopolitical order. Such statements need to be carefully considered in the light of discussion, for example, of the kind of knowledge about language which is taught, of the extent to which standard English is taught and of the kinds of access provided for students to 'appropriate' powerful discourses such as spoken argumentation. (see note 1, p.101).

5 THE ENGLISH CURRICULUM AND THE FUTURE: TEXTS AND DIFFERENCE

The imminent millennium, coinciding with a time when revisions to the existing English curriculum for schools in England and Wales can be implemented, has stimulated several layers of critical thinking about the shape such a curriculum might assume.

In *Writing the Future* Gunther Kress (1995) articulates a vision of English teaching which engages with a number of key issues in the formation of 'discourse literacy'. The main line of Kress's argument is that, in a country like Britain, we live now in an era of 'fast capitalism', a phenomenon which has surrounded whole populations across the world with rapid changes, changes to our working practices, to our leisure patterns, our media and technologies and to our language and cultural relationships. Our post-industrial society is characterised by constant change; we therefore need to see how best to work out 'productive futures' of the kind which will enable individuals to lead fulfilling lives and at the same time to ask what role education in general and English teaching and learning in particular might play in the construction of productive futures.

The subtitle to Kress's pamphlet, produced with the National Association for the Teaching of English (NATE), is: *English and the Making of a Culture of Innovation*. At the centre of this culture is an English classroom which allows children to develop by welcoming change, by understanding and appreciating cultural difference and by engaging with a wider range of literacy practices. Throughout this process of curriculum renewal and innovation English remains a subject which provides 'the means whereby we say who we are to ourselves'.

Kress lays as equal a stress on everyday texts as on aesthetically valued, canonical texts, arguing that literacy is a social practice and that we understand ourselves and the workings of our society better by not privileging Literature with a capital 'L', however culturally salient many literary texts undoubtedly are, but by giving parallel attention to the ways in which mundane texts can shape and reshape the everyday realities which make us the kinds of social individuals we are. To this end literacy is seen as a dynamic in which individuals can engage with a changing environment by critically reading and rereading, writing and rewriting its mundane but always, for the individual, highly significant texture.

For example, Kress juxtaposes a holiday home rental notice to occupants, a passage from Shakespeare's *King Lear* and regulations for members of a mother/baby swimming club, and highlights in the grammatical choices made by the writers parallel uncertainties of address and significant fractures and discrepancies between authority, control and friendly negotiability. Kress argues that the provision of grammatical knowledge should be for the purposes of helping us evaluate and understand better what we do to others and what others do to us with language, in both aesthetically valued texts and mundane texts of the kind encountered daily. It is an argument which finds echoes in Chapters 1 and 5 of this book.

Kress also stresses the need for English teachers to engage more directly and more confidently with information technology (IT), especially the opportunities afforded by word-processing and electronic mail for reaccenting our understanding and engagement with texts as linguistic processes and products, enabling a better balance of literary and non-literary work but above all generating a new relationship with the material practices of reading and writing and the ways in which they represent realities.

For example, the practices of drafting and editing can be experientially and materially enhanced by the use of word-processing programs. At the same time Kress stresses the need for an enhanced visual literacy, not simply the development of capacities for reading television or the media, important though such practices are, but an ability to read images of various kinds for a future in which the visual at all levels and in a variety of different ways will become increasingly significant.

6 CRITICAL LITERACIES: NATIONAL AND INTERNATIONAL ENGLISHES

Freedom of choice in cultural, social, political and ethical areas depends on access to the most powerful forms of writing, the most powerful forms and genres in one's society.

(Kress, 1993)

Work in genre analysis has in recent years developed an increasingly 'critical' dimension (see Chapter 3). Such work does not neglect the linguistic-structural features of core texts in the curriculum and description of such features continues; however, literacy is seen by many genre analysts as serving social purposes, as linked to social power and as a set of skills to be taught with a critical dimension that calls into question ideological and social relations. This dimension includes a critique of progressivist, student-centred process-based writing methodologies and its more 'romantic' tendencies while also recognising the dangers of a 'reactionary' back-to-basics literacy scheme based on a fixed canon of genres.

Cope and Kalantzis (1993) contains several papers which exemplify further these positions but which also offer an enhanced 'critical' perspective in two main ways: the development in writers of a more conscious oppositional awareness of social structures with an aim of seeking to change them; and a conscious recognition that literacy practices should be explicitly directed at the political empowerment of socially oppressed groups in society, in particular by identifying the kinds of genre literacy most likely to be compatible with the needs of such groups. Related studies include Baynham (1995) and New London Group (1995) in which the contributors go beyond the structural linguistic accounts of genre to include aspects of 'multiliteracies' – a term which means 'that effective citizenship and productive work now require that we interact effectively using multiple languages, multiple Englishes, and communication patterns which cross cultural, community and national boundaries' (p. 3) and where the notion of discourse literacy is extended to include mass media, multi-media and electronic hypermedia as well as the visual, the audio and the spatial.

From a perspective of international Englishes and the relationship between new Englishes and the hegemony imposed by standard international varieties, Kandiah (1995) and Parakrama (1995) have written illuminatingly on the potential for learning from the study of the social and cultural contexts of new Englishes. Taking the example of post-colonial Sri Lanka, Kandiah recognises the situation of linguistic and cultural difference and diversity with which all concerned with critical and empowerment models of literacy engage:

> It does appear that the colonial experience, negative though its impact undoubtedly was in too many ways, also bestowed on the former colonies an unintended advantage from the point of view of making adequate responses to some of the important problems of our culturally highly complex and variegated modern world . . . these places acquired a kind of complex, multi-faceted richness that makes them better endowed laboratories . . . More particularly, out of the centuries of dialectal interaction between their indigenous cultures and what came in from outside, there emerged an interesting symbiotic nature and outlook, together with language codes (including new Englishes) and other symbolic systems that naturally evolved to handle this nature and the experience they generated. This allows the users of these codes . . . a far more experienced immediacy than is possible to the users of the codes associated with the more considerably mono-type Standard Average European culture.
>
> (Kandiah, 1995: xii–xiii)

The material described here and the research by which it is underpinned take further arguments pursued in Chapter 5 and especially Chapter 4 above.

7 FUTURE PROSPECTS: LANGUAGE, DISCOURSE AND 'ENGLISH'

1. Descriptive analyses of spoken standard and spoken non-standard forms of English have tended to polarise informal, interpersonal uses of language against the formal requirements of written discourse. There is a further related tendency for the relationship between informal discourses and both personal identity and community identification to be fore-grounded in discussion. This position has been described in the foregoing postscript, alongside the patent oversimplification of the requirement that pupils correctly use the grammar of spoken English deconstructed.

On the other hand, one area in the continua from written to spoken English discourse which has been so far neglected is the use of formal spoken English for a range of communicative purposes, extending from the establishment of a point of view to more fully developed argument. The potential dangers of relativism (Chapter 4, p.60) need to be recognised. It is unduly relativistic to claim that pupils should not be required to use spoken standard English. There are socially significant core contexts of use in which forms of spoken English are required which are very close to standard written English. Competence in these spoken forms can be empowering and can enable points of view to be expressed with sufficient clarity and cogency to get things done; by contrast, competence only in more informal modes would be inappropriate to such public discourse and disabling for those unable to use more formal modes.

Two strands of research might therefore be developed: one descriptive and one empirically based on actual classroom contexts. As well as ongoing analysis of the polarities which distinguish speech and writing as different discourses, description might engage more centrally with the continua which *link* spoken and written forms. Classroom contexts might then be identified, methodologies described and examples displayed in which pupils were engaged in speaking English, in any accent, for purposes of argu-mentation, persuasion and public discussion. Curriculum statements such as: '(Pupils) should be taught to be confident users of (spoken) standard English in formal and informal situations' (DfE/WO, 1995:18) might then be better understood. To use standard spoken English in informal situations is an imposition for many pupils and likely to be resisted by teachers and pupils alike; but such an absurd requirement should not obscure the social and cultural capital which may be derived from being a more 'confident user' of spoken standard English in appropriately formal settings.

2. Several of the above chapters have explored the role of **knowledge about language** and **language awareness** in relation to literacy

101

development. (Sinclair, 1985, contributes further insights.) In the development of pupils' knowledge about language, work on the LINC project and research in general in this domain has suggested the following main points which would all benefit from further classroom evidence and further applied research:

(a) What kinds of *experiences* most effectively prompt pupils' reflection on language and language use?

(b) What is the nature of progression in KAL? For example, should teaching about smaller units of language (e.g. vocabulary) precede teaching about larger units (structure of texts)? Should the sequence be reversed? Can smaller and larger structures of language be taught simultaneously?

(c) What is the precise relationship between *implicit* and *explicit* knowledge about language? Is the natural order always implicit before explicit or can explicit teaching deepen intuitions and unconscious awareness?

(d) What are the connections between KAL and pupils' developing language use? What areas of knowledge about language most effectively stimulate language use? What kinds of interventions by teachers most effectively support such development? At what point is whole class teaching about language effective and when is it least effective?

(e) What kinds of KAL best support and underpin different genres of writing? What kinds of metalanguage are most appropriate for pupils at different ages?

(f) What differences are there between teachers' knowledge and pupils' knowledge about language? What aspects of teachers' knowledge are best withheld, or can all kinds of linguistic and metalinguistic knowledge contribute to pupils' language development?

(g) What kinds of evidence can be obtained concerning the relationship between metalinguistic knowledge and cognitive development?

(h) Should any form of KAL (or language awareness) be a separate curriculum component or should it be embedded within the core linguistic skills of reading, writing, speaking and listening?

(i) What kinds of assessment are most appropriate for pupils' knowledge about language?

(j) What kinds of knowledge about language most appropriately support the development of critical literacies? What knowledge of specific linguistic forms should be developed? For example, is a knowledge about active and passive voice, transitivity and modality central to 'critical' language awareness? Is there a preferred order to this knowledge development?

3. The dilemma which continues to affect the formulation of an 'appropriate' discourse literacy is the same dilemma which characterises all educational movements and practices which adopt a critical social perspective. Should the awareness generated of existing literacy practices be used to

resist such practices and the positions of power which enforce them? Should critical awareness lead to engagement with these practices in order to attempt to effect fundamental change to or within them? Or is conformity to existing practices a more effective strategy? Conformity leads to assimilation and to the maintenance of the existing order but the empowered have the advantage of being differently positioned and able, should they so choose, to use that position to effect change.

In the case of spoken standard English, for example, is it a more effective strategy, on the part of teachers, to attempt to resist the obvious discrimination inscribed in British National Curriculum documents against non-standard grammar in the hope that, over time, a change of attitude will prevail in which the same kind of tolerance is shown towards non-standard grammatical forms as now generally prevails regarding non-RP (Received Pronunciation) accents? Or should pupils be encouraged by their teachers to conform to these public requirements, learning in the process how to manipulate the resources of standard spoken English for their own purposes but leaving the discoursal situation intact and unreconstructed and, conceivably, paying a price individually in the loss of a certain identity with modes of language use which are communally constructed and reinforced?

The whole relationship of language, discourse and English in the classrooms of British schools is generalisable to many other pedagogic-linguistic situations and has been summarised very effectively by Susan Brindley:

> is teaching about the transmission of sets of skills, or about encouraging children to explore their own and others' language use? A related point concerns the broader sets of values that underpin different approaches to English teaching. English teaching can be seen as providing access to powerful language forms and language practices: to Standard English, for instance, or to certain formal written genres. But what are the implications for children's sense of themselves and their personal identities? Does teaching such forms and practices actually empower children, or serve to keep them more firmly in their place? Should teaching be about reproducing powerful forms and practices or questioning them?
>
> (Brindley, 1996: 228)

A development of my own position, initiated in Chapter 3, is that the knowledge about language taught in schools should be doubly directed: first, towards equipping students with an explicit grasp of the particular linguistic forms which characterise dominant discourses in standard English, written and spoken (and in such discourses specific genres – see Chapters 4 and 5 – such as argumentation and reporting will be instrumental); second, towards developing, principally on the part of teachers, a critical understanding of the strengths and limitations of such discourses so that

---

LANGUAGE CHARTER

It is the policy of_____
(insert name of institution or authority)

to enable all learners, to the maximum extent possible within available legislation and resources

    (i)   to develop their own mother tongue or dialect to maximum confident and effective use;

    (ii)   to develop competence in a range of styles of English for educational, work-based, social and public-life purposes;

    (iii) to develop their knowledge of how language operates in a multilingual society, including basic experience of languages other than their own that are significant either in education or the local community;

    (iv) to develop as extensive as possible a practical competence in at least one language other than their own.

It is our belief that the development of these four strands in combination will contribute to an effective language curriculum for Britain in the twenty-first century more than emphasis on any one of them separately at the expense of the others.

Signed: _____

Date: _____

Figure 4.

they can be manipulated for specific ends and so that they can, if necessary, be differently formulated and studied. To be deprived of access to the kinds of knowledge which can deliver competence in such genres is a serious linguistic impoverishment. It is not a compliant acquiesence in the existing social order to learn to be competent and to be able to deploy such competence. Indeed, it can be argued that nothing can be changed unless the appropriate discourses are 'appropriated'. This same point has been well made by Michael Halliday and is quoted in this same context of debate in Chapter 5 (where the emphasis is mainly on written argumentation):

To be literate is not only to participate in the discourse of an information society; it is also to resist it; it is rather perverse to think you
can engage in discursive contest without engaging in the language of
the discourse.

(Halliday, 1996: 357)

For further exploration of these issues see Cope and Kalantzis (1993),
Derewianka (1996) and for a further discussion of an anti-assimilationalist
position, Threadgold (1994).

4.   The possibilities of mobilising institutionalised action by means of
consensus on the position of languages 'other' than English in educational
establishments should not be discounted. The Language Charter developed
by Professor Christopher Brumfit of the School of Education, University
of Southampton, is one such example (see Figure 4).

Part II

LITERATURE, DISCOURSE AND 'ENGLISH'

INTRODUCTION TO PART II

The chapters in this part explore different possibilities for greater integration of language and literature in the curriculum. Central to such a pursuit is a continuing investigation of the nature of literary language and an illustration of both the creativity of ordinary language users and the creative potential inherent in so-called 'everyday' language use.

The main linking argument is that language studies can be all the richer as a result of greater attention to literary language use and that literary studies can be similarly enriched by greater attention to the creative formations and reformations of spoken and written English in a wide range of contexts of use.

Other main points established in this part are that teaching methodologies which explore texts along continua of contrast and comparison and which utilise process-based methodologies can promote greater literary under-standing and foster more effective language development both on the part of first-language users and, especially, on the part of learners of English as an additional language. Throughout this part of the book 'English' as an academic subject is seen to be impoverished if too restrictive and isolationist a view of the nature of literature and the teaching of literature is adopted; fuller inte-gration of language-based approaches to text study is seen as a positive way of democratising access to literary texts. Understanding the connection between language and literature, as in the chapters in Part I, also requires recognition of different shaping discourses and of the ideological construction of different versions of 'English'.

The 'Overview' explores some relevant theories and practices of language-based interpretation of texts.

Chapter 6 investigates the nature of literary language, its social and linguistic construction and the notion of literariness in language use.

Chapter 7 explores the communicative risks and rewards associated with metaphorical usage in a range of discourse contexts.

Chapter 8 draws on a corpus of spoken English to discuss the creativity inherent in ordinary, everyday conversation and the potential relevance of such creativity to the design of classroom materials.

Chapter 9 considers different language-based methodologies for the teaching of literary texts.

Chapter 10 investigates approaches to the teaching and study of literary and non-literary discourses in ways which illuminate the textual character of different discourses.

'Postscripts and Prospects' reviews recent developments in the fields covered by Part II and proposes topics for further research.

OVERVIEW: 'LANG' AND 'LIT': INTERPRETING DISCOURSE

There is no 'pure' act of perception, no seeing without thinking. We all interpret the flux of experience (by) means of interpretive schemata.

Benjamin Lee Whorf

There are no such things as facts, only interpretations.

Friedrich Nietzsche

Literature is what gets taught.

Roland Barthes

This overview considers work during the course of the past twenty years or so of linguistic and discourse-based approaches to the analysis and interpretation of texts. A main aim is to highlight some strengths and limitations in the different approaches but the particular focus is on two main procedures of *interpretation*: one a conscious activity of constructing meaning from the language of texts; the second less conscious acts of interpretation, subtexts as it were, which inform decisions made in the linguistic analysis of texts concerning what *kinds* of meaning are found in texts and how such meanings are warranted and accounted for.

I argue that recent discussions in discourse and cultural theory have potential for refining some of the more typical procedures of interpretation and I suggest ways of enlarging the scope of the disciplines of 'lang' and 'lit' by a consideration of the notion of literature and language *as discourse* as well as by brief exploration of related pedagogic implications. A discussion of procedures of interpretation is deliberately placed at the beginning of this section of the book because it provides a framework within which the following chapters can be read.

1 LANGUAGE, INTERPRETATION AND IDEOLOGY: AFFECT AND RESPONSE

Crucial to many of the points of entry into the analysis of texts and to the selection of analytical frameworks which attempt to account for such responses is the question of how such responses are organised in the first place. Such a field of enquiry can be described under several names but we will call it here 'affective stylistics', the term employed by Stanley Fish in a range of work culminating in the study taken as a focus here: *Is There a Text in This Class?* (Fish, 1980).

Work in affective stylistics confronts directly issues of interpretation. Such work foregrounds in particular the question of how different readers who are native speakers of the same language can make a text in that language *mean* differently. It is a question which returns us to a dilemma posed by Charles Bally, one of the originators of stylistics as a discipline:

> Thought tends towards personal affective integral expression: *la langue* can only render the most general traits of thought by depersonalising and objectifying it.
>
> (Bally, 1925)

On the one hand, style is linguistically constituted and should be subject to generalisable, consensual description: on the other hand, it is individual and can only be intersubjectively verifiable if there is recourse to potentially reductive linguistic models. Thus, support is lent to those literary critics who argue that it will only be works whose effects are limited, uniform and not especially creative which can be accounted for in terms of linguistic descriptive frameworks.

Stanley Fish's *Is There a Text in This Class?* contains an overview of developments in affective stylistics during the 1970s. In its earliest forms affective stylistics was developed to explore the extent to which interpretation could be intersubjectively attested. Fish sought to locate 'meaning' not as a static, text-immanent property *internal* to the text but rather as a dynamic, sequential, 'affective' response by the reader who processes the text. Meaning is therefore seen to be *in* the reader and created *by* the reader rather than residing in the text itself.

Fish then proceeds to pursue other related questions posed by the nature of affective responses to and interpretations of texts. For example, who is *the* reader? How do we know what readers *do* when they process a text? What kind of reading *qualifies* as productive of meaning? What if, as seems likely, readers process the language of a text in similar ways but still interpret it differently? How and why is one interpretation preferred to another and how are certain interpretations authorised and legitimised? In other words, when is an interpretation not an interpretation?

The clue to Fish's position is in the subtitle to his book which is, intriguingly, '*The Authority of Interpretive Communities*' – a term which to some extent explains why the only reader Fish ever properly studied was himself. Fish acknowledges the partiality of his earlier readings of texts (including those of major canonical authors such as Milton) by conceding that they were controlled by sets of interpretive assumptions and competences which he took

112

to be procedures shared by other 'right-minded' readers but which are, in fact, the norms of sense-making authorised by an interpretive community of professional textual critics and analysts.

In spite of claims for analogies between linguistic and literary competence, literary 'competence' is, unlike linguistic competence, *taught* not caught. It is by such means that the teaching academy can maintain an appearance of stable and consensual interpretations and, more crucially, of interpretive procedures for it is these same procedures which underlie the teaching of texts in the classroom and it is these same procedures which both limit and control – often by formal and informal modes of examination and assessment – the ways in which individual subjects in that community are allowed to interpret.

Fish argues that claims to validity in interpretation are inevitably therefore flawed and that text analysts should adopt the somewhat more modest aim of persuading others that the interpretations of texts which they offer are reasonable and that the linguistic tools they employ to provide evidence to support such interpretations are reasonable. One conclusion to this argument is that literary linguistic procedures cannot but be tinged with a degree of prescriptivism. Another consequence is that it is naive to conceal the fact that the text analyst represents a specialised community of readers with specific ideologies and an accompanying set of beliefs about the world which will be implicated in the interpretations proffered.

2 'LANG' AND 'LIT' AS SOCIAL DISCOURSE

Another question opened up by studies of reader responses is the extent to which interpretive strategies are generalisable beyond the canonical, literary texts authorised by the professional academy as objects of study. Such a question is potentially productive to explore, is of educational relevance and is especially germane in the light of the topics pursued in this part of *Investigating English Discourse*.

Relevant questions in this connection include: is there such a thing as literary language? What is the nature and function of literary tropes such as metaphor, metonymy, irony in ordinary language use, including 'ordinary' conversational exchanges? To what extent are such figures exclusively 'literary' phenomena? Can and should stylistic analysis be applied to all texts, literary and non-literary, in which there are common stylistic and textual patterns? The questions derive from positions similar to that articulated by Todorov (1981: 71):

> there is no longer any reason to confine to literature alone the type of studies crystallised in poetics: we must read 'as such' not only literary texts but all, not only verbal production, but all symbolism.

A footnote to Todorov's statement reads:

Our teaching still privileges literature to the detriment of all other types of discourse. We must be aware that such a choice is purely ideological and has no justification in the phenomena themselves. Literature is inconceivable outside a typology of discourses.

Extensions to this work include stylistic analyses and interpretations of popular fictions such as romances, Westerns, action adventures, as well as the rhetoric of advertising copy, newspaper editorials and political speeches. Implicit in all such studies is the notion that elements of literariness inhere in all constructed texts and much pedagogic benefit can be derived from comparisons and contrasts of such 'constructedness'. Carter and Nash, 1990 is a representative example of such practice and related theoretical and practical investigation is undertaken in Chapters 6–8 below.

The most natural partner to such investigations would be the extensive studies of the relationship of language, style and ideology undertaken by Fowler and others such Kress, Birch and Fairclough (see section 4, p.118). Fowler's starting point is that it is impossible to attain neutrality in linguistic description because 'linguistic meaning is inseparable from ideology and both depend on social structures' (Fowler *et al.*, 1979: 2). It is naive to suppose that literature is any different from other language use in this respect and linguistic criticism can be harnessed to unmask ideologies, and to analyse critically the ways in which reality is socially contained and politically reproduced in *all* texts.

The preceding description should not suggest that the axis between theory and practical analysis is straightforward. As Taylor and Toolan (1984) point out, for example, there are no rules proposed for relating specific surface linguistic features to specific ideological functions. Fowler *et al.* (1979) and subsequently Kress and Hodge (1981) offer a range of interpretations of, for example, passives in which the order of *actor* and *affected entity* is inverted and interpretations of nominalisations which are used to simplify or mask the ways in which processes are lexicalised for ideological purposes. (For more extensive discussion and illustration see Chapters 2 above.) However, as discussed in section 4 below, until equations between form and ideological function can be more explicitly mapped, then readers are forced to rely on the assumptions of the individual analysts, which do no more than encode their own ideological positions.

In *Literature as Social Discourse* Fowler (1981) stresses the interpersonal dimension of literature. From within a broadly sociolinguistic framework he examines writers' uses of language in so far as linguistic choices reflect and influence relations with society. Following theories outlined in Halliday (1978) and Sinclair and Coulthard (1975), Fowler gives attention to the sociolinguistic varieties or registers of language and examines how they crystallise in a range of literary texts in response to the social, economic, technological and theoretical needs of the cultures concerned. A particular focus emerges, too, on the linguistic relations produced by the text between authors and readers;

these will in turn encode, according to Fowler, the determining socioeconomic structures of particular historical contexts.

> There is a dialectical interrelationship between language and social structure: the varieties of linguistic usage are both *products* of socio-economic forces and institutions – reflexes of such factors as power relations, occupation roles, social stratifications, etc., and *practices* which are instrumental in forming and legitimating these same social forces and institutions. The New Critics and the Formalists vehemently denied that 'literature' had social determinants and social consequences, but a sociolinguistic theory ... will show that all discourse is part of social structure and enters into ... effected and effecting relationships.
>
> (Fowler, 1981: 21)

Discourse is also used by Fowler in another related but quite distinct sense. He refers to literature itself as a discourse. Here the meaning is rather more that of an institutionalised category. Literature is seen by Fowler, in terms similar to those posed by Fish (1980) above, as a discourse which is in varying degrees defined and controlled by the social institutions within which it is embedded. The urge here is to prevent literature from simply becoming a body of texts institutionally authorised by the academy, examination boards and publishers as possessing the qualities necessary for 'literature'. Fowler is anxious to demonstrate the truth of Roland Barthes's statement that 'litera-ture is what gets taught' and that claims for the universal validity of literary values are specious. What is valued as literature changes from one society, or culture within a society, to another and cannot be validated outside a study of the discourses which a society produces and lives by. Even the term 'liter-ature' itself changes, for in the eighteenth century it was used to mean writing in the broadest sense of the word and not necessarily in the sense of creative, imaginatively marked production which it has come to have under the influ-ence of culturally powerful figures such as Matthew Arnold and F. R. Leavis.

In terms of linguistic properties, too, Fowler argues that there is no special variety of language use which is distinctively or exclusively literary:

> Some of the varieties used in the constitution of a specific 'literary' text may tend to occur regularly in some, but not all, other 'literary' texts but they are not restricted to literary texts (rhyme and alliteration are found in advertisements); and 'literary' texts also draw upon patterns which tend to occur in 'non-literary' texts (conversation, news report). This stylistic overlapping and the absence of any necessary and sufficient linguistic criterion for the 'literary' text, is well known though often ignored. My suggestion is that stylistics and literary studies must take sociolinguistic variety theory and methodology seriously as a way of accounting for the specific linguistic properties of the texts concerned.
>
> (Fowler, 1981: 21)

Formalist theories of literary language may attempt to isolate 'literary' language, but such language use can be found in social discourses which are not institutionally defined as literary. And this, for Fowler, would be further evidence of the paradoxes inherent in not seeing literature as social discourse.

3 STYLISTICS AND ACCOUNTING FOR DISCOURSE

Stylistics . . . may be regarded simply as the variety of discourse analysis dealing with literary discourse.

(Leech, 1983: 151)

specifying . . . the conventions of making sense of a particular text is only the first step towards describing all the contextual features relevant to this act of interpretation. These other features – material setting, ideologies and purposes of the interpreter, his political relationship to the text and to his audience, the historical circumstances of his action and so on – all constrain the interpreter's use of shared hermeneutic procedures.

(Mailloux, 1983)

Throughout this book, and in Part II in particular, a case is made for the stylistic analysis of texts to occupy territory beyond the level of the sentence or the single conversational exchange, and to examine those broader contextual properties of texts which affect their description and interpretation. In its varied forms, discourse analysis is that branch of linguistics most directly concerned with the ways in which texts create contexts, with their organisation at this supra-sentential level and with their operation as part of a dynamic process of linguistic exchange between participants. Description provided by the field of discourse analysis allows this to be done in a systematic and rigorous manner.

Second, the analyses undertaken on all kinds of texts aim to be sufficiently detailed, explicit and **retrievable** for other analysts, working on the same texts, to check or retrieve the original analytical decisions and procedures. These other readers may not indeed share the writers' intuitions, and this may lead them to their own different interpretations of the texts; but it is regarded as essential that they should be able to follow the steps by which particular analyses are made. And because the analysis is systematic and according to clearly defined models or procedures, such readers are in a position to argue against the positions adopted in each chapter, should they wish to do so. Also, although such methods of analysis do not, of course, guarantee a single meaning or the only possible reading of a text, they do have an added **pedagogical** advantage. One of the problems with traditional methods of close reading is that the procedures of analysis and interpretation are not made particularly explicit, with the result that learning to read in this way takes place, if it takes place at all, by a kind of osmosis. Although few analysts would claim that the analytical procedures demonstrated are other than basic and preparatory to fuller interpretation, it is pedagogically appropriate that such initial procedures should not be so hidden between the lines that only a few students can gain access to them. The argument for more democratic access to a wider range of texts and the development of pedagogies which support such a process is a core argument throughout Part II, and in Chapters 9 and 10 in particular.

Third, we must also examine the extent to which discourse analysts can accommodate work in the analysis of literature in which the notion of discourse is viewed with different theoretical assumptions, and from different analytical perspectives. The question is an acute one as far as analysis of discourse as a social and political phenomenon is concerned, for discourse analysis of both spoken and written texts is concerned with language as a social semiotic. Issues of class, gender, sociopolitical determination and ideology can never be very far away from analysis of the words on the page. Discourse analysis should therefore be concerned not simply with the micro-contexts of the effects of words across sentences or conversational turns but also with the macro-contexts of larger social patterns. Much current work focuses on micro-contexts; some touches upon macrocontextual issues. One question is: how far can we go and still retain for our analysis a character which is linguistic? Another is: how far should we take into account the 'position' of the analyst and the ideologies of both analysis and analyst, which are invariably and unavoidably embedded in discourse? In our use of the term 'discourse' here we are moving in a direction common in much contemporary literary theory.

Work within alternative traditions of discourse thus takes us beyond the traditional concern of stylistics with aesthetic values towards concern with the social and political ideologies encoded in texts. The starting point for such concerns in literary-linguistic studies can be traced to Voloshinov and Bakhtin writing in the Soviet Union in the late 1920s and early 1930s:

> Existence reflected in the sign is not merely reflected but refracted. How is this refraction of existence in the ideological sign determined? By an intersecting of differently oriented social interests in every ideological sign. Sign becomes an arena of class struggle. This social multi-accentuality of the ideological sign is a very crucial aspect.
>
> (Voloshinov, 1973 edn: 23)

In other words, language does not mediate 'reality' in any simple or 'common-sense' way. Meanings are not *in* the text or *in* language but are produced *through* language. There is no easy one-to-one correspondence between words and what they refer to 'objectively' in the world. Instead, users of language or 'subjects' are positioned at the intersection of various discourses which are inherently unequal and the site of struggle. A crucial contribution to analysis of such multi-accentuality or 'heteroglossia' is Michel Foucault's argument that discourses are historically determinate. Foucault, whose influence as a critic of culture on much contemporary literary theory has been powerful, argues that there is no single right way to see things. Our knowledge and beliefs are *discursively* produced; they are not universal but social-semiotic in origin, functioning under the control of cultural shaping processes in society (Foucault, 1972). However much dominant ideologies may work to reinforce stability and resist alternative orders, any speaker of the language is part of an ongoing struggle in which different interests are embedded. How we see things depends on where we see them from, and where we see them from is a sociohistorical, culturally shaped position. The language we use does not reflect; it refracts a world which we are in but which we can contest and change. Literary discourse analysis should seek to demonstrate the determining positions available within texts, and show how 'meanings' and 'interpretations of meanings' are always and inevitably discursively produced. For example, Herman (1995) and Mills (1995) offer discursive socially based feminist interpretations of their selected texts. Carter and Simpson (1989), Verdonk (1993) and Verdonk and Weber (1995) offer related arguments for 'discourse' and 'contextualised' stylistics.

Thus, we might say that if the 1960s was a decade of formalism in stylistics, the 1970s a decade of functionalism and the 1980s a decade of discourse stylistics, then the 1990s has become the decade in which discursively based sociohistorical and sociocultural stylistic studies are a main preoccupation. The whole argument for a siting of text analysis in relation to sociopolitical ideologies and their attendant discourses leads directly to recent further work in linguistic criticism and critical discourse analysis.

4 CRITICAL DISCOURSE ANALYSIS AND THE INTERPRETATION OF DISCOURSE

Taking inspiration from work undertaken in the late 1970s and early 1980s and in particular from Fowler *et al.* (1979), Fowler (1981), Hodge and Kress (1981), Kress (1989), Pecheux (1982) and Macdonell (1986), such work has grown exponentially in the late 1980s and in the 1990s. Examples are Fairclough (1989, 1992b, 1992c), Birch (1989, 1996), Hodge and Kress (1988), Wodak (1988) and Lee (1992). There are several sources which in their review of this body of work serve as a supplement to and extension of this overview (e.g. Wales, 1989; Birch, 1996).

The focus here is on one aspect of this work: the part played by interpretive procedures in the analysis of discourse. It is an aspect of the work which bears more directly on work reviewed in this overview for, as we have seen, the relationship between linguistics, literature and text study is in part one in which the role of linguistic description in the process of interpretation is regularly brought into prominence.

In summary, critical discourse analysis (henceforth CDA) has as a main aim to uncover the insinuation of ideology and the imposition of power into texts through uses of language which ordinarily readers of texts do not notice.

Language use is social action and language is an instrument of control as well as of communication; and where there is control, according to CDA, there is conflict and where there is conflict there is politics. No act of communication can be neutral therefore and it is the task of critical discourse analysis to reveal the ways in which communication is motivated and 'interested', usually in the service of maintaining a particular power structure, either of an individual in a social situation or of a particular social class, or an ascendant culture, or a colonising power and so on.

There is thus a social responsibility on the part of linguists not exclusively to analyse textual structure but also to show how language choices are not simple choices. They need to show how such choices are made according to a series of political, social and cultural constraints. In turn, these social and institutional processes *produce* particular linguistic structures and meanings. For analysts within the CDA tradition language is not merely a reflection or reflex of social processes. The responsibility also extends to an educational purpose of enabling all consumers of texts better to understand how texts work upon them, not least because reading is by most people construed as an unproblematic, neutral and natural accessing of the meaning of a text.

In critical reviews of work undertaken within a tradition of CDA and particularly of studies by Fairclough *Discourse and Social Change* (1992b), Widdowson (1995, 1996) makes a number of charges against the practices and procedures of critical discourse analysis. Widdowson (1996) describes the studies by Fairclough as constituting a 'theory of discourse as hegemonic struggle whereby power is exercised to construct social reality by the intertextual control of discursive practices'. He criticises this position on a number of grounds, ranging from what he sees as terminological confusion in the use of words such as 'discourse' and 'text' to the more serious charges that critical linguistic interpretations are, as a result of the political commitment of the analyst, frequently reductive:

> To the extent that critical discourse analysis is committed, it cannot provide analysis but only partial interpretation. What analysis would involve would be the demonstration of different interpretations and what language data might be adduced as evidence in each case. It would seek to explain just how different discourses can be derived from the same text, and indeed how the very definition of discourse as the pragmatic achievement of social action necessarily leads to the recognition of such plurality. But in CDA we do not find this. There is rarely a suggestion that alternative interpretations are possible. There is usually the implication that the single interpretation offered is uniquely validated by the textual facts.
>
> (1995: 169)

This commitment of CDA analysts extends to a programme of correcting the social inequalities revealed by critical discourse analysis but, for Widdowson, this all too often leads to a text being made to have a single preferred interpretation because the analyst reads into the text an interpretation which will inevitably be rooted in his/her own value systems and his/her own ideological commitments and preferences. Indeed, Widdowson charges that much of the linguistic description undertaken in CDA is often insufficiently detailed to warrant the interpretations it is made to carry and that the analysis is often directed to support the interpretation which the analyst's political commitment has already prefigured – a criticism commonly made by Stanley Fish of work in traditional literary stylistics. Widdowson's position is broadly supported by Hammersley (1996).

Finally, Widdowson stresses the importance of the pragmatic function of interpretation; for him, discourse analysis is a crucial function of pragmatics since it is not possible to read what people mean directly from the texts they produce, whether spoken or written. As argued by Fish (1980: above, p.112) meanings are not contained *in* texts but are interpreted pragmatically *from* texts. In that process the value and belief systems held by each individual play a constructive but *not*, according to Widdowson, a determining or even constraining part in the assignment of meaning.

In a reply to Widdowson, Fairclough (1996) argues strongly for the invariably *social* construction of interpretation, pointing out that a focus on discourse analysis as principally a descriptive and subsequently a pragmatic-interpretive process presupposes that both the social context and the subjects involved (the sender and receiver of the message) are pre-discoursal and not 'constituted in discourse'. That is, Widdowson appears to Fairclough to be arguing from an assumption that interpreting subjects are free and 'innocent' individuals, that contexts are socially neutral and that even the descriptive linguistic frameworks adopted for analysis are value-free and do not need to be interrogated. Widdowson's position, argues Fairclough, is one which seeks to locate critical discourse analysis within the boundaries of general linguistics, disabling it from productive interdisciplinary enquiry and from engagement with other disciplines such as those in the social sciences where the term 'discourse' has developed a range of meanings largely under the influence of work by Foucault, a major influence on Fairclough's construction of discourse who would endorse the following statements by Birch:

> Meanings and values are not the property of a unique individual but are produced in a communicative struggle and interaction in actual, ideologically determined and politically motivated time . . . Traditional linguistics excludes too many important aspects of such communicative struggle, most notably the *action* and *interaction* involved amongst people and institutions in the making of meanings. This marginalises language as meaningful activity and focuses upon structural relations rather than communicative and cultural processes. Discourse is about interaction and exchange; about people and institutions; about power, status and control.
>
> (Birch, 1996: 65)

Understanding meaning in a critical linguistics/social semiotics is, therefore, about understanding social realities rather than determined truths
which are thought to preexist language.

(Birch, 1996: 80)

In a subsequent response (in what is an extended debate) Widdowson (1996)
gives particular analytical attention to a text analysed by Fairclough – a booklet
about pregnancy issued by a hospital to expectant mothers – in order to
demonstrate how different meanings can be read into and from the linguistic
particulars of the text according to the ideological predisposition of the analyst,
concluding that to arrive at a single interpretive position as Fairclough appears
to do is a form of hegemony every bit as coercive as the discourses critical
discourse analysis sets out to deconstruct.

5 CONCLUSION: THE PROVISIONALITY OF INTERPRETATION

The failure of structuralist linguistics to account for how texts mean,
and therefore for how societies and institutions mean, has been spec-
tacular. This is the legacy of a twentieth-century preoccupation with a
scientificity that has demanded explicitness and objectivity in a world
that operates, for the most part, as a denial of the explicit and objective.
It is therefore a scientificity that seeks to compartmentalise and pigeon-
hole the world into categories and classifications – structures and
relations – that allow statements to be made about idealised worlds, not
actual worlds. This is a scientific, formal convention, the convenience
of which has modelled the world as something that it is not – neat,
ordered and unproblematic.

(Birch, 1989: 150)

Why speakers or writers should wish to speak or write, what they might
want to speak and write about, and how, is not a question in linguistics.

(Kress, 1989: 67)

The above discussion calls into question the claims repeatedly made in the
literature on stylistics that stylistic analysis can deliver interpretations which
are objective or at least more objective than many traditional literary critical
accounts because evidence is supplied in the form of an explicit, retrievable
description of the language of the text. Although such a position has continued
to be subjected to radical critique (e.g. Mackay, 1996), it represents the mainstream view of those working at the interface of linguistics, discourse and
textual criticism.

What needs to be re-emphasised in such a context is that linguistic analysis
and the increasingly discourse-based procedures of analysis that are associated
with it will always represent no more than a way of reading. A practice of

121

stylistic analysis is a way of reading which is inevitably as partial and as limited, as subjective and as strategic, as any other way of reading and it is certainly compromising. It represents a compromise between scientificity (with its attendant limitations) and the pursuit of essentialist meanings which are assumed to be the inalienable property of the text, on the one hand, and a belief, on the other hand, that language is a public property which is communally and normatively shared and which can serve as a point of reference for the assessment or evaluation of preferred meanings. To adopt this position of compromise is to refuse to privilege interpretive relativism and undecidability while at the same time to refuse to assume either that there is an absolute, context-free interpretation or that the analyst can operate with a wholly essentialist, context-free linguistic model or descriptive framework.

At its best discourse-based stylistic analysis seeks to do no more than to persuade a group or community of readers that the interpretation proffered is a reasonable one for that community and that within its limits it can be validated by others by reference to the language used. The basis of the interpretation in explicit reference to language means that, if fellow travellers in this community are so predisposed, they can argue against the interpretation and offer their own. The more explicit the analysis offered the more retrievable it is and the more reasoned disagreement is facilitated. An interpretive community of readers, in the manner described by Fish (1980 and section 1 p.112 above) can then choose to prefer an interpretation according to how persuasive it is. Above all, such procedures recognise the existence of discourse, critical discourse and literary discourse, and the discoursal norms of language, to be a public and publicly analysable property. Such interpretive and analytical procedures do not claim undue authority, cannot be anything other than provisional and are bound in more senses than one to the nature of the description and analysis employed. They represent no more than a starting point for further exploration (which is why they are so pedagogically serviceable) when more historically and culturally based discursive modes can be brought into play. Such work is, as Michael Toolan has pointed out (Toolan, 1986: 139), the work of bricoleurs not engineers.

6

IS THERE A LITERARY LANGUAGE?

1 INTRODUCTION

This chapter explores the interface between language and literature. The question 'Is there a literary language?' is consistently addressed throughout, but it is one which cannot be addressed in isolation either from questions concerning the nature of literature itself or from the institutional contexts in which literature and language are taught. It will be apparent, too, that linguistics can help supply some partial answers to the main question but it will be argued that it is within sociolinguistic theories and descriptions of discourse that these answers may be most successfully located.

In one sense, literary language is the language of literature; it is found in literary texts and is, for many literary critics, an unproblematic category. You know when you are in its company. Such a position cannot, however, be as unnegotiable as it seems to be, if only because the term 'literature' itself is subject to constant change. In the history of English 'literature', literature has meant different things at different times: from elevated treatment of dignified subjects (fifteenth century) to simply writing in the broadest sense of the word (e.g. diaries, travelogues, historical and biographical accounts: eighteenth century) to the sense of creative, highly imaginative literature (with a hieratic upper-case 'L') appropriated under the influence of romantic theories of literature by Matthew Arnold and F. R. Leavis in the last one hundred years. For a fuller account of such semantic change in respect of literature, see Williams (1983) who also points out the semantic detritus of the eighteenth-century sense of the word in its use to describe the 'literature' of an academic subject, or in the collocations of insurance 'literature' or travel agents' 'literature'. Literature is subject to constant change; it is not universally the same everywhere and is as a category of text eminently negotiable. Definitions of literary language are part of the same process.

2 LITERARY LANGUAGE: A BRIEF HISTORY OF DEFINITIONS

The history of definitions of literary language in this century is a long and battle-scarred one with various interest groups competing for power over the property (properties); and each definition has itself inevitably assumed a theory of literature whether explicitly recognised or admitted to be one or not. Two main camps can be discerned and these can be grouped, rather loosely, into **formalist** and **functionalist** though the division is by no means a clear-cut one. I shall begin with formalist definitions because they are historically antecedent but also because their influence has been pervasive in the export of Russian formalism into American New Criticism, and with its subsequent import into practical criticism in Britain.

2.1 Formalism

Formalist definitions, especially those of the Russian formalists, were predicated on a division between poetic and practical language and to this extent were paralleled by I. A. Richards's opposition in his writings in the 1920s between scientific and poetic discourse. The Russian formalists shared the belief of the symbolists at the turn of this century in the aesthetic autonomy and ahistorical separateness of art and literature from other kinds of discourse, but were unhappy about the symbolists' vague subjectivity and impressionism when it came to discussions of literature.

Paradoxically, they wanted to set up a *science*, a *poetics* of literature which sought to define the literariness of literature; that is, they sought to isolate by rigorous scientific means the specifically literary forms and properties of texts. Since there is no exclusively literary content, they argued, poetics should evince a concern with the *how* rather than the *what*. Thus, the early formalists such as Shklovsky, Tynyanov, Eichenbaum and Jakobson gave special attention to the linguistic constituents of the literary medium – language – and drew on the new science of linguistics for their theoretical and descriptive apparatus. Their main theoretical position was that literary language is deviant language. It is a theory which has had considerable influence.

According to deviation theory literariness or poeticality inheres in the degrees to which language use departs or deviates from expected configurations and normal patterns of language and thus defamiliarises the reader. Language use in literature is therefore different because it makes strange, disturbs, upsets our routinised 'normal' view of things and thus generates new or renewed perceptions. For example, the phrase 'a grief ago' would be poetic by virtue of its departure from semantic selection restrictions which state that only temporal nouns such as 'week' or 'month' can occur in such a sequence. As a result, however, grief comes to be perceived as a temporal process. Deviation theory represents a definition of literary language which contains interesting insights but which on close inspection is theoretically underpowered. For example:

1 If there is a deviation then this can only be measured if you state the norm from which the deviation occurs. What is the norm? Do we not mean norms? Is the norm the standard language, the internally constituted norms created within a single text, the norms of a particular genre, a particular writer's style, the norms created by a school of writers within a period? And so on. If it is the norms of the standard language, then what level of language is involved? Grammar, phonology, discourse, semantics? This is an important question, because a deviation at one level may be norm adherence at another level. And there is a further problem in that our ability to measure and account accurately for deviations will depend on what levels of language linguists know most about. Since the greatest advances this century have been in grammar and phonology, formalist poetics has tended to discuss literariness, rather limitedly, in terms of grammatical and phonological deviations.
2 What is defamiliarising in 1912 may not be in 1922.
3 There will be a tendency to discover literariness in the more maximally deviant forms – that is, poetry rather than prose, avant-garde rather than naturalist drama, in, for example, e.e. cummings and Dylan Thomas rather than in Wordsworth's Lucy poems or George Eliot's shorter fiction.
4 It presupposes a *distinction* between poetic and practical language which is never demonstrated. It can easily be shown that deviation routinely occurs in everyday language and in discourses not usually associated with literature. Similarly, in some historical periods, literature was defined by adherence to rather than deviation from, literary and linguistic norms.

However, the idea of literary language as language which can result in renewal or in new ways of seeing the familiar cannot be as easily discounted as some of the above observations might suggest. But deviation theory needs greater theoretical and linguistic precision for the definition to hold and it needs to be considered and tested alongside complementary definitions.

2.2 Self-referentiality

Another influential formalist definition is particularly associated with Roman Jakobson. Originally connected with the Russian formalists, Jakobson subsequently moved to the United States and in a famous paper (Jakobson, 1960) he articulated a theory of poetic language which stressed the self-referentiality of poetic language. In his account, literariness results when language draws attention to its own status as a sign and when as a result there is a focus on the message for its own sake. Jakobson's notion has been clearly explained by Easthope (1983: 15):

The poetic function gets into the syntagmatic axis something which normally would stay outside in the paradigmatic axis: it does so by operating a choice in favour of something that repeats what is already in the syntagmatic axis, thus reinforcing it.

Thus, in the examples:

I hate horrible Harry or **I like Ike**

the verbs **hate** and **like** are selected in favour of 'loathe' or 'support' because they establish a reinforcing phonoaesthetic patterning. The examples cited (the latter is Jakobson's own and is a specific slogan in favour of the former American president Dwight Eisenhower, whose nickname was Ike) demonstrate that poeticality can inhere in such everyday language as political advertising slogans. The notion of self-referentiality is developed more extensively below. But we should note here that Jakobson's definition is, like definitions of deviation theory, founded in an assumed distinction between 'poetic' and 'pragmatic' language. According to Jakobson, in non-literary discourse the signifier is a mere vehicle for the signified. In literary discourse it is brought into a much more active and reinforcing relationship serving, as it were, to symbolise or represent the signified as well as to refer to it. (See also Widdowson, 1975: ch. 11 for related discussion.)

This emphasis on patterning and on the self-referential and representational nature of literary discourse is valuable; but it should be pointed out that (1) Jakobson's criteria work rather better in respect of poetry than of prose; (2) he supplied no clear criteria for determining the *degrees* of poeticality or 'literariness' in his examples. He does not seem to want to answer his own question as to what exactly makes some messages more unequivocal examples of works of art than others (see also Waugh, 1980); (3) Jakobson stresses too much the *production* of effects, neglecting in the process the recognition and reception of such effects. The reader or receiver of the message and his or her sociolinguistic position tend to get left out of account. (For further discussion, see Werth, 1976.)

2.3 Speech acts and language functions

Accounts of literary language which attempt more boldly to underscore the role of the reader interacting in a sociolinguistic context with the sender of a verbal message are generally termed speech act theories of literary discourse. Where the work of Jakobson and others can be termed formalist, these theories are more functionalist in orientation, although one of their main proponents, Richard Ohmann, might be better described as a formalist disguised as a functionalist.

Ohmann's basic proposition is that the kinds of conditions which normally attach to speech acts such as insulting, questioning and promising do not obtain in literary contexts. Instead we have quasi- or mimetic speech acts. As Ohmann (1971) puts it:

> A literary work is a discourse whose sentences lack the illocutionary forces that would normally attach to them . . . specifically, a literary work purportedly imitates (or reports) a series of speech acts, which in fact have no other existence . . . Since the quasi-speech acts of literature are not carrying on the world's business – describing, urging, contracting, etc. – the reader may well attend to them in a non-pragmatic way and thus allow them to realize their emotive potential.

Thus, the literary speech act is typically a different kind of speech act – one which involves (on the part of the reader) a suspension of the normal pragmatic functions words may have in order for the reader to regard them as in some way representing or displaying the actions they would normally perform.

The notion of a displayed, non-pragmatic, fictional speech act certainly goes some way towards explaining why we do not read Blake's 'Tyger' for information about a species of animal or Wordsworth's 'Daffodils' because we are contemplating a career in horticulture. Or why we cannot be guilty of breach of promise when that promise is in a love poem rather than a love letter (see Widdowson, 1975). It also explains to some extent why Gibbon's *Decline and Fall of the Roman Empire* (1776–88) is still widely read today or appears on literature course syllabuses in departments of English around the world, when Gibbon's statements about the Romans are, as history, either invalid or at least irrelevant.

Ohmann's theory suffers from an essentialist opposition between literary and non-literary which careful consideration does not really bear out. Pratt (1977), for example, has convincingly demonstrated that non-fictional, non-pragmatic, mimetic, disinterested, playful speech acts routinely occur outside what is called literature. Hypothesising, telling white lies, pretending, playing devil's advocate, imagining, fantasising, relating jokes or anecdotes, even using illustrations to underscore a point in scholarly argument, are then, by Ohmann's definition, literary. Ohmann's theory also does not explain either the 'literary' status of certain travel writings, or Orwell's essays on the Spanish Civil War (and Orwell would have been extremely perturbed for people to read those essays as merely pretended speech acts); nor does it explain how Thomas Keneally's *Schindler's Ark*, a piece of non-fiction, a 'novel' based on documentary research into real events and characters in a Second World War German concentration camp, won the Booker Prize for 'Literature' in 1982. Neither does it explain why detective novels, science fiction and popular romances which are fictional are not literary; nor why the prose works of Milton or Donne, which are non-fictional, are literary. Indeed, as Leitch (1983) has also argued, the distinction between fiction and non-fiction is not an absolute one since truth itself is a convention determined institutionally and to which commitments differ in different contexts. Work by Hayden White in the field of historiography also raises the intriguing possibility that the writing of history is a kind of narrative in which our interpretation of the past, indeed the facilitating of historical thought, is often made by means of 'literary' tropes. Work on metaphor by Lakoff and Johnson (1980) and others shows how so-called 'literary features' of language routinely occur outside what are commonly called literary texts. And Moeran (1984) has demonstrated the existence in advertisements of such literary-linguistic elements as allusion, intertextuality, phonetic symbolism, ambiguity, represented language and so on.

2.4 Literariness in language

The opposition of literary to non-literary language is an unhelpful one and the notion of literary language as a yes/no category should be replaced by one which sees literary language as a continuum, a cline of literariness in language use with some uses of language being marked as more literary than others. The argument in the next section will follow the one advanced in Carter and Nash (1983), and illustrative material will be provided by a range of thematically connected texts which describe different aspects of Malaysia. Although the most immediate focus is on text-intrinsic linguistic features, it will not be forgotten that whether the reader *chooses* to read a text in a literary way, as a literary text as it were, is one crucial determinant of its literariness. For example, Herrnstein-Smith (1978: 67) discusses[1] how the first line of a newspaper article on Hell's Angels can, when arranged in a particular lineation, be read and interpreted for all kinds of different literary meanings:

> Most Angels are uneducated.
> Only one
> Angel in
> ten
> has
> steady work.

3 LITERATURE, LITERARINESS AND DISCOURSE: SOME EXAMPLES

In this section some criteria for specifying literariness in language are proposed. The criteria, although based on those proposed in Carter and Nash (1983), are extended and modified in a number of ways. Reference to the criteria will enable us to determine what is prototypical in conventional literary language use, as far as it is understood in its standard, modern average Western conception; in other words, the criteria will assist in determining *degrees* of literariness and provide a systematic basis for saying one text is more or less 'literary' than another. The texts about Malaysia used in this discussion are labelled A–E (Figure 5 pp.130–2).

3.1 Medium dependence

The notion of medium dependence means that the more literary a text the less it will be dependent for its reading on another medium or media. In this respect Text B is dependent on a code or key to abbreviations used and on reference to a map or illustrations (e.g. inc.; indep.; a.; p.; cst; exp.; cap.).

To a lesser extent Texts A and C could probably be said to be medium-dependent in that they are or are likely to be accompanied by a photograph or by some means of pictorial supplement. By contrast, Text D is dependent only on itself for its 'reading'. It generates a world of internal reference and relies only on its own capacity to project. This is not to suggest that it cannot be determined by external political or social or biographical influences. No text can be so entirely autonomous that it refers only to itself nor so rich that a reader's own experience of the Malaysia it refers to (though, paradoxically, none of the places actually exist: there is no Kuala Hantu, etc.) cannot extend the world it creates. But the text is sovereign. Relative to the other writing about Malaysia, this text requires no necessary supplementation.

3.2 Re-registration

The notion of re-registration means that no single word or stylistic feature or register will be barred from admission to a literary context. Registers such as legal language or the language of instructions are recognised by the neat fit between language form and specific function; but any language at all can be deployed to literary effect by the process of re-registration. For example, Auden makes use of bureaucratic registers in his poem 'The Unknown Citizen'; wide use of journalistic and historical discourse styles is made in such novels as Salman Rushdie's *Midnight's Children* (1981) and *Shame* (1983) and in numerous novels by Norman Mailer. This is, of course, not to suggest that certain stylistic or lexical features are not appreciably more 'literary' than others; but such words as **twain**, **eftsoons**, **azure**, **steed**, **verdure**, together with archaic, syntactic forms and inversions, belong to a past literary domain. They are associated with what was considered to be appropriately elevated and decorous in poetic discourse and were automatically used as such, losing in the process any contact with a living, current idiom and becoming fossilised and restrictedly 'literary'. Re-registration recognises that the full, unrestricted resources of the language are open to exploitation for literary ends. Text D (the opening to Anthony Burgess's novel *Time for a Tiger*), for example, exploits the language more normally connected with travel brochure and geography book discourse but redeploys or re-registers it for subtle literary purposes. Here the guidebook style is regularly subverted, an ironic undercutting serving to suggest that the conventional geographical or historical presentation of the state is comically inappropriate to a world which is much more heterogeneous and resistant to external ordering or classification.

Text A

Watch "Little Asia" come alive in Kuala Lumpur, then relive the historical past of nearby Malacca.

Kuala Lumpur. Malaysia's capital city with an endless maze of colourful images. The people, the food, the sights, the sounds. All an exotic mix of European and Asian cultures. A pulsating potpourri of Malays, Chinese and Indians.

And there's more. To the south is the historic town of *Malacca*. Here, 158km from *Kuala Lumpur*, you can step into history and relive the glorious past of this ancient port.

Fish, sail, swim or simply relax on the sandy, sun-kissed beaches of *Port Dickson*, only 100km away from *Kuala Lumpur*.

Or take a scenic drive from the capital city to one of several hill resorts, set in the midst of lush green tropical jungles.

And it's all here in Malaysia. The country where great cultures meet, where the diversity of its history, customs and traditions is reflected in the warm hospitality of gentle, friendly Malaysians.

Come share a holiday in this wonderful land. Come to Malaysia. We welcome you now and any time of the year.

IT'S ALL HERE IN MALAYSIA.

Text B

Malaysia, East, part of Federation of Malaysia: inc, Sarawak and Sabah (formerly Brit. N. Borneo); less developed than W. Malaysia; p. concentrated on cst.; hill tribes engaged in hunting in interior; oil major exp., exploration off cst.; separated from W. Malaysia by S. China Sea; a. 77,595 sq. m.; p. (1968) 1,582,000.

Malaysia, Federation of, indep. federation (1963), S.E. Asia; member of Brit. Commonwealth; inc. W. Malaysia (Malaya) and E. Malaysia (Borneo sts. of Sarawak and Sabah); cap. Kuala Lumpur; a. 129,000 sq. m.; p. (1968) 10,455,00

Malaysia, West (Malaya), part of Federation of Malaysia; consists of wide peninsula, S. of Thailand; most developed in W.; world's leading producer of natural rubber, grown in plantations; oil palm and pineapples also grown; world's leading exporter of tin; nearly half p. Chinese; a. 50,806 sp. m.; p. (1968) 8,899,000.

Text C

Singapore & Malaysia. Kuala Lumpur: 2 nights. Singapore: 3 nights. Kuantan: 4 nights Plus 7 nights (optional) FREE

Day 1 Fri London/Kuala Lumpur Evening departure from Heathrow by Malaysian Airlines scheduled flight to Kuala Lumpur.

Day 2 Sat and Day 3 Sun Kuala Lumpur Arrive in the early evening and transfer to the beautiful Regent Hotel (see page 48). In this rapidly growing, predominantly Muslim city, futuristic development blends with old Moorish architecture – but there is still plenty of evidence of the 'old England' of former British colonial days, including the cricket matches which are regularly played at KL's distinguished Selangor Club.

Figure 5(a).

Day 4 Mon Kuala Lumpur/Singapore A short flight brings you to Singapore where you will be met and transferred to your hotel the Hyatt Regency.

Day 5 Tue and Day 6 Wed Singapore Two days to enjoy Singapore with its fascinating blend of east and west. Try dinner at Raffles, a harbour cruise or stroll through Chinatown – and at the Hyatt Regency in the heart of the city you are right on the doorstep of literally hundreds of fabulous shops.

Day 7 Thu Singapore/Kuantan Fly by MAS scheduled service from Singapore to Kuantan and transfer to your hotel, the Hyatt.

Day 8 Fri to Day 10 Sun Kuantan In Kuantan the atmosphere is still very local and unspoilt – ideal if you don't like crowds long, deserted stretches of beautiful sandy beach and the clear blue waters of the South China Sea. Sightseeing on Malaysia's east coast is very much a journey through local lifestyles with tours to local villages, 'kampongs' and fishing ports to observe cottage industries such as 'songket' weaving, batik printing, the moulding of silver and brass, to witness the popular pastimes of top spinning and kite flying and perhaps to visit a local market – a veritable riot of colours and aromas.

Day 11 Mon Kuantan/Kuala Lumpur/London Last day in Kuantan before leaving for the short evening flight to KL and MAS scheduled connection to Heathrow, landing next morning.

FREE WEEK OFFER

If you wish to extend your stay in Kuantan, you can have a further 7 nights at the Hyatt ABSOLUTELY FREE.

PENANG EXTENSION

3 or 7 nights After Kuantan continue north-west to the island of Penang for a further 3 or 7 nights to laze on more of Malaysia's sun-drenched beaches.

Day 11 Mon Kuantan/Kuala Lumpur/Penang Leave Kuantan for the morning MAS flight via KL to Penang and the Hotel Golden Sands.

Day 14 Thu or Day 18 Mon Penang/Kuala Lumpur/London A last full day on Penang before the short flight to KL connecting with MAS to Heathrow arriving the following morning.

HYATT KUANTAN

Located on a beautiful white sand beach, the mood here is one of peace and tranquility. The Verandah, overlooking the sea, is an ideal corner for a sundowner, there's a speciality restaurant for continental cuisine, and the Kampong café restaurant offers delicious local delicacies. You can saunter along to the Chukka Club disco and a converted sampan down on the beach provides a cosy rendezvous. There is a beautiful swimming pool and children's pool, three tennis courts, two squash courts, a sauna or herbal steam bath with a massage and the Manna Sports Centre offers windsurfing, waterskiing, sailing and sea fishing. All 185 rooms are furnished with elegant rattan furniture and subtle colours. Rooms have balconies, air-conditioning, bath and shower, television, radio, direct dial telephone, minibar, fridge, video-movies and have either seaview or mountain view (non seaview). Regency Club rooms also available.

Opinion: An excellent first-class hotel, good sports facilities and generally less-expensive than its equivalent in Penang. **N.B.** The rains in the east coast of Malaysia (Kuantan) may be prolonged and heavy during the period November to January.

Figure 5(b).

Victor Crabbe slept through the *bilal's bang* (inept Persian word for the faint unheeded call), would sleep till the *bangbang* (apt Javanese word) of the brontoid dawn brought him tea and bananas. He slept on the second floor of the old Residency, which overlooked the river.

The river Lanchap gives the state its name. It has its source in deep jungle, where it is a watering-place for a hundred or so little negroid people who worship thunder and can count only up to two. They share it with tigers, hamdryads, bootlace-snakes, leeches, pelandoks and the rest of the bewildering fauna of up-stream Malaya. As the Sungai Lanchap winds on, it encounters outposts of a more complex culture: Malay villages where the Koran is known, where the prophets jostle with nymphs and tree-gods in a pantheon of unimaginable variety. Here a little work in the paddy-fields suffices to maintain a heliotropic, pullulating subsistence. There are fish in the river, guarded, however, by crocodile-gods of fearful malignity; coconuts drop or are hurled down by trained monkeys called *beroks*; the durian sheds its rich fetid smell in the season of durians. Erotic pantuns and Hindu myths soothe away the depression of an occasional *accidia*. As the Lanchap approaches the coast a more progressive civilization appears: the two modern towns of Timah and Tahi Panas, made fat on tin and rubber, supporting large populations of Chinese, Malays, Indians, Eurasians, Arabs, Scots, Christian Brothers, and pale English administrators. The towns echo with trishawbells, the horns of smooth, smug American cars, radios blaring sentimental pentatonic Chinese tunes, the morning hawking and spitting of the *towkays*, the call of the East. Where the Lanchap meets the Sungai, Hantu is the royal town, dominated by an Istana designed by a Los Angeles architect, blessed by a mosque as bulbous as a clutch of onions, cursed by a lowering sky and high humidity. This is Kuala Hantu.

Victor Crabbe slept soundly, drawn into that dark world where history melts into myth.

....

Malacca belles greet Dr M.

Pretty lasses, representing Malacca's Portuguese community, welcoming Prime Minister Datuk Seri Dr Mahathir Mohamad who is on a two-day visit to the state.

Dr Mahathir launched on Thursday a Portuguese cultural centre, "Medan Portugis," costing $1.3 million at Hujung Pasir in Malacca Town.

He said the centre, an idea he mooted two years ago, would help the community fall back on their rich cultural heritage to supplement incomes.

Malacca, once an ancient thriving port on the west coast of the peninsula, is the home of Malaysia's Portuguese community, many of whom still live in a small sea-front enclave and eke a living from fishing. There are about 3,000 Portuguese in Malacca.

Dr Mahathir urged the Malaysian Portuguese to drop their "hang-up" over history and resolve to look ahead.

He assured them that the government has no intention of maltreating any community in the country.

In August last year, the government announced that it was allowing Malaysian Portuguese to invest in the National Unit Trust, until then preserved for Bumiputras.

Figure 5(c).

3.3 Interaction of levels: semantic density

This is one of the most important of defining criteria. The notion here is that a text that is perceived as resulting from the additive interaction of several superimposed codes and levels is recognised as more literary than a text where there are fewer levels at work or where they are present but do not interact as densely. There are different linguistic levels at work in Texts A, B and C but in D, I would argue, we have a degree of semantic density which is different from that in the other texts and which results from an interactive patterning at the levels of syntax, lexis, phonology and discourse. The most prominent of these patterns is **contrast** (contrasts exist between a simple syntax of, variably, subject, predicate, complement – 'The river Lanchap gives the state its name.' 'This is Kuala Hantu' – both of which act as a kind of frame for the first two paragraphs), and a more complexly patterned structure involving greater clausal complexity through participial and subordinate clauses, more embedding and simply longer sentences. There are contrasts, too, on the level of lexis between words of Greek and Anglo-Saxon derivation (**accidia**, **unimaginable**, **pantheon**, **dominated**, **progressive** as opposed to **clutch**, **hurled**, **sheds**, **smug**, **fat**) which is simultaneously a contrast between mono- and polysyllabic, formal and informal lexical items. The contrast is carried further into semantic oppositions marked in the items **inept/apt**, **lowering sky/high humidity**, **blessed/cursed**, **soothe away/blare** and the opposition of East and West in 'smug **American** cars'/'**Los Angeles** architect', 'call of the **East**' and '**pentatonic** tunes'.

Grammar, lexis and semantics are complemented by effects at the level of phonology. Here the plosive **b** and **p** are predominant patterns (overlapping notably with the more formal and 'ancient' lexical items, for example **bulbous, pentatonic, pullulating, pantheon, paddy-fields, pantuns, prophets**); but they exist in contrast with an almost equally predominant pattern of **s** sounds (**second, source, snakes, sleep, tigers**, etc.). This interaction of levels, particularly in the form of contrast, serves to symbolise or represent the unstated content of the passage. For example, one of the possible functions of these linguistic contrasts is to underscore the contrast between Victor Crabbe, an idealistic colonial teacher, and an alien ex-colonial territory; but between these contrasting worlds there also subsists a less clearly marked, more heterogeneous reality to which Crabbe is directly exposed.

Text D is, however, not the only passage in which an interactive patterning of different linguistic levels is foregrounded. Text A contains many such features from the phonetic symbols of: 'Fish, sail, swim or simply relax on the sandy, sun-kissed beaches of Port Dickson', or the metaphoric and phonetic constellation of: 'A pulsating potpourri of Malays, Chinese and Indians', or the almost self-referential syntactic and graphological deviation of: 'IT'S ALL HERE IN MALAYSIA' or the strategic semantic reiterations of: 'relive the historical past', 'relive the glorious past' and the contrasts between past and present figured in the juxtaposition of present and past, Malacca and Kuala Lumpur, the past tense and the eternal present of moodless clauses (the people, the food, the sights, the sounds).

Across this spectrum of texts about Malaysia it is clear that where different levels of language multiply interact there is a potential reinforcement of meaning. More than one possible meaning is thereby represented or symbolised although any activation of meanings must be dependent on a reader whose literary competence permits 'reasonable' correlations of linguistic forms and semantic functions. In this respect Text D can be demonstrated to have greater semantic density than Text B, for example. The interesting case is Text A which, as we have seen, contains an interaction of levels. The existence of these texts illustrates one aspect of a cline of relative 'literariness' and enables us to begin to talk about one text being more or less literary than another.

3.4 Polysemy

The main point here is one which has been widely discussed: the existence of polysemy in literary texts. In terms of this criterion of literariness Text B, by being restrictively and necessarily monosemic, sacrifices any immediate claims to be literary. The monosemy of the text is closely connected with the need to convey clear, retrievable and unambiguous information. This end is served by a number of means: the formulaic code of the headings, for example 'Malaysia, Federation of': the many abbreviations employed; the geographical and numerical explicitness and the extreme economy of presentation (giving as much information in as little space as possible). There is no indication that the text should be read in more than one way although the compositional skills which go into entries such as this in encyclopaedias and geography textbooks should not be dismissed. Polysemy is a regular feature of advertisements although there are no particular examples of this in Text A, which is perhaps best referred to as *plurisignifying* rather than polysemic in that it shares the capacity of many advertisements to be memorable, to promote intertextual reference and to provide a verbal pleasure which can result in frequent citation and embedding in discourses other than that for which it was originally intended. (See Moeran, 1984, especially his discussion of the Heineken beer advertisements.) Text D is, however, polysemic (in that individual lexical items in Text D have more than one meaning: **call** of the East (actual 'sound' and 'longing for'); **smooth** ... American cars ('surface metal' and, by extension, 'the personality of their owners') and **dark** world ('lack of light and mysterious', 'uncivilised', etc.). And so on.

One characteristic of the polysemic text is then that its lexical items do not stop automatically at their first interpretant; denotations are always potentially available for transformation into connotation, contents are never received for their own sake but rather as a sign vehicle for something else.

3.5 Displaced interaction

The notion of displaced interaction serves to help differentiate the direct speech acts of Text C, in which readers will, if they take the advertised holiday, actually perform the actions described in the sequence depicted in the itinerary itself, from the more indirect or displaced speech acts transmitted in Text D. In D the reader is asked to perform no particular action except that of a kind of mental accompaniment to the text in the course of which he or she interprets or negotiates what the message means. The meaning may change on rereading of course; but this is unlikely to be the case with Texts C or B, although in the case of Text A there is some scope for taking it in more than one way and this is a function of its potential literariness. A displaced interaction in a text allows meanings to emerge indirectly and obliquely. What we conventionally regard as 'literary' is likely to be a text in which the context-bound interaction between author and reader is more deeply embedded or displaced.

3.6 Discourse patterning

Criteria for literariness discussed so far have focused mostly on effects at sentence level. At the supra-sentential level of discourse, effects can be located which can help us further to differentiate degrees of literariness. Space prohibits detailed analysis at this level so the point will have to be underlined with reference to one example.

In Text D patterning at the level of discourse occurs by virtue of repetition of the particulars of place, which are concentrated in the long second paragraph. Reference to the river and town is made as follows:

> The river Lanchap gives the state its name.
> As the Sungai Lanchap winds on . . .
> As the Lanchap approaches the coast . . .
> Where the Lanchap meets the Sungai, Hantu is the royal town . . .
> This is Kuala Hantu

The main effect of cross-sentential repetition here, reinforced by repeated syntactic patterns of clause and tense, is to enact the lingering presence and progress of the river and to provide for the appearance of the town as if the reader were actually engaged in a journey through the jungle towards the town. The short focusing sentence 'This is Kuala Hantu' is thus discoursally interconnected with a number of related patterns out of which it grows organically and, in terms of the content of the passage, *actually* grows. Although there is a related patterning around the word **Malaysia** in other texts (e.g. A and B, and especially A) the discourse patterning does not reinforce content to the same extent. (For further discussion, see de Beaugrande and Dressler, 1981: 154–61.)

3.7 Some conclusions

In Sections 3–3.6 the following main points have been argued:

1 Literary language is not special or different, in that any formal feature termed 'literary' can be found in other discourses.[2]
2 Literary language *is* different from other language uses in that it functions differently. Some of the differences can be demarcated with reference to criteria such as: medium dependence; re-registration; semantic density produced by interaction of linguistic levels; displaced interaction; polysemy; discourse patterning. What is prototypically literary will be a text which meets most of the above criteria; a non-literary text will meet none or few of these criteria; that is, it will be monosemic, medium-dependent, project a direct interaction, contain no re-registrations and so on.
3 The worse excesses of paradox and the essentialist dichotomies of an absolute division into literary/non-literary or fictional/non-fictional can be avoided by positing a **cline** of literariness along which discourses can be arranged.
4 The terms 'literary' and 'non-literary' might be best replaced by the more neutral terms **text** or **discourse**.
5 The sociolinguistic and sociocultural context of the discourse is important. This point is developed below.

4 LITERARINESS, SOCIETY AND IDEOLOGY

This section stresses one further point about literariness, with particular reference to the notion of semantic density. In this connection it is worth examining Text E because it is a text which can be read as displaying some relatively dense semantic patterning at the intersection of language, society and ideology. The underscoring of these dense relations – as with Text D – is to a considerable extent depend on readers' interests, on how interested the reader is – in several senses of the word 'interest'. The degree of attention brought to its reading may depend on your 'interest' as a journalist, or a feminist interested in the presentation of women, or as a student of Malaysian history and of Portuguese colonisation, contemporary Malaysian politics or the place of minority groups in majority cultures. The density of patterning here involves, to this reader at least, less interaction of levels but a number of apparent contradictions in the passage can be interestingly analysed with reference to options taken at different linguistic levels. For example, the lexical items used to refer to the feminine 'representatives' **belles** and **lasses** might be linked to questions of the extent to which they represent that community and to the items used of the community itself, that is **community** and **enclave**. The semantic contrasts in the items used to describe their activities – **eke** out a living/**rich** heritage, **thriving** past/**fall back** on their heritage/**drop** their **hang-up** over history – can be set against the patterning of past and continuous present tenses in the passage to frame the contradiction that this community appears to be adjured simultaneously to 'draw on its rich cultural past' and 'drop its hang-up about history'. Analysis might be extended to include the kinds of verbal process options used of Dr Mahathir, **launched**, **said**, **urged**, **mooted**, **assured**, which become progressively contradictory as a set of propositions or to include the stark contrasts in time between **ancient** and **last year** when the Portuguese were allowed to invest in national unit trusts. The whole patterning of the passage can then be explored in terms of the ideology of the newspaper, the medium-dependence or non-dependence of the text on the photograph, the use of the headline, the lexical items **bumiputras** (meaning Malay-nationals), the Malayanisation **Medan Portugis** and so on.

4.1 Reading texts: the interested reader

One legitimate and major objection to the nature of the above discussion is that both the role and the relative position of the reader *vis-à-vis* the text has been underplayed. This was touched on in the previous subsection and will be developed a little here. One main problem is that of regular agent-deletion in discussions of the reading process and the discussion in this chapter is not innocent of such practice. Use of syntax such as: 'the text signals that . . .' or 'the text can be read as representing' or 'The semantic patterning here reinforces' requires to be exposed, because it is readers (not texts) who are performing these activities. And it is important not to forget that all readers will be located in a particular social, political and historical environment.

The study of the reader and the reading process is now in the forefront of research in a number of disciplines. But unanswered questions do need to be highlighted. For example: to what extent do all readers perform the same kinds of operation when they read? Are different competences required at different points in the reading process and do they differ from one to another and, if so, in what ways? Do the same processes apply to non-verbal media such as film, television, radio, etc. (MacCabe, 1984)? To what extent might the kind of attention readers bring to a text depend on the social, cultural or material functional position they adopt or are *taught* to adopt (often institutionally, that is in schools and colleges) when encountering such a text? The attention brought to bear on a text can, as I hope to have illustrated, depend on the reader's own interests and this can be further underlined by the kind of interpretive attention brought to bear by 'readers' on such texts as suicide notes, statements by politicians during elections or during times of crisis or even on the comment 'No comment'. Such scrutiny can, of course, lead to overinterpretation and there is never a reliable way in which the intentions of the sender of a message can be 'read'. The point to underline here is that semantic densities and rereadings are activated by readers and that readers are interested parties willing, in certain sociolinguistic circumstances, to do interpretive work on all kinds of discourses if it appears contextually appropriate for them to do so.

This conclusion leads to the much-debated area of the ways in which 'literature' and its interpretation exists ideologically, as it were, by courtesy of communities of socioculturally and sociolinguistically situated readers with common interests (see Bennett, 1983; Eagleton, 1983; Fish, 1980; Carter, 1985) and to the question of the extent to which Barthes's statement that 'Literature is what gets taught' (and by extension, literary language is what gets taught as literary language) is appropriate or not. It certainly requires recognition of the ideological positioning of this writer as middle-aged, white, West European, Anglo-Saxon, male, tenured university teacher writing in the late 1980s but taught within the institutional boundaries of English studies in the 1960s. Differently positioned readers may well frame different answers to questions concerning the nature of literary language.

5 INTEGRATING LANGUAGE AND LITERATURE: PEDAGOGICAL CONSEQUENCES

Discussion of the pedagogical consequences of the notion of clines of literariness in language requires a separate paper. But it can be briefly recorded here that studying texts along clines can serve to free those texts from the kinds of institutional labels which can be all too frequently assigned to them and at the same time serve to release readers from the constraints of narrowly aesthetic consideration into more regular encounter with broader, discursive issues of moral, social and aesthetic import and with the role of language in the mediation of such issues (see also Brazil, 1983). This would be the beginning of a sociolinguistic theory of discourse which would have far-reaching consequences for literature and language study, both in contexts in which language and literature are studied separately and in contexts where the integration results in a narrowly 'literary' stylistics based on canonical texts. In addition, reading and interpretation could become more inclusive operations and might even be sharpened by the resulting exposure to the kind of range and variety of texts explored in this chapter. Far from demeaning literature and reducing appreciation of literary language use, such a study would lead to an enhanced understanding of and respect for the richness of language in its multiple uses.[3]

6 CONCLUSION

The questions addressed in this chapter have resulted in the posing of further questions; and such questions can only begin to be answered by the integrated study of linguistics with other disciplines such as sociology, literary theory and reading theory in education. It is hoped, however, that a principled basis has been prepared for discussion and analysis of the notion of literariness and that it has been demonstrated that discussion of literary language cannot take place with reference only to text-intrinsic features. Literary language use has to be defined with reference to sociolinguistic theories of discourse and this chapter does no more than take a small step in that direction. But in the world of English language and literary studies stylisticians have, for better or for worse, always been those prepared to argue for the need for one small step at a time.

This chapter is a re-edited version of a paper with the same title in Steele, R. and Threadgold, T. (eds) *Language Topics: Essays Presented to Michael Halliday*, Vol. 2 (John Benjamins, Amsterdam, 1987).

7

METAPHOR AND CREATIVE RISKS

1 INTRODUCTION

In this chapter the workings of metaphor and the interpretation of metaphor are explored, with particular reference to the following two notions:

1 that metaphor can usefully be seen as a kind of risk-taking in the interests of richer interpersonal communication (hence a risk with rewards); and
2 that there is some possibility of specifying, at least for a particular standard dialect of a language (here, English), clines of metaphoricity associated by speakers with items in the lexicon. This second notion is explored while at the same time a basic tenet is maintained that metaphor interpretation must ultimately be related to language in use, i.e. to speech events, rather than simply to the lexicon.

Additionally, four main related arguments are pursued: the need to see metaphor interpretation, and the criteria used in interpretation, as emerging from the speech event in which hearers understand themselves to be participating (section 2). One consequence of this is that what a metaphor means is only *partially* predictable when detached from its interactional context. The claims for 'creativity' in metaphor understanding are then discussed (3), before elucidating, in (4), an emphasis on metaphor as risk-taking (where there is particular reference to literary examples). In the final section (5) the possibilities of specifying clines of metaphoricity are explored with reference to the possible usefulness of the concepts of collocation and culturally salient core metaphors.

2 METAPHOR IN LOCAL CONTEXT

Metaphors, along with most other examples of figurative language, can be paraphrased into more literal meanings. Paraphrasability has a troubled but useful role to play in metaphor analysis (with the proviso that we cannot assume that paraphrase can supply the *equivalent* of a *complex metaphorical evaluation*). The frequency of agreement over metaphor interpretation, and the tendency of variant interpretations to fall into clear sub-types, suggests that there is an identifiable logic or set of conventions at work. At the same time, however, 'componentialist' proposals (e.g. Levin, 1977), to the effect that metaphor interpretation is essentially the mapping of semantic features of the metaphorical term on to the literal term, with cancellation of those deemed incompatible or irrelevant, are assumed throughout this chapter to be both implausible and inadequate as responses.

What then *are* the grounds of plausibility and adequacy in metaphor interpretation? The interpretation of metaphor operates not on words as meaning-types in a fixed decontextualised lexicon, but on utterances in context, as complex exploitations of the lexicon integrated with a potentially diverse range of other dimensions to a speech event: stress, intonation, phonaesthetic criteria, deictic orientation, syntax, encyclopaedic or background knowledge, and so on. While this means that, in principle, 'anything goes' in determining the import of a metaphor and the criteria by which it is arrived at, I maintain that in normal practice this is not the case and that there is rather a mutual attending to a cluster of particularly salient linguistic clues or cues.

In support of these claims, let us turn to a metaphor discussed in Pulman (1982):

That girl is a lollipop

One reading of this, Pulman argues, is that the speaker is suggesting that the girl in question is 'frivolous'. Since it is hard to see how [+FRIVOLOUS] can be a core semantic feature of the word 'lollipop', Pulman cites this, very reasonably, as one example highlighting the implausibility of the feature-mapping theory of metaphor interpretation. He proceeds with a brief account of how an addressee might go about analysing the above utterance (1982: 88). Pulman's account of the interpretive steps runs as follows:

1 The utterance is not a literal description; so
2 Is it a description asserting similarity (e.g. of physical appearance, or of function – pacifier of children)? If seemingly not,
3 then we might attempt to construe the metaphor as an evaluation: asking ourselves perhaps what sort of thing a lollipop is. Well, it is a sweet associated with children. What would it mean to transfer associations of sweets and children to this girl? That she behaves like a child? Perhaps. Is that a good thing or a bad thing for an adult in our culture under normal circumstances? A bad thing, we assume. How might we describe the way children behave with respect to the way adults behave – frivolous? Does that property make sense when applied to this candidate? If yes, then this is what the speaker could have been intimating.

(Pulman, 1982: 88)

One objection to this usefully explicit account concerns the notion that evaluation only seems to be brought to bear on construal where more neutral descriptive interpretations do not seem to apply. Pulman's ordering of the steps of conversational reasoning implies that literal description and similarity descriptions are prior and non-evaluative. But on the contrary, it seems more reasonable to argue that speakers invariably assume implicit or explicit evaluations in utterances: metaphor is then used when speakers wish to foreground their evaluations of things without the bald, on-record effect of conventional (literal) approval or disapproval.

Relatedly, it seems more reasonable to suppose that we *habitually* ask ourselves (in Pulman's words) 'what sort of thing' the referent of any term is. This evaluative (and not merely descriptive) reflection is presumably undertaken whenever we interpret signs in discourse. And we may often make these moves without any confidence that we are able to judge whether or not a speaker's applying that particular evaluation to this topic 'makes sense' (to use Pulman's terms again). Our interlocutors may, typically, be just and reasonable in their descriptive evaluations, but that is irrelevant to the interpretive task, which is to derive an interpretation of the utterance which seems reasonable in the assumed larger context. An often neglected feature of this situated interpersonal guesswork is that there are considerable *risks* involved, for both the producer and the addressee of the metaphor. A creative metaphor is a foregrounded exemplum of what is inherent and problematic in all normal interaction: when confronted by particular metaphors, or by discourse in general, we often do not have the prior knowledge of the topic that the formulation of step 3 above assumes – a knowledge which, it might be argued, would render our interlocutor's informative evaluation superfluous.

Thus, an interpretation of **lollipop** in the above utterance as meaning 'frivolous' certainly seems possible and reasonable. But at least two other important interpretive moves are involved in reaching it, besides and in addition to those cited above:

1 External and prior to the steps of this reasoning under 3, Pulman has made an undeclared judgement as to 'what sort of thing' a girl is (as of course he must). Specifically with reference to age, his girl is not even a teenager, but an adult (tell feminists that that isn't evaluative!). The 'frivolous' reading simply won't emerge if the girl is understood to be an infant.
2 While lollipops are associated with and evocative of children, and while we are invited to ascribe characteristics of children to the girl, these moves alone will not lead to the 'frivolity' estimation, as 'frivolous' is not normally accepted as a reasonable description of children, or of their behaviour as compared to that of adults. Such estimations can also often seem to be subculture specific.

In our arrival at an interpretation of any utterance we may attend to many aspects of that utterance (over and above the semantic associations of the metaphorical focus embedded in it), as well as of the extratextual context we impute. Thus, in relation to 'That girl is a lollipop', other contextually richer interpretations might include the following:

1 phonaesthetic effects in the word lollipop, which might connote playfulness
  or childishness for some speakers (for some speakers, a word of seven
  phonetic segments that is three ways echoic, as this one is, may invariably
  sound childish, presumably on the basis of auditory similarities to babbling);
2 the distal deictic **that**, which, given the absence of co-text, is sufficient to
  draw us to impute a negative evaluation of the topic of comment, the girl,
  by the speaker;
3 the possibility that **that**, in speech, might be contrastive as well as deictic,
  that evaluative comparison might be being made;
4 the possibility that, in speech, the intonation contour might cue or direct
  us towards a particular evaluation of the girl;
5 the fact that, given the sexist world we live in, evaluative interpretation
  may be quite constrained by the age and, especially, the sex of the speaker.
  Can we get the 'frivolous' reading if, as may be the case, the speaker is a
  six-year-old girl?

The extra work involved in metaphor interpretation is very probably triggered
by the interpreter perceiving some anomaly, in the interpreter's own understanding of how the world is – his/her belief systems and personal encyclopaedia. This role played by anomaly is commonly highlighted in quite
introductory textbooks:

> Anomaly provides the basis for one of the most versatile and widely
> used foregrounding devices, metaphor.
>
> (Traugott and Pratt, 1980: 207)

Once an anomaly is suspected, the interpreter may adduce evidence from
many quarters beyond the commonest associations of the metaphorical term,
in attempting to understand the message the speaker intends to convey. And
as Pulman notes, the triggering anomaly will not be pan-contextual, but is
perceived *in the given circumstances*.

If our understandings of what sorts of things girls and lollipops are are
various, what kinds of understanding are prompted by the following
metaphoric utterance?

> Their legislative programme is a rocket to the moon.

This metaphoric use may be based on an assessment that, by inference, the
programme is adventurous, far-reaching, fast-moving, and so on (Cohen, 1979:
70), but the interpretation would rest almost entirely on the interpreter's
favourable disposition to rockets on the moon. Ecologists, animists, astrologers,
anyone appalled by the expense of space exploration while so many millions
on this planet are destitute, anyone suspicious that such exploration is merely
preparatory to a perilous 'militarisation' of space, may intend (as speaker) or
infer (as hearer) a more complex critical evaluation. This example, like the
'lollipop' example, shows that there are always the traces of ideology in

metaphor if we have eyes to see them and if evaluation and knowledge of the world are involved.

But if we do judge that the statement amounts to praise of the programme, the judgement cannot be simply on the basis of retaining such features of **rocket to the moon** as 'fast-moving' and 'far-aiming'. Those features would not distinguish the above from the following:

> Their legislative programme is a rocket to a dead planet.

although it is clear that they do need to be distinguished. It is the entire phrase, **rocket to the moon**, and not just the word **rocket** that is the metaphorical term, and this will give rise to different evaluative associations from those of another phrase even when there is referential identity.

3 CREATIVITY

The questions whether metaphor interpretation is truly creative, and how such posited creativity can be demonstrated in empirical testing, remain vexed and persistent ones in the literature. They are the focus of Pulman's paper. By creativity in metaphor construal he means interpreters' 'inventive' ascription of new features to a word, features not apparently previously or intrinsically associated with that word, and their use of them in the arrival at an inter-pretation. Pulman attempted to test for this creativity by means of a simple exercise. By first asking informants to 'write down everything you would need to know' to use certain words appropriately (e.g. **slums**, **disease** and **city**) and then later asking them to provide full interpretive paraphrases of metaphorical sentences which employed the same words (e.g. 'Slums are a disease of the city'), he hoped to uncover the extent to which we either mechanically adhere to our general understanding of words reflected upon in isolation, or creatively depart from that understanding, when interpreting metaphors. Responding creatively, in this approach, is the ability to judge unforeseen associations of a word to be more appropriate in a given metaphorical context than all the previously declared associations.

Whether the results of Pulman's test support the hypothesis that metaphor interpretation is creative (in the sense specified above) is questionable.[1] In the majority of cases, it seems that informants were relatively uncreative in their glossing of metaphorical foci. Only two of the five metaphorical terms used in the text were interpreted by most informants in a more creative way (i.e. using words with weak or non-existent semantic relation to those of the description-in-isolation). The terms were **horse**, in

> John is a horse when he eats

and **pluck**, in

> He plucked the thought from the air

'Creativity' is hardly surprising here? If the first of these is understood as an odd version of the more familiar idiom in 'John eats like a horse' then both utterances involve idioms rather than live, creatively, interactively interpretable metaphors. Such idioms are not open to the sort of analysis we are seeking to clarify as being at work in metaphor. The decontextualised description of a horse is hardly more likely to allude to the animal's implied voracious eating habits than a description of posts will mention their deafness, or of cats and dogs that they have a habit of arriving in torrential downpours from the skies.

The format and objectives of Pulman's test are attractive, and although creativity is not revealed by this data this may be in part due to use of the wrong sort of test sentences, ones, for example that are not fully metaphorical. On the other hand, it would be unwise to place too much weight on the findings. Incongruence of paraphrase and prior description is only significant if that description is indeed a full and fair record of informants' understanding of the specified words. If our background understanding of words includes knowledge of their regular collocations and contexts (e.g. that slums are often spoken of as an urban disease), the sort of knowledge that we cannot be bothered to specify, or do not see as relevant, in response to a request for a description of 'everything you need to know to use this word appropriately', then all we can hope of the test is that it may confirm that we delve deeper and range more adventurously, even in short paraphrases of words we judge to be metaphorical.

But the broader objection to Pulman's test must be that it explores only one characterisation of creativity and possibly a misleading one. Creativity is implicitly defined as departure, in terms of lexical characterisation, from previous descriptions of terms. But we might also consider (and test for) creativity as the successful and appropriate selection of *particular* terms, from all those associated with an item, in construal – and the noticeable agreement among informants selecting these terms, not others. For it is clear that while a dictionary or thesaurus or informant can supply numerous paraphrases or near-synonyms for a word, these glossing items are not *themselves* regularly paraphrases of each other: our creativity may lie in successful selection of the appropriate paraphrases and disregard of the contextually inappropriate and semantically remote competitors.

4 INTERACTIONAL RISKS AND REWARDS

Metaphor is a creative risk-taking with the less conventional or usage-enshrined associative possibilities of the language – risky because your addressee may not 'get' your metaphor, may merely think you a liar or an idiot or needlessly obscure. If we emphasise that fully metaphorical utterances are a creative risk-taking by speakers, we ought to be able to point to some of the rewards that make the risks worth taking. Each of the motivations for using metaphor has its own rewards: subtle indirect informativeness often 'gets people thinking', sorting things out for themselves without being insulted or talked down to; being entertaining often results in the speaker gaining friends and influencing people, coming to be held in high regard, and so on. These various rewards are perhaps united in involving an increased identification or affinity between speaker and addressee(s). Risky metaphor that 'hits it off', 'gets through' from speaker to addressee, effects a more than everyday intersubjective accord and interpersonal intimacy between the parties.

Literary texts have long offered a safety-net for metaphorical risk-taking, for they are the legitimate arena of the fictitious. Indeed, in many cultures, it may be part of the definition of a literary text that it demands no adherence to literal truth, as such 'truth' is perceived by a community of language users. In a literary text, depending on the genre, it is accepted and even expected that Alices disappear through looking-glasses and Gullivers converse with talking equines. Thus, the metaphor-maker takes a well-calculated risk when he/she embeds the most daring and original, the most creative of metaphors, in a literary text. Sylvia Plath recognises this in a poem simply titled 'Metaphors':

> I'm a riddle in nine syllables,
> An elephant, a ponderous house,
> A melon strolling on two tendrils.
> O red fruit, ivory, fine timbers!
> This loaf's big with its yeasty rising.
> Money's new-minted in this fat purse.
> I'm a means, a stage, a cow in calf.
> I've eaten a bag of green apples,
> Boarded a train there's no getting off.

The poem is a construct of metaphors, each metaphor emphasising some aspect of a pregnant woman: her size, shape, ungainliness, fecundity, value, the inevitability of her transformation. Yet its risk is obvious; these metaphors form a maze, a riddle, and one possible conclusion to a guessing game of this kind is a failure on the part of the audience to arrive at the right conclusion, or, even, at any conclusion at all. But if the audience fails to ferret out meaning, the lack of success is not theirs alone. It is also the metaphor-maker's. A riddle without a solution, at least a possible solution, is no riddle at all. If, in the first instance, the metaphor-maker can convince her audience that the metaphor is plausible, that it admits of a possible solution, they might be tempted to reread the text in order to seek an answer. However, if the metaphor is initially judged too impenetrable, too bizarre, too implausible, the audience may reject the possibility of a solution. This would amount to a rejection of the text itself and a failure of communication between author and reader. Metaphor-makers therefore tread a tightrope which, if successfully traversed, rewards them with a greater intersubjective accord but, when unsuccessfully attempted, punishes with an ignominious fall into incoherence.

Like language, of which it is a special part, metaphor is an instrument of communication. When the tool of language is employed in our everyday discourse it works, on the whole, most efficiently when we obey the rules for its use – that is, when we communicate our messages with neither too much brevity nor too much prolixity. There are many metaphors in any language whose use is consonant with these rules. Metaphors which have grown to have a fixed meaning in the language (e.g. 'a heart-to-heart talk', 'all in the same boat'), may actually *assist* conversationalists in conveying their meanings more effectively since they pithily encapsulate a sentiment or thought that might prove difficult to spell out in non-metaphorical language.

To this extent, the pragmatic rules that guide our everyday conversation also guide our employment of metaphor in conversation. But the use of such fixed metaphorical collocations offers no major rewards to conversationalists. Although they may help communicate meaning effectively in our daily discourse and may even demonstrate that their users possess a certain facility with the language, their use does not credit the users with any 'creative' grasp of language. These metaphors are 'low-risk' because conversationalists do not intend to convey any *additional* meaning by using them: addressees need do no extra deductive reasoning in their interpretation.[2]

Indeed it may be questioned whether a violation of Grice's (1975) maxim of quality (which is supposed to trigger the chain of reasoning that enables us to arrive at a metaphorical paraphrase or 'additional meaning') occurs in any but the most trivial sense when this type of metaphor is used. For, in such cases, metaphors actually stand for specific and immutable meanings (e.g. a heart-to-heart talk = an intimate conversation). Risk of misunderstanding, incomprehension or the possibility of using deductive reasoning to arrive at a conversationalist's meaning can only arise in cases where an interlocutor happens not to be familiar with some idiomatic usage in the language. This accidental risk, in everyday interaction, that one's interlocutor simply does not know a phrase or sentence to be an idiom, clearly cannot be a feature of novel or creative metaphor. High-risk metaphors are especially created when metaphor-makers deliberately invite their audience to solve a riddle.

Hence the role of paraphrasability in metaphor. The metaphor-maker artfully designs his or her message, setting the audience the task of perceiving the design or, at least, some aspects of it. If they succeed in this task, they have some version of a paraphrase. Indeed, it is precisely in this sense that messages derived from violations of Grice's maxims are 'paraphrases', that is, meaning *deduced* from the literal content of the utterance plus background encyclopaedic and contextual information. However, since the deductive paths to a solution are, in principle, infinite, depending upon the various knowledges that individual interpreters bring to their tasks, a creative metaphor, also in principle, eludes a definitive interpetation. Similarly, violation of Grice's maxims may in theory be interpreted in a variety of different ways. A rich range of alternative, complementary, or even conflicting interpretations characterise a creative metaphor.

In contrast, a low- or no-risk metaphor has a single paraphrase that is wholly adequate and often enshrined in the lexicon. For, although a low-risk metaphor may superficially resemble a high-risk metaphor in that it is paraphrasable, this kind of metaphor has a 'paraphrase' only in the sense that every other word in the language has a paraphrase. Indeed, in most cases, the meaning of a low-risk metaphor is *more* easily paraphrasable than that of single morpheme words in the language because this meaning is non-negotiable, particularised and fixed in our common lexicons. Compare, for example, the negotiable meaning of very ordinary lexical items such as **girl** and **work** (Is work defined in opposition to **play** or **leisure**? Must it be productive?) with the relatively fixed meaning of dead metaphors like **to spill the beans** (to reveal something secret) and **to jump out of the frying pan into the fire** (to exchange a difficult situation for a worse one).

The concept of paraphrasability does have a role to play in the analysis of metaphor. A paraphrase is a formulation of concealed meaning and there is a cline from most definite to agreed-upon paraphrasability to least definite paraphrasability, which parallels the cline of metaphoricity upon which we may place low-risk metaphors towards one end and creative metaphors at the other.

For the reasons mentioned earlier, it may be that Grice's maxim of quality is most consistently violated in literary texts, which are authorised fictions. Further, the conventions which in different cultures govern the reading and writing of various genres of literature help contextualise creative metaphors so that plurality and complexity of interpretation are positively encouraged amongst audiences of literary texts. Their knowledge of these conventions tells the audience that the riddles posed in literary texts must be linguistically sophisticated and deserving of a complex response. Although creative metaphors are found in our everyday conversation, there is more than just a statistical correlation between frequency of creative metaphors and literary texts in particular.

Metaphors embedded in a literary text are by convention assumed to be creative, so that the reader conventionally presumes that the writer has put some effort into the construction of the metaphor. Indeed, as evidenced by the sorts of metaphor which appear in literary texts, the most 'creative' metaphors are not generally the most spontaneous; they are instead the most well considered and thoughtfully constructed, inviting the readers to draw upon a complex variety of knowledges (knowledge of literary conventions, knowledge of syntactic structures, knowledge of semantic and pragmatic rules, and so on).

In contrast, we know inductively of the metaphors which arise in our everyday conversation that, even if creative, they are often produced on the spur of the moment and are therefore less likely to be carefully constructed. Dead and frozen metaphors abound in our everyday speech; but the presence of dead metaphors that have not been reworked in some fashion would be noticeable in a literary text, and would be one of the criteria by which an audience might dismiss the text. A literary text is conventionally required to be creative and original: if it employs metaphor as one of its techniques, the audience expects these metaphors to be creative. Consider the following examples:

1a She made my mouth water.
1b She made my eyes water. (said of a beautiful woman by a private eye in a sub-Chandleresque TV series)
2a I'm melting! (said on a hot summer's day)
2b The rivers sweat from the melting hills.

In the two examples above, (b) in both cases occurs in some kind of 'literary' text. Both 1a and 1b have, roughly, the same bare paraphrase: 'She was very desirable.' But whereas 1a by idiomatic convention has this *fixed* interpretation, 1b must be deductively interpreted in a more complex fashion. First, we need to know the conventional paraphrase of the idiom in 1a in order to deduce that 1b is not meant to be interpreted *literally* but *metaphorically* since 1a is recognised by convention to be a metaphor, albeit a dead one. Second, we need to know that the predicate in 1a expresses desirability. Our need to *use* this knowledge is reinforced by the text itself which informs us that the words are spoken about a beautiful woman by the male hero of the TV series. Third, we must draw on a more general knowledge of the world, which tells us that eyes are directly concerned with appraising appearance and that it is standard for watering eyes to connote pain and discomfort. Only by combining all these sorts of knowledge are we able to arrive at a possible interpretation that the woman described by the speaker is not only desirable but perhaps unattainable, thereby causing him pain. As we can see, 1b requires far more complex interpretation than 1a in order for us to arrive at a satisfactory paraphrase.

Example 2b is much less explicit in the way it draws upon metaphor idioms that already exist in our everyday language. Yet knowledge of such ordinary metaphorical underpinnings is necessary if we are to achieve a satisfactory paraphrase of Ted Hughes's new and creative metaphor. We know of course that rivers do not literally sweat and that the hills referred to are unlikely to be melting literally since the moon exudes little heat and this poem is, at one level at least, a description of the effect of the harvest moon on the landscape. But where do we go from here? Even to begin to paraphrase the poetic metaphor, we need knowledge of the phrase 'rivers of sweat' and the expression 'I'm melting', as well as knowledge of the context in which these idioms are generally used (for example on a hot summer's day). Perhaps we also need access to that other common metaphorical idiom 'pouring with sweat', for Hughes's metaphor condenses our knowledge of all these well-known idioms so that we are forced towards a fresh solution, another paraphrase. From what we know of the contextual use of idioms like 'rivers of sweat' we gather that the hills are personified, 'melting' (i.e. sweating) as humans do under the heat of the sun. But it isn't the sun but the *moon* that is the subject of this poem, so we still have to explain why the hills have become hot enough to melt.

At this point, the co-text gives us a clue. Earlier in the poem we read:

> The harvest moon has come . . .
> Filling heaven, as if red hot, and sailing
> Closer and closer like the end of the world.

These lines establish that the moon certainly *appears as if* it is 'red hot' and threatening, though it may not literally be so. They therefore direct our attention to one particular aspect of the 'melting hills' – their appearance. The rivers flowing down the hills glisten in the light of the harvest moon like sweat on bodies. We now have some simple equations:

hills	=	bodies
rivers	=	sweat
moon	=	an awesome presence

These enable us to reach a final stage in the solution to the puzzle posed by the compressed metaphor in the poem. The landscape is animated by the appearance of the harvest moon and behaves *as if* it is human. It is a human reaction, we know, to respond and 'melt' when confronted with an overwhelming presence; it is human to sweat, to cry out:

> The gold fields of wheat
> Cry 'we are ripe, reap us!' and the rivers
> Sweat from the melting hills.

Both examples discussed above emphasise that creative metaphors in literary texts often contrast dramatically in complexity of paraphrase with low-risk metaphors, yet constantly draw upon such metaphors of everyday communication.

5 CORE METAPHORICAL VOCABULARY

High- and low-risk metaphors are similar in two important and related ways. Both types of metaphor, indeed *all* metaphors, are essentially evaluative, whether the target of evaluation is a person, or feeling, or object, or whatever else. In order to fulfil this general function, they often call up especially the connotative meanings of metaphorical vehicles. Intermediate between frozen and novel and creative metaphor (as in poetry), where rather peripheral, recondite or topic-specific associations may be invoked, there seems to be a large domain of moderately creative metaphorical usage, drawing on shared and accessible evaluative connotations. Within this domain, a core set of metaphorisable terms seems to be apparent.

These core terms, such as **head, heart, tree, jewel, key, door, hand**, and so on, have easily accessible and widely agreed upon conlexical items which seem to become enshrined – at least in synchronic usage – as particularly relied-upon 'counters' to be used in a variety of familiar metaphors. It is not that these *cannot* appear in creative metaphors (anything can), but that they do appear with striking frequency in everyday metaphors. (For a more extensive description of 'coreness' in vocabulary see Carter, 1987: ch. 2; Carter and McCarthy, 1988.)

It is perhaps worth remarking on the pervasiveness of metaphor in lexical relations generally. Many collocations appear to depend on a process of metaphorical extension (e.g. **soft water**, **to harbour doubts**) and numerous fixed expressions require or may at one time have required analogy-seeking interpretive strategies. By institutionalising an analogised sense, we can re-use the idea of a door as an entry, as access, which can be left open or sealed, and so on, in very many everyday metaphors: an open-door policy, at death's door, to close the door on further negotiations, etc. Reddy (1979) is an exemplary demonstration of the pervasiveness in English of institutionalised conduit metaphors, in which our ways of speaking about time, emotions, the workings of communication and the mind, and so on, predominantly involve spatial images of a channel along which materials flow.

An emphasis on the fact that the constituents of conventional metaphors of today may have hardened from malleable, creatively posited interpretations at some earlier stage of the language, is simply a reminder that core cultural metaphors become, like the rest of the lexicon, determinate and institutionalised developmentally. Changing cultural and hence communicative needs may tend to shift particular items deeper within or rather further away from our notional core of common metaphorical items. Items once creatively metaphorical may become progressively frozen (or dead metaphors, in conventional terminology) and as a result have an increasing likelihood of finding their way into the lexicon and of having a conventional meaning fixed to them.

A seminal early article in this area, from a lexicological perspective, is that of McIntosh (1966), which explores the varying 'patterns' of use and 'ranges' of occurrence of words. 'Patterns' are comparable with the patterns of syntax, in that certain collocations are allowed but others are not (**soft water**, **soft drink**, **mild steel**, **gentle slope**, *****mild water**, *****gentle drink**). A 'range' refers to the span of collocates contracted by a lexical item. Similar to our own observation above, McIntosh points to the 'range-extending tendencies' of certain items such as **key** (e.g. **key move**, **key policy**) which will allow of metaphoric combinations, though it is sometimes difficult to demarcate exactly what are fixed figurative extensions and what are more creative exploitations of the range-extending tendencies of these more core items. For example, which examples of **fat** here are the more creative and which are merely fixed expressions: **fat man**, **fat child**, **fat belly**, **fat chicken**, **fat salary**, **fat bank balance**, **fat book**, **fat chance**? McIntosh offers a framework by which the collocational and colligational properties of words can begin to be measured:

There is the possibility of four obviously distinct stylistic modes: normal collocations and normal grammar, unusual collocations and normal grammar, normal collocations and unusual grammar, unusual collocations and unusual grammar.

(McIntosh, 1966: 149)

This could be cast as a continuum with familiar standard language use at one end of the scale and the nearly indecipherable at the other end. Between these two poles lies the usage relevant here, involving degrees of individual and creative risk-taking.

It is not clear whether there is a roughly delimitable set of core, productive and culturally salient vocabulary items that predominate in conventional and creative metaphors. But it seems probable that an especially prominent role is played in everyday metaphor – and perhaps literary metaphor too – by words denoting a language community's 'basic-level concepts' (in the sense of Rosch et al., 1976, and Rosch, 1977). Rosch has argued that taxonomies of real-world objects are sub-categorised into levels of abstraction, on the basis of the preponderance of shared attributes. Three levels are particularly identified, on the basis of informant tests: a superordinate category (e.g. 'animal') where few common attributes are reported, a basic level ('dog', 'cat', etc.) where all instances of a category are judged to have many attributes in common, and a more specific, subordinate level ('tabby', 'Manx', 'Siamese', etc.).

Various tests of recall and discrimination seem to confirm that basic-level concepts are the most vividly grasped, most discriminable, most usefully differentiated items in our taxonomies. This is the level at which we get such terms as **dog, cat, apple, orange, chair, car,** and so on. Part of Rosch's argument concerns the reliable co-occurrence of bundles of attributes in objects (wing and feathers – but rarely fur – in birds): in this respect this is an exploration of clustering patterns of semantic attributes that somewhat parallels McIntosh's commentary on patterns of clustering in lexis. Some sort of process of attribute transfer or adducement, in metaphor production and interpretation, is acknowledged throughout the literature. But with reference to the kind of attributes that focus on basic-level concepts, it is suggested here that it is usually those attributes that are characteristic rather than any thought to be defining, that are usually more relevant to metaphorising.

Whether Rosch-type basic-level concepts are the 'standard material' used in much everyday – and more creative – metaphor is a question which can only be speculated upon here. But it is interesting to note just how common such concepts are as metaphorised objects in the Plath poem quoted earlier: **elephant, house, melon, loaf, purse, cow, apple, train.** By contrast with the basic-level, superordinate terms, though often usable in metaphors, are such general terms that they may give rise to undesirably stock or clichéd utterance: **mental furniture, the fruits of one's labours, a tool of the**

bosses, **syntactic trees**. And subordinate terms are just too specific to be regularly useful in metaphor (**honeydew melon**, **African elephant**, **terraced house**). With reference to the claim at the end of the previous paragraph, subordinate terms are chiefly more *defining*, but no more usefully characterising than basic-level terms.

Also in need of further research with reference to metaphor production are the exciting cognitivist and universalist aspects of Rosch's theory. Such enquiries should proceed within a social-semiotic orientation, in the expectation that community-based cultural determinations strongly affect formation and use of basic-level concepts. An invaluable beginning in just this area is the work of Lakoff and Johnson (1980). One preliminary observation we may risk is that the relative prominence of basic-level concepts in metaphorising may depend crucially on the area of human activity that the taxonomy categorises. For example, one of the taxonomies cited in Rosch (1977: 215) is that of musical instruments, with 'guitar', 'piano', 'drum', etc. as basic-level concepts: while we do drum information into people and blow our own trumpets, our intuition is that these terms are far less productive, in metaphors, than items in the other taxonomies. Conversely, other taxonomies which less readily yield a basic level, such as human body-parts, are intensely metaphorically productive. A further point to consider is Rosch's notion of a prototype or best example among any set of basic-level concepts. It is reasonable to suggest that it is unlikely that the prototypical exemplar in a taxonomy is the most used in the more creative metaphors we risk things by.

This chapter is a rewritten version of a paper entitled 'Clines of metaphoricity and creative metaphors as situated risk taking' first published in *Journal of Literary Semantics*, 17, 2 (1988). The original paper was co-written with Rukmini Bhaya and Michael Toolan and I am grateful to my co-authors for allowing me to use the original paper as a basis for this chapter.

8

DISCOURSE, CONVERSATION AND CREATIVITY

1 INTRODUCTION

This chapter examines some practical and pedagogical issues in the design and implementation of materials at the interface of language and literature, with particular reference to the teaching of English as a second or foreign language. In order to achieve this practical focus, theoretical issues are necessarily never far from the forefront of discussion. There are therefore core questions such as: what is literature? What is literary competence? What kind of materials development is best suited to teaching which enhances both linguistic and literary competence? Such questions, as we have seen in Chapter 6, are not new but answers to the questions, however preliminary and provisional, must continue to form the basis for any prospectus for further development in this field.

A main point in the argument is that an extension of fuller *language awareness* and of the enhanced interpretive skills which should go with it are instrumental to a prospectus for future materials development. In particular, it is argued that course books for the teaching of English should exploit the opportunities provided by recent work in the domain of language awareness and that, if language awareness becomes a more central component in all course books, then the need for *separate* books which seek to integrate language and literature will not exist to the same degree.

Much of the data illustrated here is drawn from the CANCODE project, a corpus-based project designed to collect and analyse samples of everyday conversational discourse (see p. 91 above). The project data exemplifies in places considerable creative facility with language on the part of many speakers; greater awareness of such creativity in ordinary language can be a valuable starting point for an enhanced language and literary awareness. In order to build towards the overall argument the chapter begins with a brief review of materials development at the interface of language and literature study during the past ten years or so.

1.1 Literary materials 1983–93

During the 1980s materials for the teaching of literature in the context of English language teaching have operated according to a number of common theoretical and strategic principles. Among the underlying theoretical assumptions are first that literature is made from language, and that sensitivity to language use is a strong basis for the development of an understanding of literary texts and, particularly in the case of non-native users of a language, often a secure and practical way to unlock the different levels of meaning in such texts. Second, suitably selected literary texts can provide a motivating and stimulating source of content in the language classroom, serving as a basis for discussion and interpretation in which the response of the individual learner is encouraged. Third, the skills of decoding literary texts are transferable to most language learning contexts in which meanings, because they are not always immediately transparent, have to be experienced, negotiated, or 'read' in the sense of interpreted between the lines. Such principles stress the mutual reinforcement and support of literary and linguistic skills and underlie an essentially integrated view of language and literature.

Pedagogically, two main principles can be isolated: an activity principle and a process principle. An activity principle means that students are more than merely passive recipients of interpretations generated by a teacher or assimilated from books of literary criticism. Instead, students actively participate in making the text mean. In this activity they are supported pedagogically by a range of strategies of the kind widely used in the EFL classroom: rewriting, cloze procedures, jumbling texts, role-play, prediction tasks, and so on. A process principle means that students are more likely to appreciate and understand texts if they experience them directly as part of a process of meaning creation. Process-based approaches are learner-centred and seek to encourage students to respond to the text not exclusively as a complete artefact or finished product but rather more to the text as an unfolding process in which the relationship between form and meaning is shown to be central. The learner-centred activities outlined above serve also to stress the unfolding and evolving nature of the reading and interpretation of literary texts. Skills in interpretation are likely to be more successfully fostered if both activity and process principles operate at the same time. For further discussion see Carter and Long (1991: ch. 1) and for specific illustration Chapters 9 and 10 below.

The materials developed during these years have had different inflections according to context, purpose and audience. For example, some more advanced materials have involved learners in more linguistic-stylistic analysis (e.g. Carter and Long, 1987); some materials (e.g. Gower and Pearson, 1986) have been more traditionally literary in orientation, providing detailed reference to literary and cultural history. Some materials have been more eclectic, drawing on a wider range of literary and non-literary texts to encourage the building up of literary competence through interaction with the text, the textbook and others in the class (e.g. Boardman and McRae, 1984; McRae and Pantaleoni, 1991).

All these materials are characterised, however, by being additional or supplementary to mainline language course books. They reflect a teaching context in which language courses and literature courses are taught separately and in which integrated courses in language and literature are not integral to either. In the remainder of this chapter a main argument is for the need to build upon the advances of the past decade but at the same time to switch the focus to the place of language awareness in language and literacy development and to the place of literary texts in all language course materials.[1]

1.2 Some core questions

In order to provide such a focus, some core questions have to be posed. The main ones are: What *is* a literary text and how does it differ from other kinds of text? What is the relationship between literary uses of language and everyday uses? What is literary competence and how does it differ from general linguistic competence? What is literacy development and are there major differences between literacy development in a first language and literacy development in a second or foreign language? Is there such a thing as pre-literary competence (that is, a set of skills basic to the development of a subsequent fuller literary competence)?

The provision of answers to such leading and complex questions depends on many more years of extensive research than have currently been undertaken, but continually to pose the questions is a necessary part of all processes of text selection, materials design and of competence testing in relation to language and literature in language learning.

2 BASIC MATERIAL: THE ARBITRARINESS OF THE SIGN

It can be safely assumed that colour words are among the first words learned in a language (see Wyler, 1992: 43ff.), allowing as they do a necessary contact with the identity of things and providing the language user with a vital means for distinguishing and differentiating within the material world. **Red**, **yellow**, **green**, **black**, **white**, **brown** and **blue** are thus central to the semantic structure of the lexicon of English, and the words are normally assimilated both early in a learning sequence and with relative ease. The centrality and coreness of such words often means, however, that they are extended into a range of compounds and combinations which result in changes in meaning. It also means that such words are available as basic signs for states of mind and feeling, for marking core cultural properties and for shaping attitudes and interactions, usually through processes of idiomatic extension. Taking a core word such as **green**, therefore, we can have the meaning of green as a core colour, as in the first example, but also:

green	=	She is wearing a green skirt.
green	=	They are playing on the green.
Green Cross Code	=	Children must follow the 'Green Cross Code' when crossing the road and when green means go.
green light	=	Give somebody the green light.
greens	=	Eat up your greens (green vegetables) and you'll be healthy.
Greens	=	I'll always vote for the Greens (the Green party) because of their concern for the environment.
greenhouse	=	Tomatoes should normally be grown in a greenhouse; 'the greenhouse effect' is altering weather patterns across the world.
green	=	She's rather green about such things (innocent, inexperienced).
green	=	You've done well to pass the examinations. I'm very green (envious).
green	=	In contrast with 'orange' as the colours of Catholic Republicanism and Protestant Unionism, respectively, in the conflict in Northern Ireland (e.g. an Orangeman).

In a first-language learning environment such meaning extensions to the word **green** and its morphological derivatives are learned in the process of naturalistic exposure to the language in its cultural contexts; in most second- or foreign-language learning environments the specifically cultural, idiomatic and, to a considerable extent, simply *arbitrary* meanings of the sign are normally withheld on the grounds that they are problematic for learners, for the most part reappearing only in upper-intermediate and advanced learning contexts. However, to tidy up the language to this extent may be simultaneously to remove opportunities for recognising and interpreting non-literal forms and meanings in ways which lay a valuable basis for reading and interpreting a variety of texts, including literary texts. McRae (1991) has explored this domain with particular reference to differences and distinctions between referential and representational language. And as we shall see in section 2.2 below, the productivity that results in the derivatives of **green** within prevailing socio-cultural frameworks is immanent in everyday conversational interaction, not just in literary creation.

One essential element in the literariness of language is that there is no single or simple one-to-one correlation between the language used and the meanings produced. Meanings have to be read from the language and the context of use. Such a process of negotiation also pays due attention to the arbitrariness inherent in many language forms, which may require a reorientation to what was supposed to be their point of reference in the world, even a relearning of the frames of reference within which differently possible worlds are created. The process may also require an understanding that more than one meaning can exist as part of the message. To know the word **yellow** is also to know its associations with cowardice; to know the word **blue** is also to know that in English its plural in nominal form ('the blues') is connected with feelings of depression as well as with an associated style of music from the deep South of the United States; to know the word **green** is to know the colour, its natural, vegetative associations *and* its additional considerably more non-literal, representational and arbitrary meanings.

Idioms, metaphors, proverbs and other extensions to what is assumed to be the core of a language are frequent across all languages and may, indeed, be in themselves more core than the construction of language courses would suggest. They are often embedded within the cultures which are intrinsic to that language and therefore do not readily translate between and across languages. But awareness of such features and interpretations of them allows access to these cultural embeddings, providing in the process opportunities for interpreting meanings which are communicated with varying degrees of indirectness and obliqueness.

As a preparation for subsequent reading of complete literary texts such awareness is valuable in this connection but the language learner is also learning that words have extended meanings as well as learning those meanings themselves, that meanings often have to be negotiated, that language is something to be learned *about* as well as learned, and that language is not just a fossilised code but a productive resource of great creative potential.

2.1 Playing with words

The simultaneous holding of more than one meaning within the communicative layers of a message is basic to a very wide variety of language use, from everyday conversation to the most elaborate literary texts, and in the context of language and literacy development may therefore be better included in the language course and not separated off into the literature course or into more advanced supplementary materials. Very young children possess the capacity for telling and receiving jokes which depend for their effect on a recognition of creative play with patterns of meaning. For example, first-language learners of English encounter in the school playground creative exchanges such as the following:

Q: What is black and white and read all over?
A: A newspaper.

They can also give varying explanations for a newspaper headline such as the following:

General flies back to front

– both instances of which depend on recognising dual meanings created by the phonology (read/red) and syntax of English (front is both a noun and a preposition).

Advertising language also depends crucially on creative play with language and on the cultural discourses of society within which the language is embedded (see, in particular, Cook, 1992; also Moeran, 1984; Tanaka, 1992). For example, an advertisement for a motor car which states that it is 'A car for the 90°s' holds simultaneously together the possibility that it is a car in which you can travel at great speeds (90 m.p.h.), that it is particularly suited to very hot weather (90 degrees – the temperature reaches the nineties Fahrenheit), and that it is ultra modern and in tune with expectations for the decade (the 1990s). To provide learners with such a text and working collaboratively with them to decode it is also to provide them with an especially rich set of possibilities for learning language, for learning about language and for the development of literary competence. All the texts discussed so far have required some engagement and interaction on the part of the reader/interpreter; the reader has been positioned, as has been remarked in several chapters of this book, in a creative conversation or dialogue with the text.

So-called ordinary, everyday discourse is frequently patterned creatively so that it is memorable and striking, displaying a play with the more stable forms of language in ways which make them less stable. In the process the limits of idioms, fixed expressions and other pre-patterned regularities are stretched and creatively deformed and reformed. The names of shopfronts are a good example of this creative design, playing with common collocations and idioms in order to make language used to describe the products they offer part of the presentation. Here are examples of a chain of health food shops in Southern Ireland:

Nature's Way
Mother Nature
Back to Nature
Open Sesame
In a Nutshell
Wholesome Foods
The Whole Story
Fruit and Nut Case
Naturally Yours
Grain of Truth
Simple Simon
Nature's Store
Just Natural

Most of these words and phrases (many of them fixed expressions or idioms) are connected with nature and a simple way of life and are creatively exploited to promote the sale of food which is either organically grown or which is defined as having particularly health-giving properties. For example, words like **grain, nut, nutshell, store, whole** and **wholesome, sesame (seeds)** are all words used to describe specific foods or specific qualities associated with such food; and they are then combined into fixed expressions such as 'in a nutshell' or 'grain of truth', which draw attention to themselves as expressions and are made memorable by their unusual association with the sale of health food products. The examples here illustrate a basis for awareness of literary and cultural uses of language. Terms such as 'literary' and 'cultural' are used with a small 'l' and a small 'c' (see McRae, 1991). In other words, creativity and cultural embedding are not the exclusive preserve of canonical texts but are pervasive in the most everyday uses of language (see also Alptekin and Alptekin, 1990; Gibbs, 1994 and from the point of view of practical language teaching resources, Prodromou, 1990). Further related examples are discussed in Chapter 10.

2.2 Creativity in conversation

It is not just in the more deliberately planned contexts such as journalism, joke-telling and advertising that we find embedded cultural references, extended uses of linguistic forms, metaphors and idioms, and language in general being creatively manipulated. Everyday conversation reveals uses of language that are strongly associated with criteria for 'literariness', that is with the uses of language that characterise texts held by members of given speech communities to be 'literary'. One of the more negative aspects of the communicative movement in language teaching that has dominated the last couple of decades is an overemphasis on the transactional uses of language (i.e. the transacting of information, goods and services) at the expense of interactional uses (i.e. for the creation and reinforcement of social relationships) and creative uses. In McCarthy and Carter (1994) in particular that trend is criticised in an attempt to formulate what a language-teaching syllabus based on a notion of language as discourse would entail. However, the communicative urge has been a double-edged sword, and the very desire for authenticity in communication has led language practitioners to look more and more towards real spoken data, where day-to-day creativity and cultural embedding leap to the fore again.

Empirically based studies in discourse analysis continue to reveal the pervasiveness of creativity in everyday discourse and to recognise that so-called literary tropes such as metaphor and metonymy (as well as figurative imagery in general) play a seminal part in the construction of interpersonal relationships. Recent studies by Tannen (1989), McCarthy and Carter (1994), Brazil (1995) and McCarthy (1997) recognise that casual conversation intrinsically creates a space within which speakers can fulfil what would appear to be a basic need to insert a more personal or personally evaluative position into the ongoing discourse. It is as if the relationships which are so important a part

160

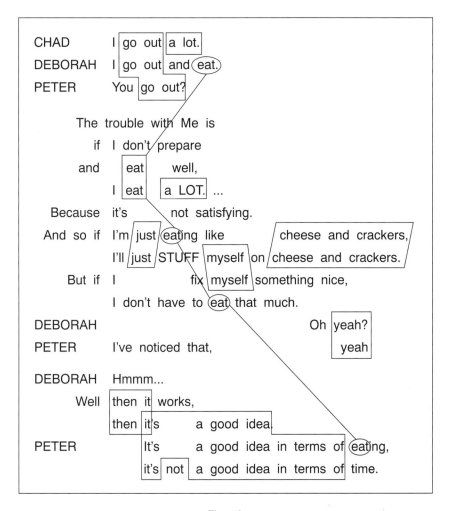

Figure 6.

of casual conversation cannot be fully realised without an element of verbal play and inventiveness; and it is as if verbal play and creativity in talk are in essence interactive and interpersonal in character, that a fundamental casual conversational strategy is to engage and involve others and that there is an underlying recognition that, although, as Cook (1996) suggests, casual conversation is often a space-filling discourse, it comprehends so much more than the transfer into the space of information.

Tannen (1988: 71) has commented extensively on this feature of conversational discourse and with particular reference to repetition (see Figure 6). Crystal (1995: 413) has summarised and himself glossed this position in a clear and helpful way, drawing on the above data examined by Tannen herself in her book *Talking Voices* (Tannen, 1988):

Crystal (1995: 413) comments:

> Not only does it readily admit linguistic deviance, it displays many of the formal features which are traditionally thought to be 'literary', such as metrical rhythm, syntactic parallelism, figurative language, alliteration and verbal repetition . . .
>
> The literariness of a conversation is not immediately obvious . . . Transcribed in a conventional manner, it is difficult to see anything of interest taking place. Laid out differently, several patterns begin to emerge and a more informed comparison can be made with the crafted conversation of drama. Only the lexical patterns are shown: several other links can be found between certain grammatical words (*I*, *if*) and there are signs of phonological repetition too (*in terms of time, lot/not, just/ stuff/much*).

(For a study which also parallels poetic structure with language structure in a non-literary event – livestock auctions – see Kuiper and Haggo, 1984.)

In the following extract from CANCODE data, a not dissimilar pattern of phonological echo and lexical repetition occurs (is the relationship between 'bob' and 'Bob' in the fixed idiom 'Bob's your uncle' accidental?) alongside a further creative extension of an idiomatic phrase ('to get/have a finger in every pie').

B: Yes, he must have a bob or two.

A: Whatever he does, he makes money out of it. Just like that.

B: Bob's your uncle.

A: He's quite a lot of money tied up in property and things like that. He's got a finger in all kinds of pies and houses and things. A couple in Bristol, and one in Cleveland I think.

Further scrutiny of naturally occurring, informal conversational data of the kind collected as part of the CANCODE project appears to refute the notion that speakers are not normally creative in their daily uses of language and that certain fixed linguistic structures, idioms in particular, cannot be unfixed. Instead, numerous examples show that speakers can engage in creative play with idiom: here are two teachers talking about their classes:

A: The second year I had, I started off with 37 in the class, I know that, of what you call dead wood, the real dregs had been taken off the bottom and the cream, the sour cream in our case, up there had been creamed off the top and I just had this dead wood, I mean it really was and he was so impressed with the job I did with them and the way I got on with them and he immediately said, how do you feel about taking a special class next year? And I took one from then on.

B: Rather you than me.

The idiom structure here is creatively transmuted in the play with **cream** (which is good) and **sour cream** which is not good and between metaphors of **down** and **dregs** which are not good and **up** and **top** which are good. Here idiomatic and fixed expressions are used almost in the manner of extended metaphors but they are deployed in order to comment on the world in some way rather than to describe it. They are frequently evaluative in a manner which confirms Gibbs's hypothesis (see Gibbs, 1994) that idioms are never just neutral alternatives to semantically equivalent, literal transparent expressions. They nearly always display a marked interpersonal orientation.

Irony and sarcasm are also common features of much conversational discourse. Indeed, fixed expressions can be deployed to critically ironic purpose; as in the following conversational extract from CANCODE data (based on the phrase 'And pigs might fly' – a fixed phrase used to frame an unlikely event), when a friend, who is notoriously unreliable at remembering to repay debts, promises to repay a small loan the following day:

A: Thanks I won't forget this time. Till tomorrow OK?
B: Brian, can you see those pigs over my left shoulder, moving slowly across the sky . . .
[*A and B burst into laughter.*]

As in this example, the witty, ironic effects depend on shared knowledge; here both participants are aware of the phrase 'And pigs might fly' which is 'echoed' by B and which needs to be interpreted indirectly by A by drawing on such mutual understanding.

Ironic utterances are to an extent culture-specific and may cause problems for learners who are not suitably acculturated: in Britain, for example, remarks about the weather are frequently given an ironic preface such as:

Lovely day, isn't it?
Warm enough for you?
Just right for a day on the beach

– all of which refer to weather which is cold and inclement and which require a listener to work out that the referential propositions advanced do not obtain directly or literally. The listener furthermore interprets the speaker as making a critical, evaluative comment on current meteorological conditions. Irony belongs within a range of contextually generated effects such as sarcasm, satire, understatement and hyperbole which produce meanings that are non-literal and that require listeners to make indirect, interpretive inferences.

That such communicative features are common in conversations (particularly in informal casual discourse) reinforces the view that ordinary language can be pervasively unordinary and can involve the creation and interpretation of patterns which enjoy a family resemblance with those more usually designated literary.

2.3 Morphological creativity

Another kind of creativity which students of literature have to contend with, especially in modern poetry, is morphological creativity, whereby derivational potential is creatively exploited. Vizmuller-Zocco (1985) sees lexical derivation as belonging to 'that linguistic competence which is based on creativity', while Howden (1984) sees the native speaker's knowledge of existing derived words and what the potential for choice is as centrally important; she also stresses the interrelationships of meaning set up by new combinations of stems and affixes. Such creativity is surprisingly common in everyday talk, and can be used as the basis of a bridge towards its more daunting manifestations in literary texts. Here are some examples from the Nottingham University CANCODE Corpus (see above, p.91) of speakers exploiting the **-y** suffix in non-institutionalised word-forms to create diffuse and evaluative meaning:

> [*B, who is preparing food, has asked A to get her a bowl.*]
> *A*: You said you wanted the little ones as well. Want the little ones?
> *B*: Not really . . . sort of **salady** . . . that fruit bowl would be ideal.

> [*A is describing some newfangled shoelaces she has bought.*]
> *A*: They're well sort of like lycra, **elasticky** sort of stuff.

> [*A and B are deciding where to go for the evening.*]
> *A*: Cos there's a really nice place me and Myra go to.
> *B*: Oh I don't want a romantic **mewsy** pub

On another occasion, using the **-ing** inflexion, a speaker 'derives' a verb from a noun while telling a story of a dangerous game he and his friends played as children, rolling down industrial spoil heaps inside old lorry tyres. He intensifies the nightmarish rolling movement:

> *A*: And you'd just roll, like **circusing** right the way down and get right up the top.

This is not inherently different from the poet Seamus Heaney's morphological creativity in describing the flight of a snipe: 'as he **corkscrews** away / into the vaults / that we live off' ('The Backward Look').

In another extract in the corpus, two women are assembling a portable baby-cot which involves twisting the metal parts until they become rigid. Note how speaker B uses morphological creativity, this time with a prefix (instead of using the more conventional 'loose' or 'slack'), to satirise her own mistake in the twisting movement:

A: There, that's solid now.
B: I think I've made it **unsolid** . . . sorry . . . I've done it the wrong way round, have I.

We find parallels of this in poetry, with the 'hot **unasking** sun' and 'the friendless and **unhated** stone' in W. H. Auden's poem 'As He Is'. To make such parallels between conversation and literary text is, as stated several times in this book, not to demean literary text in any way. As Widdowson (1975: 36) points out, it is the randomness of such occurrences in conversation as opposed to their *patterning* in literary text which is the significant difference. What the literary and conversational contexts cited have in common is their ability to bring together elements that are normally separated in the language code, to borrow again an observation from Widdowson (ibid.: 57). It is this common property that the teaching of literature and language can exploit.

Morphological creativity can be combined with satirical cultural reference too, as in this extract where a hostess (speaker A) is apologising to her dinner guests (one of whom is speaker B) that they are a little short of home-grown vegetables. The extract reinforces with real data our comments above on the breadth of lexical extension and shared cultural reference that accrues to a basic term such as **green**:

A: And so I'm afraid we're a bit sort of erm challenged **greenwise**.
B: **Greenly** challenged.
A: We're **greenly** challenged so erm sorry about that.

Here we have the morphological creativity of **greenwise** and **greenly** combined with an oblique cultural reference to phrases such as **visually challenged**, **physically challenged**, etc., as current 'politically correct' euphemisms for 'blind' and 'disabled', just as being 'green' (growing one's own vegetables organically, etc.) is a politically correct stance. The pun works on several levels, and it is significant that the joke is jointly created by the two speakers, emphasising the high degree of shared cultural knowledge and convergence. Along the scale from everyday conversational punning to literary text we find parallels in journalistic satire. The following example is taken from a recent newspaper article on left-handedness:

> These . . . figures come from a survey held by the Left-Handers' Club . . . the national mouthpiece of the **dexterously challenged**.[2]

The importance of awareness of multiple meanings has also been mentioned. Speakers play on these spontaneously by exploiting the real, immediate context for humorous effects, just as ready-made jokes exploit fictitious contexts. In the next conversational extract, a group of young female students are taking tea together, and two such ambiguities are exploited within a very short stretch of text:

A: Yeah, did you ever do . . . erm erm . . . oh what was she called erm Cynthia.
B: Did I ever do Cynthia.
A: [*laughs*]

B: [*laughs*] Can't say, did you.

. . .

A: Oh this is wonderful, Bakewell tarts.

B: Tea and tarts.

A: [*laughs*] tea and tarts.

B: [*laughs*] tea with

A: Tea with tarts [*laughs*] . . . tarts with tea.

'Do' is exploited for its sexual ambiguity and 'tarts' for its meanings of (a) a sweet pastry item and (b) a slang term for a prostitute.

These examples are some of the many kinds of linguistic creativity that one finds in a corpus of everyday conversation. They have in common with literary language that language is being made to 'stick out' from its context of use. Casual conversation is classically marked by a high degree of automatic and unconscious routine language use, but, now and again, speakers make their language draw attention to itself in some way, displacing it from its immediate context, a phenomenon Widdowson (1992: 26) has argued to be a fundamental characteristic of poetic language. It can therefore be argued that to use in the language class only those types of dialogue that are transparent and transactional and devoid of richness, cultural reference and creativity is to misrepresent what speakers actually do and simultaneously to lose an opportunity for interesting language awareness work of the kind which may be an ideal precursor to enhanced literary awareness.

2.4 Semantic density: grading the text

It is clear that some instances of language require a greater effort of processing. One reason for this is that they possess a greater semantic density. Stretches of language or texts such as the advertisement for 'A car for the 90°s', involving as they do a greater element of creative play with language and a layering of patterns at different levels, generally demand more processing effort than the semantic reordering of the word **green** as a colour to the phrase 'on the green' in which the word refers to a stretch of (mostly) green parkland. Similarly, idioms such as 'bumper to bumper', as in 'the traffic was bumper to bumper', are semantically transparent when compared with idioms such as 'to smell a rat' or 'to be on the ball'. Proverbs such as 'don't cry over spilt milk' allow real-world analogies to be drawn or semantic extensions to be made in a relatively more straightforward way than is normally the case with proverbs such as 'every cloud has a silver lining', which involve more indirect and metaphoric processes of decoding and interpretation.

The following examples of the names of shopfronts for hairdressers' shops in Britain involve varying degrees of creative play with language (and are indeed essentially *literary* in such verbal play), and require competence in recognising a multilayering of effects; but some names are more semantically dense

166

and require a greater processing effort than others which are less oblique and less multilayered in the creation of meaning:

Highlights	Brush Strokes
Way Ahead	Cut Above
Headlines	Hair Comes Linda
Shampers	Hair and Share Alike
Cut 'n' Dried	Headcase
New Wave	

'Way Ahead', for example, is more transparent in its straightforward link between hairdressing and 'head' and its suggestion that hair styling in this shop puts you at a social advantage over others, as does 'Cut Above', from the idiom 'to be a cut above the rest', meaning to be superior, though this example demands more idiomatic knowledge, as does 'Cut 'n' Dried', a patterned semantic equation between the idiom and cultural behaviour (a confident, no-nonsense approach) as well as a literal link between cutting and drying hair. 'Shampers' too requires a specific cultural knowledge of the drinking of champagne (colloquial word 'shampers' and its phonetic analogy with shampoo) in contexts of high living. 'Brush Strokes' obliquely suggests 'art', while 'Headcase' (meaning 'crazy', 'lunatic') suggests a zany, youthful environment, and so on.

As we have seen (above, section 2.1), proverbs, idioms, metaphors, jokes and texts such as newspaper headlines, advertisements and some titles/names for shops involve language use which is central to the culture patterned in and through that language. A further processing effort is therefore required in the case of those texts which invoke specific frames of cultural reference, for without the relevant cultural knowledge interpretation becomes a much more testing procedure. For example, children's jokes such as:

Q: Waiter, we're getting hungry. How long will the spaghetti be?
A: Each piece is about 15 centimetres.

Q: What's the difference between a teabag and Everton?
A: A teabag stays in the cup.

demand knowledge which is culture-specific (knowledge that Everton is a Liverpool-based football club with a poor FA 'Cup' record; or knowledge that spaghetti consists of long strips of pasta in addition to the linguistic knowledge that 'long' can be both an adverb of time and an adverb of measurement.

Jokes are generically diverse and range from straightforward verbal punning as in the instances above (p.158) to jokes which allude to or reproduce specific sets of sociocultural assumptions. Thus, in the following example:

British Rail announces: Coffee up 20p a slice

the comic equation of coffee (a liquid) with the word 'slice' (normally applied to pieces of bread or to cake) together with the sizeable cost of the increase combine to reveal much in public attitudes to British Rail; for example, that British Rail is believed to provide a poor but expensive service; that food and beverages served on British Rail are expensive and of poor quality; that the coffee, in particular, is barely drinkable and is more like bread or cake in its consistency (see Chiaro, 1992).

And some texts allude in ways which require specific literary knowledge. For example, a camping shop with an advertising slogan:

Now is the winter of our discount tents

may only be processed on one level by readers not acquainted with a key speech from Shakespeare's *Richard III* (for this and further similar examples, see McCarthy, 1992).

On the other hand, some effects produced in conventionally identifiable contexts such as poetry are less semantically dense. Poems by Dylan Thomas which contain phrases such as 'all the sun long' or 'once below a time' (based on the fixed phrases 'all the day long' or 'once upon a time') obtain their effects from, for example, a basic substitution of 'sun' for 'day', creating a suggestion that the sun shone through the day. Alternatively, titles such as Dylan Thomas's 'A Grief Ago' allow grief to be measured in temporal terms by substitution of a noun describing the emotion for the more usual noun measuring time such as hour, week, month or year. Recognising such patterns is instrumental to understanding the effects which such patterns produce. Producing them, as a British actress did recently in a television interview (commenting that a 1950s film she had appeared in was 'four husbands ago'), is a marker of a linguistic inventiveness and creativity which all 'ordinary' language users possess.

In this section it has been suggested that texts from various sources can be utilised to promote the development of skills of interpreting, inference, reading between the lines, that such texts could be included as a natural and normal component in language teaching materials at all but the most elementary levels, and that such texts can be graded and thus appropriately sequenced according to the relative degrees of processing effort required of them.

3 LANGUAGE AWARENESS: OPENING A DOOR TO LITERARY COMPETENCE

The above arguments are for learners to engage earlier in second- or foreign-language learning processes with samples of non-literal, representational language. Such engagement entails processes of interaction with and inter-pretation of language use. A necessary prerequisite for this kind of interaction and interpretation is a fuller awareness of language itself as a medium. This requires of learners that they become more reflective as learners, that is, that they become more conscious of texts and stretches of language as containing messages which need to be negotiated for meaning. In addition to interpreting language use they need to be aware of how they have made interpretations and to reflect on interpretive procedures, learning, in other words, how to learn better to interpret and engage with such texts as a result of more conscious operations.

The orientation here is parallel to that advocated by, among others, Ellis and Sinclair (1989) who have constructed teaching materials designed to enhance both awareness of the nature of the language system being learned and consciousness of the learner's own procedures for learning the language. Ellis and Sinclair's work underlines that a more conscious reflective language learner is a more effective language learner. For further arguments on the relationship between language awareness and language learning, see Donmall (1985); Hawkins (1987); James and Garrett (1992); Carter (1994); Bardovi-Harlig *et al.* (1991); Holborrow (1991).

4 CONCLUSION

One of the main theoretical and practical implications of this chapter is that the term 'literature' is not defined in any exclusive sense. The position adopted here is close to that established by Carter and Nash (1990), exemplified with comparisons of conversational data and literary texts by McCarthy (1994a, 1994b), and developed more fully in pedagogy by McRae (1991) and McCarthy and Carter (1994: ch. 4). It is that of recognising the co-existence of literature with a capital 'L' (canonical literature) and of literature with a small 'l' (the latter is the title of McRae's 1991 book – examples of texts, ranging from proverbs to jokes, to advertisements, which can be read as displaying literariness). Such a position may be felt by some, especially teachers of literature, to demean texts valued by a cultural community as of canonical status; the argument here is that, far from demeaning literary texts, it reveals and endorses the creativity inherent in much 'ordinary' everyday language use.

Literary uses of language and the necessary skills for its interpretation go routinely with all kinds of text, spoken and written. Literature exists at many different levels for different people in different communities but it is argued here that literary language is not simply any use of language. The main argument in this chapter is that literary language will always be patterned in some way and will involve a creative play with these patterns. The patterns may also involve words or structures which are representational and not intended to be read literally. The patterns invite involvement on the part of a reader or hearer who then has an option to interpret the text as the context and circumstances of the language use appear to him/her to demand. This patterned, representational 'literary' aspect of language is central to language use, though it will of course occur with greater density in some texts than others. The sooner language learners can come to appreciate this central component of language, the sooner they appreciate that they themselves and other users of language are essentially creative. In the future pedagogies and related tests for literary language development are likely to be all the richer for recognising this reality.

This chapter is a rewritten version of a paper entitled 'Discourse and creativity: bridging the gap between language and literature' in Cook, G. and Seidlhofer, B. (eds) *Principles and Practice in Applied Linguistics: Studies in Honour of H.G. Widdowson* (Oxford University Press, Oxford, 1995). The paper was co-written with Michael McCarthy, to whom I am grateful for allowing me to draw on the original source.[3]

9

TEACHING LANGUAGE AND LITERARINESS

INTRODUCTION

The main aim of this chapter is to argue that in the teaching of English as a second or foreign language, opportunities should be sought for more extensive and integrated study of language and literature than is commonly the case at present. The first half of the chapter discusses some language-based **study skills** which I consider important preliminary activities to reading literature. Although the study skills I discuss are language-based, I am not claiming that understanding the language is the same as understanding the literature. For this reason, I stress that these skills/activities are preliminary and pre-literary. In the second half of the chapter I discuss the use of a linguistically based model in application to a literary narrative. I claim that studying models like this can contribute much to the development of literary competence. Such language-based analysis can also have considerable benefits for the study of the language and thus aids the integration of language and literary study; again, however, we must exercise caution, since language and literature are separate **systems** or phenomena, although literature is made from language which is its primary medium and is, therefore, of considerable significance in our reading of literature. For this reason, I consider that the use of linguistic models enables us to work on the **literariness** of texts rather than on texts as 'literature'. Recognition of literariness is one of the most fundamental components in literary competence.

Other related aims of this chapter are as follows. It is suggested that for students of a foreign literature linguistic models and pre-literary linguistic activities can:

(a) aid recognition of and sensitivity to the nature of **language organisation** in related discourse types in the target language;
(b) lay a basis for **interpretation** of texts by analysing closely key structural features of the language of that text;
(c) explain the literary **character** of particular texts (in this instance, narrative style in a short story);
(d) point to features of **literariness** in texts by simultaneous application of

171

relevant models to non-literary texts *and* to texts conventionally considered literary;

(e) promote **learner-centred language activities** which are relevant for general language development.

1 LANGUAGE TEACHING STRATEGIES

In this section a number of teaching strategies are proposed. They have no special claim to originality; indeed, language teachers will probably recognise them as part of their everyday tools of the trade. They are employed in the belief that they can assist the preliminary or pre-literary process of understanding and appreciating the text in question. It is clear that another text may require different strategies and also that any adequate teaching of a literary text goes beyond language teaching techniques, however widely used and principled they may be. However, it is claimed in the case of short narratives like Somerset Maugham's 'The Man with the Scar' that the strategies are broadly generalisable. The text is printed at the end of the chapter.

1.1 Prediction: what comes next?

This requires careful preparation before the story is read in class. The technique is for the teacher to stop the reading at key points and to elicit predictions of how the narrative will develop. In the case of 'The Man with the Scar' a number of 'stopping places' can be suggested.

(a) The title can be omitted and, after the story has been read, students can be invited to predict what it should be.

(b) At the end of the first paragraph, students might be asked to predict, on the basis of the information supplied about the man, what the story is going to be about. This can be an important stage in sensitising students to the function of the opening of the story in an interpretation of the whole. This opening bears an interestingly oblique relation to the rest of the text.

(c) In the second narrator's narrative a cut-off could occur at lines 85–86: 'She flung herself into his arms and with a hoarse cry of passion . . . , he pressed his lips to hers'; or at the question of the general in line 101; and/or at a point which elicits a prediction of the reaction of the general to the action of the man in slitting the throat of his wife (line 105): 'the general stared at him for a while in silence'.

(d) The end of the story also allows an interesting predictive focus at the point where a question is asked about the man's scar in line: '"But how then did he get the scar?" I asked at length.'

These are all key points in the development of the plot. This is not the place to discuss in detail the nature of predictions made. Each class will produce its own varied responses. The teaching point to underline is that a heightened degree of attentiveness to the story can be brought about by prediction. There is increased involvement as a result of the natural desire of seeing one's own expectations fulfilled or contravened.

Features of the structure of the story can be highlighted for subsequent discussion. A firm basis is laid for exploring such questions as: why did the man do what he did? Was he right or wrong in so doing? Did the general torture him more by allowing him to live? Prediction exercises lend themselves particularly to work in pairs or small groups, with individuals being invited to justify their own or the group's verbal prediction by close reference to the foregoing text and to their own individual experiences of human behaviour. Some groups persist in their preferences for outcomes alternative to those given by the writer, and they can be encouraged in this so long as evidence and support is forthcoming. Such activities can be a basis for stimulating and motivating class oral work and discussion. There is no reason why in some cases this should not be done in the students' own language, but the target language should be used wherever feasible.

In the face of 'gaps' (see Rimmon-Kenan, 1983: 125–7) in the narrative, such as some conclusion or evaluation of the behaviour of the man with the scar on the part of the first narrator, prediction serves the function of allowing that gap to be filled by the reader. However, prediction activities should be used sparingly. Not all texts lend themselves to this kind of macrostylistic work. Most lyric poems, for example, or texts where descriptive states are evoked, do not benefit. But texts with a strong plot component, where the next step in the action can be significant, do force readers to predict. And the best narratives will contain the seeds of their own development, so that readers have to read back as well as project forward. This is the case, I want to assert, with 'The Man with the Scar', where an additional advantage of prediction exercises is that they draw attention to the dual narrative structure of the story.

1.2 Cloze procedure

This is, as many language teachers know, a form of prediction. The focus is on individual words or sequences of words, rather than on stretches of text. There is also an inevitable concentration on microstylistic effects which can be of a subtle and complex kind in some stories. Teachers will need to give careful attention to the number of words deleted, to the relative multivalency of the chosen items, to the linguistic competence of a group, and, perhaps, to preparatory activities on non-literary texts in order to give practice in contexts where a greater degree of predictability may obtain (though predictability is not the exclusive preserve of the non-literary text; indeed, 'literary' effects can be produced by predictable and unpredictable elements). Items which might be deleted from this story include:

(a) line 102 'I —— her.'
(b) line 106 'It was a —— gesture,' he said at last.
(c) from the title: 'The Man with . . .' (e.g. a scar; lottery tickets; a grudge?).
(d) line 10 '. . . strolling leisurely round the bar offer —— for sale'

and so on.

Lexical prediction can be made during a reading or after the story has been read, and preferably after some preliminary discussion. It can be used as well as, or instead of, structural plot-based prediction. Reasonable and supportable predictions require students to be alert both to the overall pattern of the story and to the immediate verbal context in which the deleted word occurs. Some students are assisted if the first letter of the word is given or if a list of words – from which an appropriate choice is to be made – is supplied by the teacher. For example, with reference to (b) above, if students are asked to choose from a list of words as follows:

'It was a —— gesture,' he said at last.
brave noble foolhardy futile ignoble

then they are being asked to focus on words which have resonances across the whole story. To justify and account for their decisions they are being asked to demonstrate careful and close reading of the story.

As with structural prediction, such 'lexical' prediction can lead to the kind of individual and group involvement with the text as well as to the kind of oral language practice which are not usually engendered by exposition from the teacher. Structural and lexical prediction can be employed jointly, and interesting oral and group language can emerge from asking students to delete words for other classes to predict. (For an interesting history of cloze methods in language teaching – some with obvious possibilities of transfer to the literature class – see Soudek and Soudek, 1983.)

1.3 Summary: what's it all about?

A strategy designed to focus attention on the overall point or meaning of the story is to ask students to produce summaries of the text. Indiscriminate use of summary has its dangers, and instructions need to be fairly precisely formulated, because otherwise there is a danger of committing the heresy of paraphrase by suggesting that there is a paraphrasable meaning to the story. The technique should be seen rather as an enabling device for students in their personal process of interpretation or engagement with the text.

It is useful to impose a word limit for the summary (in a range, say, of 25–40 words, in the case of a story as short as 'The Man with the Scar'), and to ask initially for a summary which is not an interpretation of the story but rather an account of *what happens*. The reasons for this are mainly three-fold:

(a) An imposed word limit makes the exercise a useful one linguistically. Much syntactic restructuring, deletion, and lexical reshaping goes into meeting the word limit. The teacher can do much here to foster integrated language and literature work.

(b) A word limit enforces selection of what is significant. Does the summary, for example, include reference to the 'scar' or to the man's run of bad luck at cards prior to the execution? Is the story's political background brought into the foreground? Students learn that even a summary of what happens is in one sense an interpretive act.

(c) Students come to see that a summary of what happens is not a reason for valuing our reading of short stories by writers such as Maugham. There is, of course, more to it than this. But they should also come to understand the difference between plot and theme, evaluate the role of plot in a story like this, discuss why there appears to be no clear indication that we are to read this as any more than an account of what happens. That is, the title (in one sense a summary) is strangely oblique and there is minimal thematic pointing by the two narrators – especially in their dialogue at the close of the story. Summarising the story means that attention can be focused on *how* it is narrated as well as on what is narrated, and questions can be generated about the structure and shape of this kind of narrative. Such work points to an introduction of the kind of linguistic model for narrative structure described below.

A related linguistic and literary exercise is to invite students to compare and criticise alternative summaries. Here are three recently produced in my own class (structured limits were not always met, but the effort to conform is valuable for all):

> A man with a scar now lives a life of misery because, when facing an execution, he killed the woman he loved and was pardoned.
> A man received a scar from a burst ginger-beer bottle. He was a general and was to be executed but is now a lottery ticket seller.
> A political exile from Nicaragua ensures his own survival by murdering his wife in a sufficiently 'noble' way. He impresses his executioners but becomes emotionally scarred.

Note that summaries can also be supplied by the teacher for comparison.

1.4 Forum: debating opposing viewpoints

One advantage of a story such as 'The Man with the Scar' is that it is a relatively open text, sufficiently inexplicit in its meanings to allow for students to be asked to debate opposing propositions:

A *The man calculated that to murder his wife was the only way he could survive execution. He deserved the scar he got, but life is a lottery.*

B *The man was so devoted to his wife that he knew their life could not be lived alone.
He thought they should both die together. The scar is the surface sign of a deep emotional
wounding at his loss. He did not deserve this kind of scar, but life is a lottery.*

'Forum' is not a technical term but suggests the inherent potentiality of literature to mobilise among students discussion and debate with each other.
The exercise is one which lends itself to small group-based activity with groups
being allocated to the defence of either one of the propositions, even if this
may not be their own personal view. The group (and then its spokesperson)
adduces evidence from a combination of world knowledge and the text in
question to support points relevant to the 'argument'. The other groups listen
and try to provide counter-examples. Either the whole class can participate
or a section of the class can be assigned the task of judging and then voting
for which propositions they consider to have been most persuasively argued.
The whole exercise is a stimulus to oral language work through role-play and
can be prepared for accordingly; from a specifically literary-textual viewpoint
students learn that texts *of any kind* do not easily allow of singular or unitary
interpretation.

1.5 Guided rewriting

Guided rewriting is another widely employed language teaching strategy. It is
aimed at helping students to recognise the broader discoursal patterns of texts
and the styles appropriate to them. It involves the student in rewriting stretches
of discourse to change its communicative value.

In the case of standard language teaching procedures this can involve
rewriting a set of instructions as a description, or turning a lecture transcript
into academic prose. The basis for the strategy is to provide practice at
expressing intents within contexts according to clearly specified information
about audiences and purposes. In the case of a literary text it is, of course,
much less easy to specify such parameters, but it is claimed that, as a general
rule, it can be productive to focus rewriting exercises at the beginnings of
texts, since it is here that the kind of 'information' conveyed can have most
impact on readers. It is also claimed that the re-writing of one style into
another should help students to begin to discern a writer's communicative
effects and to explore the connections between styles and meanings: furthermore, such investigation can be especially illuminating when openings to
literary and non-literary texts are juxtaposed.

An illustration can be provided by the following newspaper narrative report
together with the opening to 'The Man with the Scar':

'Dingo' Appeal Rejected

by DENIS WARNER in Melbourne

Three Federal Court judges in Sydney yesterday dismissed Mrs Lindy Chamberlain's appeal against her conviction in the 'dingo baby' case.

What is a dingo? Why inverted commas? The reader assumes it is an appeal against conviction in a court. But conviction for what?

The place names indicate that the case and presumably the crime took place in Australia.

But what is the 'dingo baby' case?

They ordered 35-year-old Mrs Chamberlain to be delivered to the Berrinah Jail in Darwin as soon as convenient to resume her sentence of life imprisonment with hard labour for the murder of her infant daughter Azaria at Ayers Rock in Central Australia.

Background begins.

As soon as the appeal was dismissed, Mrs Chamberlain's lawyers applied for a stay of the imprisonment order, but this was refused. The lawyers later sought leave to appeal to the High Court which may hear her application for renewed bail on Monday.

The case began with the disappearance of Azaria from a tent in a holiday park near Ayers Rock in August 1980. Mrs Chamberlain maintained that the baby had been taken by a dingo (Australian wild dog).

We are told what a 'dingo' is, and what happened. We can now explain the inverted commas in the heading.

New baby

After two inquests she was found guilty of murder at a trial in Darwin but was released on bail after the birth three weeks later of her fourth child, Kahlia.

Further background is provided.

Mrs Chamberlain maintained her composure throughout yesterday's brief court session. Her husband Michael, a 38-year-old Seventh Day Adventist minister, also appeared calm after hearing the court dismiss his appeal against his conviction for

177

disposing of nine-week-old Azaria's body.

The husband, under a suspended sentence as an accessory after the fact, left court with Kahlia and church officials for his living quarters at an Adventist college.

At the Darwin trial, the jury unanimously decided Mrs Chamberlain slit her daughter's throat in the family car at Ayers Rock. But the prosecution never found the body or a murder weapon.

(From The *Daily Telegraph* [London] 30 April 1983)

Here the teacher uses the newspaper report to generate questions which are not immediately answered by the text (see marginal comments to the text). It is a report in which the reader is presumed to know certain information. If the reader does not have access to this information, then it is not until the background is supplied that it begins to make sense. The following rewriting exercises would be designed to sensitise students to the different ways in which information is structured for readers in different texts:

1 Rewrite the text ' "Dingo" Appeal Rejected', deleting all references to the background in the case and all information concerning the 'characters' in the case (including the definition of a 'dingo').
2 Rewrite the same text, bringing as much background as possible to the first two paragraphs of the report.
3 Rewrite the opening paragraph of 'The Man with the Scar', including as many details as you can invent about the man, his name, age, where he is from, how he got his scar, why he is selling lottery tickets in this bar, and so on.

Teachers will doubtless be able to construct for themselves numerous related activities. (Chapter 5 contains further discussion of rewriting in relation to the notion of discourse literacy.) What can students and teachers hope to gain from this kind of examination? It is to be hoped that the following learning takes place:

1. Students begin to manipulate or, at least, practise manipulating bits of English text. This is a linguistically based, language improvement exercise, but it is useful to consider such activities in the light of an article by Brazil (1983: 165) where he concludes:

Possibly the best way of fostering a pupil's sensitivity to literature is not by feeding him more and more literature but by encouraging him to see literary language as continuous with, and deriving its power to move from, his total language experience.

For example, here is an 'alternative' rewritten opening to 'The Man with the Scar', produced by a small group of German students of English. It is based on exercise 3, above:

> Emmanuel Montes was always noticed on account of a broad, red scar which ran in a great crescent from his temple to his chin. He was forty-two years of age and widowed. He frequented the 'Palace Hotel' in Guatemala City where he tried to sell lottery tickets to the guests although he was an exile from Nicaragua and not really at home here. He often looked miserable and indeed his life had been a sad one. He had been subjected to the kind of absurd quirks of fate that made the selling of lottery tickets somehow appropriate. For example, his scar was caused when a ginger beer bottle accidentally burst open at the bar. However, he was a noble and dignified figure and I learned from an acquaintance of mine a story which well illustrated both his loving devotion to his former wife and his sense of self-sacrifice if fate demanded it.

2. Students learn that different texts have different communicative values based, in part at least, on the different ways in which readers are expected to go about making sense of what information they are given.

In a literary text the only place the reader can turn for the resolution of background information is the text itself, or at the very least to the other texts to which this text might allude. Such allusiveness or 'intertextuality' takes two main forms: either there is reference to other works which the reader may be expected to know, or the writer assumes that the reader is conversant with certain literary conventions which govern how the story is to be read (for example, in a 'whodunnit' we do not know the motivation for the murder, but we know that the immediate suspect is unlikely to be the person named as the killer in the final act of the drama). It is predominantly the case, there-fore, that unlike other sources, *literariness* is marked by the extent to which the material is read as largely self-referential. Seeking the reason why the man is selling lottery tickets or has the kind of scar he has is an active interpretive process which involves the reader in constructing the necessary 'information' from the story itself.

However, another significant mark of literariness can be the way in which the omission of certain expected propositions or background information is assigned thematic significance. For example, we consider a number of ways to interpret 'scar' when the 'normal' explanation is not forthcoming, or we start to equate the absence of names and defined places in the text with an anonymous, featureless scenario for the story. We begin to question the constant repetition of the word 'lottery' and the references to the man's luck. This text, in particular, seems to require to be read with an additional semantic overlay in these key places. The author does not allow his narrators much overt comment and the reader is made to infer more. Literary texts differ in the degree of information supplied to a reader. In a non-literary text, however, information omitted is not generally assumed to be relevant.

2 A linguistic model for narrative structure

This model is one developed by William Labov and his associates (Labov, 1972) working on Black English Vernacular (BEV) in New York. Oral narratives (whose skilled execution is highly prized in Black communities) were collected. Initially, they were examined in the context of a study set up to investigate the notion of linguistic 'deprivation' in such communities and its educational implications. It was discovered not only that the collected narratives regularly exhibited evidence of considerable facility on the part of the narrators in the use of English (though according to the rules of BEV, and not standard American English), but also that the narratives most highly prized had structural properties in common. The structural features extrapolated by Labov were not, however, highlighted by intuition but were observed to correlate with particular linguistic forms and stylistic patterns. Such observations make it easier to work with Labov's model. Unlike some narrative models where it is difficult to retrieve the analyst's decision to assign a part of the narrative to one category rather than to another, Labov's model is generally more attestable. The marking of structural properties in terms of defined language forms also has considerable advantages for integrated language and literature study.

The structural properties isolated by Labov can be described as follows (see also Figure 7, p.182):

1 **Abstract**. This is a short summary of the story that narrators generally provide before the narrative commences. It 'encapsulates the *point* of the story'. Not all, but most, natural narratives have an abstract.
2 **Orientation** is an essential constituent in helping the reader/listener 'to identify in some way the time, place, persons, and their activity or situation'. It can include 'an elaborate portrait of the main character'. Orientation can be marked by *many past progressive verbs*, and, obviously, *adverbial phrases of time/manner and place.*
3 **Complicating action** contains narrative clauses. Such clauses have a verb which is simple past or simple present. They are the minimal units of the narrative and are temporally ordered, in that 'a change in their order will result in a change in the temporal sequence of the original semantic organisation'. For example, 'The girl got pregnant. The girl married' is a very different story if the clauses are reversed.

180

4 **Evaluation**. Like the basic narrative clause, this is a most important element in narrative. Culler (1981: 170) argues that narrative clause and evaluation correspond to the *fabula* and *sjuzet* of early Russian and Czech formalist analyses, but he omits to point out that Labov's definitions help to eliminate much critical fuzziness. Evaluation can take many shapes and be marked by a number of different linguistic forms:

A **Evaluation: Commentary**

   1 *External*: comments by the narrator external to the action and addressed directly to the interlocutor.

   2 *Internal*: comment is embedded:

     (a) the evaluative comment occurs to the narrator or character at a specific moment of the action;

     (b) comment is addressed to another character;

     (c) evaluative remarks are attributed to a third party.

B **Sentence-Internal Evaluation Devices**

   1 *Intensifiers*: e.g. gestures, expressive phonology, repetition, interjection, etc. In other words, a host of available stylistic-expressive rhetorical means.

   2 *Comparators*: generally speaking, a 'comparator moves away from the line of narrative events to consider unrealised possibilities and compare them with events that did not occur'. Realised linguistically by *inter alia* negatives, futures, modals, comparatives, questions.

5 **Resolution**: this contains the last of the narrative or free clauses which begin the complicating action.

6 **Coda**: the coda should provide a sense of completeness, signalling that the story has ended and has been evaluated by bringing 'the narrator and the listener back to the point at which they entered the narrative'.

1	Abstract	What was this about?
2	Orientation	Who, when, what, where?
3	Complicating action	Then what happened?
4	Evaluation	So what?
5	Result or resolution	What finally happened?
6	Coda	

It is clear that to satisfy the demands of a full literary analysis which accounts for as many features of narrative organisation as possible requires considerable refinement of the Labovian model. For example, the category of **evaluation** might be studied further to investigate the notion of embedded comment and how this is stylistically realised, or the range of 'stylistic-expressive-rhetorical' means available as 'intensifiers' might be explored; or the kinds of features which might make up a reader's 'orientation' to a main character (e.g. the omitted information here).[1]

However, we should also be alert to the dangers of relying too heavily on a model. Teachers will, of course, decide for themselves the extent to which such

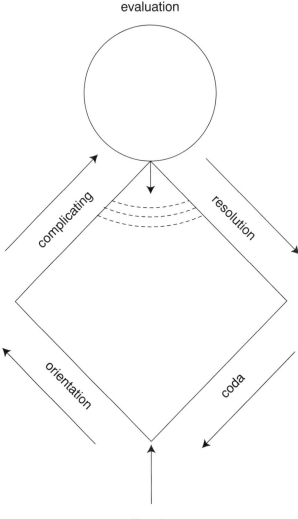

Figure 7.

a model needs to develop according to the aims of a particular lesson or syllabus. In any case, it is often not until a model is seen in relation to the working of a particular text that areas for refinement can be isolated. Indeed, it is a key principle of working with models in such contexts that they should not be seen as finite or self-complete but rather as hypotheses to be tested against data. This gives a distinctly *investigative* edge to their pedagogic application.

It is interesting to attempt to characterise the structure of the Maugham story in terms of Labov's model and to explore the extent to which such a structure might embody or correlate with the themes of the story, and to ask whether it can account for the nature of readers' experience of the story. Such a description is a challenging one, since a number of readers of this story have commented that it produces a feeling of 'so what?' This is reported as connected with their feeling that the story does not have a proper ending, that the title is odd, and that it seems difficult to work out the point of it all. (For example, why does the story end with reference to 'ginger ale'?) It is clear, then, that the meanings of the story are not easily or overtly extractable but are communicated in an embedded or indirect way to the reader. In this respect, the story is typical of many modern – even modernist – short stories. (Hemingway, Gertrude Stein and Saki provide many comparable examples.)

The structure of the story may be best analysed by working chronologically through Labov's categories. It will be recognised, however, that many narratives do not simply proceed in an orderly fashion from 'abstract' to 'coda'. Particularly in the case of the category 'orientation', there is much gradual unravelling, with orientational information embedded within other categories or within different features in the structural sequence.

2.1 Commentary: narrative style, interpretation, and 'The Man with the Scar'

Abstract: There is no obvious 'abstract', with the possible exception of the title. We are not told what the story is to be about or why we should be reading it. The title, 'The Man with the Scar', is not in itself of any particular significance, though it is natural, in the search for plot-based information, to want to enquire who he is and how he came to get the scar. (Is it, for example, possible that 'scar' may not mean simply a physical scar, though this is what is initially focused as the 'theme' for the first paragraph?)

> It was on account of the scar that I first noticed him, for it ran, broad and red, in a great crescent from his temple to his chin.

Orientation: Most of the information here centres on 'the man' and his physical features. This is puzzling, because there seems subsequently to be no point to much of this information. Very little is revealed by the narrator about *who* he is as an individual. In fact, throughout the story 'the man with the scar' remains nameless and without an identity. We might conclude that what the man represents may be more significant for the reader than the man himself. Very little is revealed by the first narrator (the 'I' figure in the story) about the man's character, except perhaps that he is sometimes 'the worse for liquor'. The second narrator – an acquaintance of the first narrator – subsequently reveals that he is 'an exile from Nicaragua'. The setting for the telling of the narrative is noticeably featureless and bare. Information of an orientational kind – i.e. concerning who, what, where – is not marked. It is notably absent from the story's opening paragraph where such information is conventionally supplied.

Complicating action: This is particularly dense in the second narrator's narrative which reveals a sequence of almost uninterrupted narrative clauses with few intervening structural features. This constitutes a significant proportion of the action of the story.

Evaluation: The action appears not to be evaluated by either narrator, though it could be said that the general's comments on bravery are evaluative of the action. Though we are, of course, dealing with a translation, the first narrator ('I') comments that the 'high-flown language' of the story told to him 'suits the story', though it is not clear whether we should regard this as a positive or negative evaluation.

Resolution: The action is in one sense 'resolved' by the second narrator when reporting the action of the general in pardoning the life of 'the man with the scar'. There is, however, no resolution of why we have been told the story of the conversation between the narrator and his acquaintance.

Coda: There is no *overtly* signalled coda. In fact, the way in which both narrators converge to return the reader to the point at which the narrative was entered with a refocus on 'the scar' is perplexing in its circularity. Rather than any distinctly extractable 'message' about the man, the final 'sequence' (even 'resolution') of the action serves almost to trivialise the story, most particularly in the way it is conveyed by the first or 'I' narrator who is presented as an 'outsider' to the action in more senses than one.

We might note here briefly that appreciation of such structural effects of narrative shaping can be fostered, in a manner which involves extending activities described above, by asking students to write their own 'endings' to the story. By 'doing it themselves' students can begin to appreciate from the inside, as it were, the relationship between narrative structure and how different readers might come to understand and interpret the story in different ways. See Appendix 1, p.191 for examples.

2.2 Literariness and language use: questions and topics

The question of what is specifically literary about certain texts is a complex and problematic one. The answer may be a primarily sociological one and lie with the disposition adopted by the reader towards the text. In terms of actual words employed, there can certainly be no quantitative distinction between literary and non-literary texts. However, differences in the way language is used are discernible, though it has been argued that such distinctions may be less a case of yes/no decisions than one of a gradient or cline of literariness (for fuller discussion see Carter and Nash, 1983, 1990 and Chapter 6 above). In the language and literature classroom it is necessary to approach such issues with an open mind and to work in the first instance from the benefits which, it was argued above, accrue from the language study of literary and non-literary texts in juxtaposition.

What follows here is a list of suggestions for discussion, topics for investigation, and issues to be raised. Such exploration is particularly suited to group or pair-based work/projects, but the question of how explicitly or abstractly such points are discussed in the classroom or remain within the conceptual underpinning of teachers' overall strategies is best left to the discretion of the individual teacher. Collectively, however, it is claimed here that engagement with these questions and the related activities can enhance the quality and depth of students' response to language, to the varied communicative values of texts, and to the different functions of linguistic items, patterns and structures.

Although aims and objectives are harder to specify, the more advanced the language learner becomes, the more such competence becomes that more usually associated with the native speaker. It is clear, therefore, that the questions and topics will need to be handled selectively:

1 Groups can be invited to apply Labov's model to a range of different narrative types such as jokes, anecdotes, children's stories, travelogues, reports of incidents in newspapers, journals, etc. Among the questions to be answered might be:
   - What do narratives have in common? (Remember Labov's model is based on *spoken* discourse.)
   - What are the stylistic differences between different narrative discourses?
   - What is the effect of narratives such as 'The Man with the Scar' which are in part patterned on the expected frame and in part a deliberate break with expectations?
   - Is it a signal of literariness in the narrative for the reader to be confronted with a break in frames?
   - Why do some narratives play with order or 'chronology' of events?
   - Is Labov right about the sequence – Abstract: Orientation: Complicating Action: Evaluation: Result or Resolution: Coda?
2 Within a narrower focus, 'orientation' can be studied along the lines described in the previous section. An additional purpose with this context of 'literariness' is to explore the extent to which readers respond (or are invited by the author/narrator to respond) to the absence of 'expected' features of orientation. In a non-literary or 'informational' text information omitted is either assumed to be known or is deemed irrelevant but, as has been suggested above, the reader of a literary text plays a generally more productive role by assigning some kind of semantic significance to 'gaps' and indeterminacies in the expected frame. This leads to greater involvement with the language of the text (where, unlike informational text, every word may be playing a significant part); it can mean that attention to the textuality of the text is much more self-conscious. Exercises such as these

are designed to try to raise and extend such self-consciousness. They can also teach directly or teach awareness of the kind of **interpretative procedures** required in reading different types of discourse (see also Short and Candlin, 1986).

3   In an ostensibly non-literary text like a newspaper report, the representational or referential functions of language are preponderant. In a text like 'The Man with the Scar', repetition, pattern, and relations between words are important. We become more involved with *how* the story is told and with the *attitude* of the narrator towards what is said. Students can thus be asked to find instances of such 'pattern' in 'The Man with the Scar'; for example, what appears to be the attitude of the two narrators towards the narrative of the man with the scar? Close reference to the text in support of answers should be demanded.

4   Finally, the use of a narrative model such as that developed by Labov, together with pre-literary language activities such as, in particular, summary and prediction, can focus attention on the *form* and *shape* of the text. It can provide a basis for an analysis of how far the form of the text reflects, embodies or otherwise enacts the meanings contained in it. The lack of explicit 'evaluation' and 'coda' in the narrative of the first narrator, for example, may be mimetic of a lack of moral interest or perception which reflects aspects of the character of the narrator himself. Or the model can be used to compare stories from different periods, and students can be invited to question why certain texts (nineteenth-century texts, for example), do have rather more explicit moral directions or codas for the reader. Note, for example, the codas in the final chapters to Jane Austen's *Mansfield Park* (1814) and George Eliot's *Middlemarch* (1871–2). Or students might examine why a narrative such as Fielding's *Joseph Andrews* (1742) contains abstracts for almost every chapter.

3 SUMMARY

It has been a main point of argument in this chapter that, where feasible, opportunities should be sought to integrate language and literature teaching activities. It is recognised at the same time, however, that to examine the language of the text is to examine only one feature of literary organisation and of what makes up a work of literature.

From a pedagogic viewpoint a number of issues have been debated, some more explicitly than others. It has been argued that basic language teaching strategies can provide a 'way in' to a text, can help raise questions about its meanings, and can begin to sensitise students to its linguistic-structural organisation. This is especially so if the language-based teaching strategies are student-centred and activity-based and can involve students in the production and generation of problems, questions, bases for interpretation, and so on. It is hoped that the suggested procedures outlined in the second section are of this order. Some teachers may wish to concentrate on this kind of integration only.

A linguistic model is introduced so that frameworks can be set up within which some questions are solved and some more precisely formulated. They exist as hypotheses to be applied to the text and then reviewed, refined and revised in the light of experience of their use. In this sense, they should not be seen as fixed and immutable. It is the responsibility of the teacher to decide how explicitly to introduce the model in the classroom, whether to introduce models *in toto* or in part, or whether to use them for their own guidance only. Much depends here on the experience of the students, their acquaintance with formal linguistics, the aims of the particular lesson, the nature of the design of the literature syllabus, etc. Models should inform the literature class to some degree and, since literary texts are made from language, the more linguistically principled they are, the more systematic the approach to literary text study.

Students need to be made aware of and given practice in the relevant procedures for making sense of the kind of reading *processes* required by different texts. This can very often involve inferential procedures of a complex kind and varies according to the kind of control exercised by the author, the kind of assumptions made by the author, and the purposes the author has in conveying the information. It is, therefore, suggested that students be given practice at reading closely a range of texts in which they will face such styles of presentation. It is often in textual openings that such issues can be most effectively and practically focused (Davies, 1995).

Models are useful, finally, in so far as they enable students to generalise across a range of texts and to move beyond an interpretation of a single text (though such activity is in itself an interesting and motivating one) and appreciate and use the language associated with different discourse types. Linguistic models provide the best means of sensitisation to and acquisition of relevant procedures.

Finally, I may have given the impression that no work on literary texts can begin until these skills and competences have been developed. That is clearly not true. We must also beware that such activities do not inhibit responses to the text or prevent students bringing their own experiences to bear on the formulation of that response. Foreign- or second-language learners are capable of fuller responses to the text than is often realised and all responses need to be developed into fuller articulacy. Some of the language activities and work with models on the literariness of texts can aid such development, and responses can best develop with increased response to and confidence in working with the language in a variety of integrated activities, with language-based hypotheses and in classes where investigative, student-centred learning is the norm. From this pre-literary linguistic basis and integrated with the development of the kind of reading competence and appreciation outlined, students can explore the wider questions of background, author study, influence and literary tradition; they can raise evaluative questions, compare and contrast works with each other, supply information to supplement the hypotheses and investigations, and so on. Such contextual and literary issues can precede linguistic study. The view adopted in this study is that language study should be the *first* step in an integrated programme. I hope this chapter will contribute something to fuller understanding of this context of integrated language and literary work.

This chapter originally appeared as 'Linguistic models, language and literariness: study strategies in the teaching of literature to foreign students' in Brumfit, C.J. and Carter R. (eds) *Literature and Language Teaching* (Oxford University Press, Oxford, 1986).

APPENDIX 1: THE MAN WITH THE SCAR

It was on account of the scar that I first noticed him, for it ran, broad and red, in a great crescent from his temple to his chin. It must have been due to a formidable wound and I wondered whether this had been caused by a sabre or by a fragment of shell. It was unexpected on that round, fat and good-humoured face. He had small and undistinguished features and his expression was artless. His face went oddly with his corpulent body. He was a powerful man of more than common height. I never saw him in anything but a very shabby grey suit, a khaki shirt and a battered sombrero. He was far from clean. He used to come into the Palace Hotel at Guatemala
10 City every day at cocktail time and strolling leisurely round the bar offer lottery tickets for sale. If this was the way he made his living it must have been a poor one for I never saw anyone buy, but now and then I saw him offered a drink. He never refused it. He threaded his way among the tables with a sort of rolling walk as though he were accustomed to traverse long distances on foot, paused at each table, with a little smile mentioned the numbers he had for sale and then, when no notice was taken of him, with the same smile passed on. I think he was for the most part a trifle the worse for liquor.

I was standing at the bar one evening, my foot on the rail, with an acquain-
20 tance – they make a very good dry Martini at the Palace Hotel in Guatemala City – when the man with the scar came up. I shook my head as for the twentieth time since my arrival he held out for my inspection his lottery tickets. But my companion nodded affably.

'*Que tal, general?* How is life?'

'Not so bad. Business is none too good, but it might be worse.'

'What will you have, general?'

'A brandy.'

He tossed it down and put the glass back on the bar. He nodded to my acquaintance.
30 '*Gracias. Hasta luego.*'

Then he turned away and offered his tickets to the men who were standing next to us.

'Who is your friend?' I asked. 'That's a terrific scar on his face.'

'It doesn't add to his beauty, does it? He's an exile from Nicaragua. He's a ruffian of course and a bandit, but not a bad fellow. I give him a few *pesos* now and then. He was a revolutionary general, and if his ammunition hadn't given out he'd have upset the government and be Minister of War now instead of selling lottery tickets in Guatemala. They captured him, along with his staff, such as it was, and tried him by court-martial. Such things are rather summary in these countries you know, and he was sentenced to be shot at dawn. I guess he knew what was coming to him when he was caught. He spent the night in gaol and he and the others, there were five of them alto-gether, passed the time playing poker. They used matches for chips. He told me he'd never had such a run of bad luck in his life; they were playing with a short pack, jacks to open, but he never held a card; he never improved more than half a dozen times in the whole sitting and no sooner did he buy a new stack than he lost it. When day broke and the soldiers came into the cell to fetch them for execution he had lost more matches than a reasonable man could use in a lifetime.

'They were led into the patio of the gaol and placed against a wall, the five of them side by side, with the firing party facing them. There was a pause and our friend asked the officer in charge of them what the devil they were keeping him waiting for. The officer said that the general commanding the government troops wished to attend the execution and they awaited his arrival.

'"Then I have time to smoke another cigarette," said our friend. "He was always unpunctual."

'But he had barely lit it when the general – it was San lgnacio, by the way: I don't know whether you ever met him – followed by his A.D.C. came into the patio. The usual formalities were performed and San lgnacio asked the condemned men whether there was anything they wished before the execu-tion took place. Four of the five shook their heads, but our friend spoke.

'"Yes, I should like to say good-bye to my wife."

'"*Bueno*," said the general, "I have no objection to that. Where is she?"

'"She is waiting at the prison door."

'"Then it will not cause a delay of more than five minutes.'

'"Hardly that, *Señor General*," said our friend.

'"Have him placed on one side."

'Two soldiers advanced and between them the condemned rebel walked to the spot indicated. The officer in command of the firing squad on a nod from the general gave an order, there was a ragged report, and the four men fell. They fell strangely, not together, but one after the other, with movements that were almost grotesque, as though they were puppets in a toy theatre. The officer went up to them and into one who was still alive emptied two barrels of his revolver. Our friend finished his cigarette and threw away the stub.

'There was a little stir at the gateway. A woman came into the patio, with quick steps, and then, her hand on her heart, stopped suddenly. She gave a cry and with outstretched arms ran forward.

'"*Caramba*," said the general.

80 'She was in black, with a veil over her hair, and her face was dead white. She was hardly more than a girl, a slim creature, with little regular features and enormous eyes. But they were distraught with anguish. Her loveliness was such that as she ran, her mouth slightly open and the agony of her face beautiful, a gasp of surprise was wrung from those indifferent soldiers who looked at her.

'The rebel advanced a step or two to meet her. She flung herself into his arms and with a hoarse cry of passion: *alma de mi corazón*, soul of my heart, he pressed his lips to hers. And at the same moment he drew a knife from his ragged shirt – I haven't a notion how he managed to retain possession of it – and stabbed her in the neck. The blood spurted from the cut vein and

90 dyed his shirt. Then he flung his arms round her and once more pressed his lips to hers.

'It happened so quickly that many did not know what had occurred, but from the others burst a cry of horror; they sprang forward and seized him. They loosened his grasp and the girl would have fallen if the A.D.C. had not caught her. She was unconscious. They laid her on the ground and with dismay on their faces stood round watching her. The rebel knew where he was striking and it was impossible to staunch the blood. In a moment the A.D.C. who had been kneeling by her side rose.

'"She's dead," he whispered.

100 'The rebel crossed himself.

'"Why did you do it?" asked the general.

'"I loved her."

'A sort of sigh passed through those men crowded together and they looked with strange faces at the murderer. The general stared at him for a while in silence.

'"It was a noble gesture," he said at last. "I cannot execute this man. Take my car and have him led to the frontier. *Señor*, I offer you the homage which is due from one brave man to another."

'A murmur of approbation broke from those who listened. The A.D.C. tapped the rebel on the shoulder, and between the two soldiers without a

110 word he marched to the waiting car.' My friend stopped and for a little I was silent. I must explain that he was a Guatemalan and spoke to me in Spanish. I have translated what he told me as well as I could, but I have made no attempt to tone down his rather highflown language. To tell the truth I think it suits the story.

'But how then did he get the scar?' I asked at length.

'Oh, that was due to a bottle that burst when he was opening it. A bottle of ginger ale.'

'I never liked it,' said I.

190

The following 'endings' to 'The Man with the Scar' were produced by Singaporean students of English. They were written to the following instructions after the students had been introduced to the Labovian narrative model: 'In not more than fifty words write an "ending" to "The Man with the Scar" in which elements of either "evaluation" and/or "resolution" and "coda" are present.' Some examples are printed below. They were discussed with different groups. Discussion tended to focus on 'endings' in which the writer had clearly considered reference to the scar, gambling (lottery) and the man's drinking to be of significance. The degree of moral approbation/disapproval expressed in 'codas' also provided much debate.

1 'I have not liked it since,' replied my friend. 'You should have seen the accident. There was an explosion. A big glass fragment lodged itself in his face, for he was standing nearby. Perhaps this is justice. He traded his wife's life for his own. His conscience is salved now.'

2 'You mean the scar on his face? That's nothing. It's the other one – the indelible scar in his heart – that's more sinister. That biggest gamble in his life was lost dearly. You notice that he never refuses a drink? Poor fellow! No amount of brandy can drown his sorrow.'

3 I walked away and reflected on the deplorable physical and social condition of the man with the scar. Could that be the price he has to pay for double-crossing his fellow revolutionaries and for his seemingly 'brave' act of killing his wife in order to cover up for his misdeeds?

4 Since then, whenever I came to the bar, I bought some lottery tickets from the general. The scar on his face moved me to do so. Moreover, the deep gash reminded me of the fatal wound that love forced itself to inflict.

10

TEACHING DISCOURSES IN
DIFFERENT WAYS

1 INTRODUCTION

In this chapter I argue for a more comprehensive definition of stylistics as a discipline and demonstrate that different kinds of teaching strategies need to be accommodated within this broader framework. A short and linguistically 'simple' poem is then analysed. Here I hope to show that the poem affords considerable possibilities for integrated language and literature work and that much that is of pedagogical benefit can be derived from not limiting the nature of this integration either to any one mode of interpretation of the text or to any one model of stylistics as an activity and discipline.

1.1 The nature of stylistics

Given that stylistics is essentially a bridge discipline between linguistics and literature it is inevitable that there will be arguments about the design of the bridge, its purpose, the nature of the materials and about the side it should be built from. Some would even claim it is unnecessary to build the bridge at all. In such a situation there is always a danger that stylistics can become blinkered by too close an affiliation to a single mode of operation or to any one ideological position. There is already a considerable division in the subject between literary stylistics (which is in many respects an extension of practical criticism) and linguistic stylistics (which seeks the creation of linguistic models for the analysis of texts – including those conventionally thought 'literary' and 'non-literary'). Such divisions can be valuable in the process of clarifying objectives as well as related analytical and pedagogic strategies, but one result can be a narrowing of classroom options and/or a consequent reduction in the number and kinds of academic levels at which stylistics can operate. For example, literary stylistics can be more accessible to literature students because it models itself on critical assumptions and procedures already fairly well established in the literature classes of upper forms in schools, whereas the practice of linguistic stylistics tends to require a more thorough acquaintance with linguistic methodology and argumentation.

I thus wish to claim here more comprehensive ground for stylistics as a discipline and to argue that it can be effectively taught at a wider range of levels. A helpful starting point may be to suggest that the practice of stylistics comes about at any point of intersection of the language of a text with the elements which constitute the literariness of that text. This is not to say that literariness is an absolute; rather there are degrees of literariness which operate along a cline which includes texts not conventionally assumed to be literary (see Chapters 6 and 8 above). One danger inherent in a purely literary stylistics is that the selection of texts for analysis can reveal certain unexamined presuppositions about what constitutes literature and can lead to statements that features such as, say, allusiveness or semantic play characterise the domain of literature. A linguistic stylistician may rightly point to examples from advertising copy such as these for Guinness and the British Leyland Mini:

> You can't see through a Guinness (semantic play)
> Nips in and out like Ronald Biggs (semantic play and allusion)

and argue for more precise analytical models for determining the nature of literature or 'literariness' although, conversely, he or she may not be interested in a detailed interpretation of what a text means for them or how exactly it produces the responses it does. In reality, there is more overlap between linguistic and literary stylistics (and their sub-varieties) than I give credit for here; but, for the purposes of the development of linguistic and literary competence in the classroom, divisions must be highlighted in order that an argument for greater catholicity can be advanced.

I shall now work through the following short text and point to some ways in which it might be explored in the classroom from within an expanded framework for stylistics. I shall outline six main approaches (see 2.1–2.6 below). 'Six' is no magic number; there can be more and, alternatively, different approaches can be conflated in different ways. The purpose here is to point to some distinct ways in which a literary text can be taught by integrating its study with a consideration of its properties of language and to explore the different pedagogical purposes of the different approaches. The points are ordered but that should not mean that one is necessarily prior, either logically or procedurally, to another:

Off Course

[1] the golden flood   the weightless seat
     the cabin song   the pitch black
     the growing beard   the floating crumb
     the shining rendezvous   the orbit wisecrack
[5] the hot spacesuit   the smuggled mouth-organ
     the imaginary somersault   the visionary sunrise
     the turning continents   the space debris
     the golden lifeline   the space walk
     the crawling deltas   the camera moon

[10] the pitch velvet   the rough sleep
      the crackling headphone   the space silence
      the turning earth   the lifeline continents
      the cabin sunrise   the hot flood
      the shining spacesuit   the growing moon
[15]   the crackling somersault   the smuggled orbit
      the rough moon   the visionary rendezvous
      the weightless headphone   the cabin debris
      the floating lifeline   the pitch sleep
      the crawling camera   the turning silence
[20]   the space crumb   the crackling beard
      the orbit mouth-organ   the floating song

(Edwin Morgan, 1966)

2 APPROACHES TO STUDY AND TEACHING

2.1 Teaching the grammar

Most striking here is the consistent pattern of nominal groups across the whole text. In each case the structure is that of *d m h* where *d* = definite article, *m* = modifier and *h* headword. The predominant modifier of the headwords in the nominal groups of this poem is an epithet. But they are not all of the same type. We distinguish in English (though by no means exhaustively) between three main types of epithet:

e^a = qualitative epithet; e.g. marvellous, interesting, strong
e^b = colours; e.g. red, blue
e^c = classifying epithet; e.g. classical, wooden

The usual order for these is *a b c*; so that you cannot normally have 'a red, classical, wonderful vase' but you can have 'a wonderful, red, classical vase'. In addition to these epithets English allows numerals, past and present participles (e.g. shining [line 14] and smuggled [line 15]) and other nouns (e.g. the space walk [line 8] – sometimes called nominators) to act as modifiers in the nominal group. What kind of exploitation of these features is made in the text?

Epithet ordering rules do not really surface since only one modifier occurs at any one time. Morgan employs a mixture of modifiers including colours (the **golden lifeline** [line 8]), nominal modifiers (the **cabin debris** [line 17]) and participles (e.g. lines 3 and 5). In terms of classes of epithet classifying epithets (e^c) seem to predominate: e.g. the **weightless headphone** (line 17); the **floating lifeline** (line 18); the **imaginary somersault** (line 6), even to the extent that the majority of participles are of a classifying kind. In fact, the golden lifeline may be seen to describe a characteristic of the lifeline as much as it does its colour. Thus, one cumulative effect of the use of

194

this structure is that a number of objects are classified and reclassified. Occasionally, a particular qualitative contour is imparted to the things seen but the predominantly defining procedure suggests something more in the nature of an inventory (the run of articles reinforces this) or, more specifically, a ship's log with only occasionally the kind of qualitative reaction allowed in line 6: the **visionary sunrise**. I shall return to a discussion and fuller 'interpretation' of these features in another section.

Other key structural features which should be noted are the absence of a verb and the particular use to which the participles are put. One main result of the omission of a verb is that there are no clear relations between objects. Objects either do not seem to act upon each other nor to have a particular 'action' of their own. Verbs generally work to establish a clear differentiation between subject and object and to indicate the processes contracted between them; a resultant effect here is that processes between things become suspended and weightless. The poet's suspension of some of the normal rules of grammar can be seen in part, at least, to contribute to this effect.

Yet this observation can be countered by a recognition that there are verbs in the poem; for example, the participles already observed (e.g. **crawling** [lines 9 and 19]; **floating** [lines 3 and 21]; **growing** [lines 3 and 14]) are formed from verbs. The difference between the two verbal items in the following phrases:

the world turns
the turning world

illustrates the point that in the participial form the 'verbs' work both with a more defining or classificatory function and to underline a sense of continuing, if suspended, action. The present participles convey a feeling of things continuing endlessly or, at least, without any clear end.

From a teaching or classroom viewpoint there is much that can be done with the above observations. They can be used in the service of fuller interpretation of the text; they can form the basis of discussion of the function of different parts of speech; and, more specifically, the text can be used to introduce and form the basis of teaching some key structural features of English syntax such as nominal group organisation, participles and verbal relations, etc. There is no reason why a literary text cannot be used to illustrate such features. In fact, one real advantage of such a framework is that grammatical forms are not learned in a rote or abstract way or in relation to made-up examples; instead, grammar is taught in action and in terms of its communicative features (cf. Widdowson, 1975). We are made to ask both what is grammatical and, practically, what specific job a grammatical form can do in addition to what the semantic relations are which underlie noun-phrase sequences. This can be of direct value to both native English language students and second- or foreign-language learners of English.

2.2 Teaching the lexis

One procedure here involves discussion and definition of what the individual words mean; it is a conventional and time-honoured procedure and is clearly of most practicable use to second- or foreign-language students. However, the introduction of the notion of lexical collocation can be rather more instructive. Here we are asking more direct questions about 'the company words keep' and exploring the different degrees of acceptability in the semantic fit between lexical items: in this case, between modifier and headword. Such exploration can teach more to learners of English about the meaning of words than dictionary-type definitions; we are forced in relation to this text into explaining, precisely, why **crackling headphone** (line 11) contains items which sit more comfortably alongside each other than **crackling beard** (line 20) or why **smuggled** has a greater degree of semantic compatibility with **mouth-organ** (line 5) than with **orbit** (line 15). Idioms are explained, e.g. **pitch black** (line 2), as well as the extent of convertibility of idioms, e.g. the **pitch sleep** (line 18) or the **pitch velvet** (line 10); the range of meanings or associations carried by particular words can be discussed in relation to collocations such as the **rough sleep** (line 10); the **rough moon** (line 16); and the possibilities of metaphoric extension can also be investigated through the uses to which items like **crawling** or **crackling** are put e.g. the **crawling deltas** (line 9); the **crackling somersault** (line 15); the **crawling camera** (line 19); the **crackling beard** (line 20).

One central insight into the structure of the poem which should emerge as a result of such lexico-semantic analysis concerns the concentration of metaphoric extensions, semantic incompatibilities and generally unusual collocational relations in the last six lines of the poem. It is almost as if the typographic inlay at line 15 signals a markedly changed set of relationships between objects and their classifications even though both object and attribute remain fixed and finite. There is thus a basis laid for further interpretive investigation and for conjunction with the syntactic analysis above. From a linguistic point of view students start to appreciate the interpenetration of different levels of language organisation in the creation of meanings; they can also learn about how words work, the network of relations they can contract, and something of the nature of figurative language. Students of English can be engaged in more basic lexicographic work and may, indeed, be asked to write dictionary entries for some of the keywords in the text. Again the emphasis throughout is on how the words mean and on their particular communicative values. Such strategies are given a special focus by the kinds of dispositions of words found in many literary texts.

The orientation of the first two approaches has thus been on the uses of literary text for language teaching. Literary text can be a 'way-in' for the teaching of structures of the language. It would not be an overt aim of this approach to explore the literary meanings released by the text, although I would hope that a sound basis has been prepared. But by varying degrees of indirectness students can learn something of the nature of the exploitation of the rules of language involved in the creation of a literary text; they are being encouraged to recognise linguistic patterns and changes to those patterns and to ask what the functions are of the features they observe. They are at one point of the intersection of language and literature study and are engaged in a rudimentary form of stylistic analysis.

2.3 The teaching of text as discourse

The point of this area of work in stylistics and its teaching is to invite recognition of how a text works as a whole. It involves an investigation of the discoursal properties of a text. There are many ways in which textual discourse can be defined but for our purposes here it should consist of a notation of the ways in which smaller units of language (such as the *d m h* structure here) combine with other linguistic semiotic properties to make up, cumulatively, the elements of a whole text. The notation or definition should be able to account for our ability to discern and respond to such various discourses, from a set of instructions for opening a can to a novel, although some units of discourse are rather easier to specify than others. Correspondingly, such description should provide the basis for a differentiation of different kinds of discourse.

From a classroom viewpoint one of the most instructive and helpful means of distinguishing textual discourse is analysis through a juxtaposition of one discourse with another. In the case of 'Off Course' it may be useful to set it alongside texts containing instructions, or inventories, or lists of participants at a meeting, or even perhaps a recipe: in other words, texts which can be shown to contain linguistic conventions of a similar nature to the poem under consideration. One main aim here should be to focus attention on the nature of the textual organisation of 'Off Course'; as a result, the following features may be discerned:

1 Readers could be uncertain as to how they are to read it. Across? Or down? The typography is not a reliable guide in this respect.
2 The lineation is unusual. There is an unexplained indentation at line 15. The second column lacks the order and patterning of the first column although there is an equal space between noun phrases in both columns.
3 Repetition of words is a marked feature although there is never repetition with the same collocational partner. A criss-cross patterning occurs across columns, with modifiers sometimes turning up elsewhere as headwords (e.g. 'camera' in lines 9 and 19).
4 The relation of the title to the text is not a direct one. Compare this with: 'Chicken and Vegetable Broth'; 'How to Use the Pump'; 'Shopping List', etc.
5 The poem has no punctuation.

Figure 8.

Appreciation of the discoursal organisation of the text can also be stimulated by analogy with other texts in which particular forms of language, common to both texts, are used in different ways and for different communicative purposes. For example, the use of verb forms in 'Off Course' can be compared with the use of similar verb forms in the above leaflet appeal on behalf of an environmental organisation (Figure 8):

In this text a simple present-tense verb form is used in key places at the beginning and end of the text, while the list contains verbs in the present progressive form which are foregrounded by fronting to the beginning of each line. The effects here contrast with 'Off Course' by indicating the enduring, permanent and unchanging nature of the action of joining the organisation and, in the present-progressive-dominated section, by indicating the continuing value of the work undertaken by the organisation and by its members.

Once again the discernment of features such as these can be used to augment an interpretation of the text. But it can also be stylistic analysis of the kind that aids recognition of different styles of discourse and their different functions. Such work can be of particular use to the second- or foreign-language learner who in some cases may have to learn totally new sets of conventions for different discourses. How explicitly he or she needs to learn this depends on the teacher's assessment of the needs of the class and the overall aims and objectives of the group's learning, but it can also be valuably underlined how different kinds of literary discourse can create their own rules for their reading, or can set out deliberately to disorientate a reader and how all literary discourse, however unusual, requires reference to one or other set of norms in order to create effects at all. Learning about the nature of literature involves learning about some of its operations as discourse.[1] Learning about its operation as discourse is one essential prerequisite for reading the sort of concrete poetry of which 'Off Course' is a notable representative.

2.4 Creative writing

One of the advantages of teaching concrete poetry is that it will often contain uncomplicated syntactic structures of the kind which can provide a real anchor for students' own writing. Much creative writing is undertaken with the provision of a stimulus drawn from a theme or 'experience'. A stylistic approach to creative writing seeks the provision of models based either on a whole text or on a particular linguistic structure(s). The informing principle here is that students, especially those with minimal experience of writing, should have to work within the discipline imposed by a stylistic form. Asking students to write a poem using only a *d m h* structure provides a starting point and thus encourages confidence, teaches that all writing involves linguistic discipline, provokes questioning of the relationship between a stylistic form and the 'shape' of an experience or subject for exploration and can provide incentives for innovation which will always and necessarily be patterned in relation to norms, whatever the degree of their 'imposition'. I am not denying that content can be a most valuable starting point but am suggesting, in the case of second- or foreign-language students of English and inexperienced native-speaker writers, that an anchoring of the activity in style and form can be especially beneficial as a starting point.

One of the interesting features of poems written by my own students to the structural pattern of 'Off Course' is the relationship between this *d m h* pattern and the number of poems about death or suicide. The very fact that writers are not allowed to use verbs establishes a connection between their absence and feelings of unrelatedness, disorientation, no clear goal-directedness and so on. Such work may therefore be usefully antecedent to the process of interpretation of the text. Here is an example of such writing produced by a Japanese student of English:

The stone top
The damp echo
The cold wind
The held breath
The fading foothills
The small trees
The missed turning
The hopeless face
The chinks of light
The life-line sky
The greening moss
The cold echo
The stone steps
The lost recourse
The pelting rain
The howling winds
The stone tower   The stone body

For more examples of the use of creative writing in language and literary study see Carter and Long (1987: unit 5).

2.5 Interpreting the text

For some people this is where we should arrive as well as the whole object of arrival. I have taken a long time to get here in order to try to demonstrate how much linguistic awareness can be derived from an examination of the language of a text as language and to challenge a prevailing view that literary texts cannot 'merely' be used for purposes of developing language competence. A stylistic approach to textual or literary interpretation is no more or less than another approach and is valuable only in the sense that it is a valuable activity for some students (but not necessarily for all). It would be wrong for our teaching of stylistics to be dominated wholly by the development of interpretive strategies; otherwise stylistics can become a restricted academic activity both ideologically and pedagogically.

Put in a crude way, stylistic interpretation involves a process of making equations between, or inferences about, linguistic forms and the meanings contracted by the function or operation of these forms in a literary context. The whole issue of what precisely is involved in this is very complex and stylisticians are committed to debates over what goes on in the process and over how particular interpretive facts can be established in a verifiable way.[2] These issues cannot be addressed directly here although perspectives are given in the overview to Part II of this book (pp.111–122).

200

One of the 'equations' that can be made in relation to 'Off Course' is between the omission of verbs and an impression of weightlessness and suspension in which objects appear to be located in a free-floating relationship with each other and with the space surrounding them. The absence of verbal groups in the poem equates with and produces a sensation of the weightless, suspended condition of outer space where objects float about according to laws different from those which are normally obtained on earth.

Another central point, and one confirmed by conclusions reached in previous sections and through different approaches, is the way in which the text shifts 'off course', so to speak, at line 15. From about line 10 to the end of the text no new headwords or modifiers are introduced. The same features recur but in different combinations, resulting initially in something of a loss of identity of the objects concerned. But from line 15 the collocations of modifier and headwords become increasingly random or even incompatible (see section 2.2, above). So the connections in our 'inventory' between object and its attribute/classificatory label seemingly get more and more arbitrary and void.

The typographical 'arrangement' of the text means that at the end we are left in an unpunctuated, unending space of free-floating connections where the mind perceiving these features in this 'stream-of-consciousness-like' progression is apparently as disconnected and 'off course' as the objects themselves.[3] What was previously an embodiment of a disorientation in gravity-free conditions has now become a more profound dislocation. Where for the most part the lines up to line 15 represent a clear and definite, even if constantly changing, categorisation of things, the remaining lines succeed only in embodying the sense of a world and/or mind shifting out of control.

2.6 Comparing texts

Texts are usually compared on the basis of related or contrasting themes; and there is little doubt that particular features of a text are placed in sharper relief through a process of comparison. A further dimension can be added by comparing texts which are constructionally and formalistically related. A stylistic examination of a text can provide a systematic and principled basis for grading texts for comparison or for further analysis. These texts can then be progressively introduced to students on the basis of linguistic accessibility.

Literary stylistic work can be enhanced by such comparison, as can be seen from a comparison of 'Off Course' with texts which have finite verbs deleted and/or exist as strings of nominal groups. Among the most interesting 'juxtapositions' are: Louis MacNeice, 'Morning Song'; George Herbert, 'Prayer'; Theodore Roethke, 'Child on Top of a Greenhouse',[4] Ezra Pound, 'In a Station of the Metro'. Prose passages organised in this way include the opening to Dickens's *Bleak House* (1852–3) and the opening to Isherwood's *Goodbye to Berlin* (1939). We should explore here the similar and different effects produced in different literary contexts by the same linguistic procedures. Also, what other 'concrete' poems work in this way? What are the relations between verblessness, the unmediated presentation of objects and the literary movement of imagism?

As demonstrated by Cook (1992), poetry and advertisements can also be productively compared as discourses. Indeed, a marked trend in advertising discourse is for advertisers to construct texts which contain features of language more normally associated with the spoken rather than with the written language.

One example discussed by Cook (ch. 3) is for Subaru cars. It is a written text but it has speakerly features:

1 'mind you', 'what's more', 'which means', are markedly spoken rather than written discourse markers.
2 several clauses are without main finite verbs;
3 use of tags (e.g. don't you think?)

The following advertisement (Figure 9), also for a Subaru car, and which bears a family resemblance to the advertisement discussed by Cook, illustrates further the dialogic character of many advertisements. Here ellipsis of the main finite verb is pervasive but there is also subject ellipsis (again particularly in structures involving 'it' and 'there' as subjects: for example, 'Pulls like a dream'; 'Feels right'; 'Precise'). There are also elliptical structures in which the verb 'have' is deleted: (It has) 'Clean burn. Sweet torque'. The text also displays complements and adverbial phrases which function almost as if they were replies to questions: 'On good roads'; 'Rotten roads'; 'Instinctively sure-footed'. (For discussion of spoken grammar see pp.57 and 91.)

Although in this example there is little or no direct opportunity for thematic comparison, there are stylistic similarities to be compared and contrasted with the poem 'Off Course', not least the extent to which verblessness creates an immediate and involving style, the poetic, imagistic character of the advertisement (note the way it appears to be constructed in stanzaic units) and the differences between texts accompanied by visual images and texts in which visual particulars have to be imaginatively supplied by the reader.

Comparison of texts moves the focus more centrally on to the essentially literary nature of the text (though the underpinning is consistently by linguistic means) and allows questions to be generated concerning differences between literary and non-literary discourse, prose and poetry, between writers from the same period writing in similar ways, and between different literary movements and allows these questions to be generated at an appropriate level of abstractness (Bex, 1996; Hughes, 1996). One seminal insight students should derive is that the same linguistic forms can function in different ways to produce different meanings according to context and according to the nature of the overlay of effects at other levels of language organisation. Interpreting such 'meanings' is no simple matter of one-to-one correlation between form and function.

Figure 9.

3 TEACHING THE 'NATURE' OF LANGUAGE THROUGH LITERATURE

There are several ways in which such investigation might be done. One, which has already been touched on, involves an examination of differences and similarities in the way language is used in literary discourse compared with other discourses. The focus here is on the specifically literary nature of the object; but this can be reversed and questions generated about the nature of language itself with the literary context providing an impetus to those questions. To underline that each of the stylistic approaches described here exists in a relationship of mutual support to the other approaches I shall then examine some possible implications of a description of the 'nature' of language for an 'interpretation' of 'Off Course'. The position adopted here is that literature can be used to advance the academic study of language as a human and cultural phenomenon. No direct connection is sought at this juncture between teaching about language and the development of language skills, although the whole area of such a potential connection is in need of investigation by language teachers and researchers and is one to which stylisticians, in particular, could valuably contribute.

An article relevant to such considerations is one by Michael Riffaterre (1973). It is entitled 'Interpretation and descriptive poetry' and is an analysis of the nature of language in poetry. Riffaterre's central point concerns what he terms the 'referential fallacy'. This is the view that the connection between a word and some object or referent is no more than arbitrary and that in poetry it is more often the case that words point to each other as much as they do to 'things'. The basic tenet is that of De Saussure and his view of the arbitrary nature of the sign. This is lucidly explained by Culler (1976: 19):

> There is no natural or inevitable link between the signifier and the signified. Since I speak English I may use the signifier represented by dog to talk about an animal of a particular species, but this sequence of sounds is no better suited to that purpose than another sequence. tod, tet or bloop would serve equally well if they were accepted by members of my speech community. There is no intrinsic reason why one of these signifiers rather than another should be linked with the concept 'dog'.

The interesting thing about 'Off Course' and poems like it is that it affords opportunities for making such insights available in a direct and accessible way. Linguistic awareness can be derived from the study of literary texts. If the words in 'Off Course' such as spacesuit, continents, debris, lifeline, etc. are no more than arbitrary representations of their referents then what are the other relations within which they exist? If the words in their organisation in this text do more than refer to some external reality of knowable 'things' then what are the internal relations? What is language doing in this poem? What does the poem help us understand about the nature of language? How might answers to the questions affect the nature of our 'interpretation' of the poem's meanings?

'Off Course', like many concrete poems, draws attention to its own status as language artefact. In fact, the way in which objects acquire different attributes in a network of free-floating links and associations confirms its status as an artefact in which words contract patterns with other words. Not all the patterns are arbitrary but the way words change partners and positions works almost as if to underline their arbitrariness. In a sense, the poem becomes something of a metaphor for an aspect of the nature of language. The suspension of clear syntactic relations and subsequent loss of 'orientation' emphasises the poem as word and allows us to conclude that the poem is also 'about' its own language.

In section 2.5 the text was interpreted in terms of a spaceship or at least a consciousness associated with the spaceship going 'off course'. This meaning for the poem is conventional in that it is predicated on an assumption that there is a neat, unquestioned and commonsense fit between a reflecting mind or consciousness and a knowable or imaginable world referred to in and by the vocabulary of that text. The analysis was made with reference to the confirmation of intuitions about the poem's 'meaning' by appeal to the linguistic facts of the text. An outcome of the kind of work at the interface of language and literature outlined in this section is to put into question taken-for-granted presuppositions about such 'facts' and 'meanings'.

For example, as a result of this focus on the self-referential and arbitrary properties of words, it may now be possible to conclude that the discovery of such 'arbitrariness' on the part of the consciousness at the centre of the poem serves to free perception from the normal and conventional coordinates of one-to-one correspondences. This squares with the comments of some of the students with whom I have discussed this poem that, far from getting more disparate in tone, the text becomes more interesting and imaginative linguistically while the persona seems to be on the verge of quite new and original perceptions. So that we are 'off course' in one sense, 'on course' in another. Others point to the fact that if we read down rather than across the columns we enter a realm where things shift in and out of focus in a similarly liberating manner. Whatever our position, such exploration should lead us to conclude that the text offers no single position from which it is intelligible just as it is in the nature of the language we are investigating not to remain referentially static or fixed perpetually in one place. To quote again from Jonathan Culler's discussion of De Saussure's theories of language (1976: 113):

> One might say that Saussure's theory illustrates the 'otherness of meaning'. What my words mean is the meaning they can have in this interpersonal system from which they emerge. The system is already in place, as the ground or condition of meaning, and to interpret signs is to read them in terms of the system.

This kind of approach, when allied to a process of textual interpretation, cannot be viewed simply as a recipe for 'anything goes' but rather as an aid to recognition that meanings occur only by courtesy of the conditions or systems under which those meanings can be conferred. It leads to an 'opening out' or pluralisation of interpretive possibilities.[5]

3.1 Studying the 'nature' of literariness

There is no space to deal adequately here with all the very complex issues raised by this kind of study. (For further discussion see Chapters 6 and 8 above.) But it is an approach which is part of a wider approach to the question: 'what is literature?' In turn, this issue is ignored all too often in the pursuit of further interpretations of established 'classics' by 'great writers' in the 'tradition' – and almost every question here begs a series of further questions. Since this seems to be a discourse of queries it may be appropriate to list some of the questions about literariness which can be explored within a framework of stylistics as a discipline and which may thus, in varying degrees, be effectively integrated with our other designs for a more comprehensive and inclusive stylistics.

Two basic questions are: what is it in the organisation of the language of a text which makes it a literary text? how and why does it differ from other discourse types? Comparative textual investigation is going to be primary here and in its relation to the poem 'Off Course' we may want to return here to such features of the text as the way punctuation is used, the nature and function of the repetitions and parallelisms, the role of the title and of typography, the way it displays its own language, the interpenetration or convergence of different linguistic levels in the creation or constitution of meanings. This may lead to further exploration of plurality of meaning in literary discourse (the hyperactivity of the signifier), of how different literary discourses and different kinds of reading are socially constituted and of how different cultures can impose different kinds of 'reading'. Again the questions can be raised at various stages of a student's development in language and literary studies and are relevant to those various stages in the case of both native-speaking or foreign-language students. It has been the aim of this chapter to argue that the integration of language and literary study for mutual benefit and synthesis at a range of pedagogical levels can develop if the sort of policy for a comparative stylistics, initially outlined in sections 2.1–2.6, is given further consideration and exploration.

This chapter is a rewritten version of a paper entitled 'What is stylistics and why can you teach it in different ways?' in Short, M.H. (ed.) *Reading, Analyzing and Teaching Literature* (Longman, Harlow, 1989). The chapter also draws on Carter (1994).

POSTSCRIPTS AND PROSPECTS

Is not *literary* language the name we give to a diction whose frame of reference is such that words stand out as words (even as sounds) rather than being, at once assimilable meanings? The meaning of words is not unimportant, of course; it is deviation from normal use that suggests something is wrong with speaker or hearer, with the source or the receiver. For instance, two persons (voices) may be trying to get through at the same time; or perhaps we have come in at the wrong point, and cannot follow. To call a text literary is to *trust* that it will make sense eventually, even though its quality of reference may be complex, disturbed, unclear. It is a way of 'saving the phenomena' of words that are out of the ordinary or bordering the nonsensical – that have no stabilised reference.

(Geoffrey Hartmann, 1981: xxi)

The grouping of chapters in Part II represents a field of enquiry which has developed vigorously and which continues to regard the attempt better to define literary language and literariness in language as a process which enables basic questions to be asked about the nature of language and the nature of literature. A number of research directions have been pursued, each of which offers possibilities for further development. These main directions can be listed as follows:

1 **The Everydayness of Figurative Language**
2 **Pleasure and Verbal Play**
3 **So Just What *Is* Literature?**
4 **So Just What *Is* Language?**
5 **Relevance to Education and Pedagogy**
6 **New Englishes, New Literatures**
7 **Prospects**

1 THE EVERYDAYNESS OF FIGURATIVE LANGUAGE

Increasingly, empirically based, investigative studies of language continue to reveal the pervasiveness of literariness in everyday discourse. These studies parallel the kind of explorations undertaken in Chapters 6–8 and by Carter and McCarthy in relation to their CANCODE spoken discourse research (McCarthy and Carter, 1994; Carter and McCarthy, 1995; McCarthy, 1997). However, whereas the data collected in relation to the above chapters are treated in an essentially descriptive vein and within a broadly sociolinguistic and functional view of language, several of the more recent parallel studies adopt a more distinctively cognitive orientation.

An inspiration for much ongoing study of figurative language is work by Lakoff and Johnson which issued in their seminal study *Metaphors We Live By*, published in 1980 and continued in further studies by Lakoff and Turner (1989) and Turner (1991). The starting point and continuing emphasis of this research are that human language and the human mind are not *inherently* literal.

In writings by cognitive linguists there is less emphasis on the deviant nature of figurative language and correspondingly less attention to the ways in which such language examples depart or 'deviate' from the norms of language use. Instead, figurative language is seen neither as deviant nor as ornamental but as ubiquitous in everyday speech. Discussions of figurative language proceed on the assumption that the fundamental roots of language are figurative.

1.1 Metaphors and minds

Such an assumption and the research paradigms which follow from it present a radically different and indeed contrary set of beliefs to the beliefs about human thought and language which have traditionally dominated the disciplines of the humanities and social sciences in the Western intellectual tradition. Raymond Gibbs, in what is probably the most seminal of the studies in the field – *The Poetics of Mind: Figurative Thought, Language and Understanding* (Gibbs, 1994), – has argued for a 'cognitive wager' which contrasts with the more standard 'generative wager'. The **generative wager** hypothesises that explanations of language and of language universals in particular are structure dependent and that linguistic constructs are autonomous of general conceptual knowledge. The **cognitive wager** of Gibbs and other cognitive linguists aims to show that there is no autonomous language faculty and to illustrate that language is not independent of the mind. Gibbs argues that *figurative* schemes of thought structure many fundamental aspects of our ordinary, conceptual understanding of experience.

An example of this position is provided by Gibbs with reference to the polysemous word **stand** which has a range of everyday meanings: for example, 'He couldn't stand the pressure', 'The law still stands', 'The barometer stands at 29.56', 'The house stands in a field.' Gibbs points out that the *basic* meaning of **stand** is one of a physical movement or a physical act. Other meanings of **stand** extend this basic sense, often metaphorically, to convey meanings of verticality, resistance to attacks (as a result of 'standing firm', remaining vertical in the face of attempts to unbalance or knock you down) and endurance (to remain upright): for example, 'He stands over six feet tall', 'He stood up to all the attacks against his theory', 'The law still stands.'

One interesting conclusion from these examples is that there is a link by metaphoric extension between physical action and mental representation. The figurative often has an origin in physical, bodily experience and the figurative framework of everyday thought motivates a surprising number of meanings in this and other examples: so that phrases such as 'to take a stand on something', 'to uphold' (principles/the law), to remain an 'upright' person derive from the same underlying, conceptually coherent domain. Traditional studies in lexical semantics attempt to uncover the componential set of features underlying each separate word **stand** and begin from an assumption of literalness. Cognitive linguists put 'the body back into the mind', arguing that 'metaphor, and to a lesser extent metonymy, is the main mechanism through which we comprehend abstract concepts and perform abstract reasoning . . . [and that] metaphorical understanding is grounded in nonmetaphorical preconceptual structures that arise from everyday bodily experience' (Gibbs, 1994: 17). While traditional lexical semantic studies search for literal meaning on the grounds that literal meaning best reflects the truth values of an objectively determined external world, cognitive linguists such as Gibbs recognise that so-called literal language is itself constituted by fundamental processes of figuration.

1.2 Language, poetry and the poetics of mind

Gibbs summarises this developing view of the poetics of mind and the new cognitive approaches to language as follows (Gibbs, 1994: 16–17):

- The mind is not inherently literal.
- Language is not independent of the mind but reflects our perceptual and conceptual understanding of experience.
- Figuration is not merely a matter of language but provides much of the foundation for thought, reason and imagination.
- Figurative language is not deviant or ornamental but is ubiquitous in everyday speech.
- Figurative modes of thought motivate the meanings of many

linguistic expressions that are commonly viewed as having literal interpretations.

- Metaphorical meaning is grounded in nonmetaphorical aspects of recurring bodily experiences or experiential gestalts.
- Scientific theories, legal reasoning, myths, art and a variety of cultural practices exemplify many of the same figurative schemes found in everyday thought and language.
- Many aspects of word meaning are motivated by figurative schemes of thought.
- Figurative language does not require special cognitive processes to be produced and understood.
- Children's figurative thought motivates their significant ability to use and understand many kinds of figurative speech.

Studies by Gibbs and others (Johnson, 1987; Sweetser, 1990; Lakoff and Turner, 1989) raise key questions for our understanding of the nature of literary language. Metaphor has always been seen as a fundamentally literary property as a result of the apparent propensity of its users to create new insights into human experience and values; and metaphorisation has conventionally been regarded as a liberating process in which divergent and de-automatising ways of thinking are made possible. Gibbs offers an alternative mapping of creative metaphoric processes by illustrating the extent to which poetry can depend on basic underlying metaphors which structure our everyday experiences.

In the case of love poetry, for example, one of the prototypical ways in which ordinary language use construes love is in terms of a basic metaphor of *love as a nutrient*. That is, love is conventionally described in terms of the energy and sustenance it provides. For example: 'They were kept going by their love for each other'; 'She's been starved of affection for too long'; 'hungry for love'; 'I was given new strength by her love.' Other everyday metaphorical construals are of love as a force which can cause a loss of control: for example, 'She's crazy about him'; 'They are quite besotted with each other'; 'He was burning with passion'; 'addicted to love'; 'sexual obsession'; 'She pursued him relentlessly.' Sometimes these two basic metaphoric frameworks converge so that the nutrient itself can be intoxicating. Gibbs cites a poem by the American poet Emily Dickinson in which he illustrates how the poet's description of the experience of love is founded upon such familiar, everyday metaphoric concepts:

> I taste a liquor never brewed –
> From Tankards scooped in Pearl –
> Not all the Vats upon the Rhine
> Yield such an Alcohol!
>
> Inebriate of Air – am I –

And Debauchee of Dew –
Reeling – thro endless summer days –
From inns of Molten Blue –

When 'Landlords' turn the drunken Bee
Out of the Foxglove's door –
When Butterflies – renounce their 'drams' –
I shall but drink the more!

Till Seraphs swing their snowy Hats –
And Saints – to windows run –
To see the little Tippler
Leaning against the – Sun –
(Emily Dickinson, 'I taste a liquor never brewed')

One one level there is a transposition here between the poetry that is in everyday language and the everyday language that is in poetry; but there is on another level a uniquely artistic instantiation of the metaphor of love as nutrient which neither entirely constrains nor entirely liberates the poet's representation of experience. Of course, Dickinson's representation embodies an imaginative and creative response which extends the basic metaphor in divergent ways, overlaying it with phonetic patterns of rhythm and rhyme and with lexical patterns which reinforce and make more semantically dense the poem's propositions; but what is often seen as the uniquely creative expression of an idea is in this and in many other literary instances also a deployment from part of a common, everyday metaphorical stock.

Gibbs's work on metaphor implicitly accepts the notion of a *cline* between creative and everyday metaphors in ways parallel to that outlined in Chapter 8. But he has less to say on processes of the contextual interpretation of metaphor and on what the communicative 'risks' are when metaphors are creatively extended, especially in literary contexts. Gibbs does, however, provide evidence to support the speculation on p.152 above 'as to whether there is a roughly delimitable set of core, productive and culturally salient vocabulary items that predominate in conventional and creative metaphors'.

1.3 Literariness and non-literalness

A not uncommon response to the above line of reasoning is, however, to point out that the metaphors we live and think by are often dead metaphors or at least metaphors which have been overused and that the creative artist is one who can transform our ways of seeing by displacing ordinary, stale and overstrained expressions with metaphoric choices which introduce new 'schema-refreshing' perceptions. Gibbs's position in such now standard debates is that supposedly dead metaphors often have roots which are alive

211

and which actively work to provide a framework for us continually to make new understandings.

An example is the verb **see** which is one of the most common verbs in English. One of its most frequent metaphorical meanings, however, which is substantiated by major computational lexical studies of semantic patterns such as the COBUILD project, is that of understanding. **See** in the sense of understand or know is three times more frequent than the sense of **see** as visual perception by the eye. Examples of such a metaphor would therefore be 'I see what you mean', or 'They've seen the point at last!' The shift from physical action to metaphorical entailment has taken place over time and has indeed now become dead. But Gibbs would argue that metaphoric extensions of various kinds remain possible which keep the relationship alive, and that both poets and ordinary people make use of the same figurative schemes of thought. A poem such as Margaret Atwood's 'This is a photograph of me' contains for example, a chain of words ('see', 'look', 'scan') to do with seeing the photograph of the poem's persona in terms of penetrating below the surface of personality to understand and develop 'insight' into the nature of a personality who is on the verge of suicide by drowning and the reader is made aware of the dangers inherent in 'closing their eyes' to such a situation.

Although metaphor is a major mode of conceptual organisation in language, Gibbs and others also explore the role of other figurative expressions such as metonymy, irony and sarcasm, idioms and proverbs, indirect speech acts and oxymora as basic, endemic constituents of language, concluding that an easy facility with such expressions by speakers of a language is indicative of the *poeticality* of much everyday discourse and suggestive of universally poetic components of the human mind. And to make such a claim, Gibbs argues, is not inconsistent with saying that figurative thought functions for the most part unconsciously and automatically in people's daily processing of linguistic meaning. Cognitive linguists stress that figurative knowledge motivates people's use of and understanding of both ordinary and literary language and that the 'easy facility' with metaphorical modes is necessary because so much of ordinary language use is figuratively patterned.

A final example can be taken from examination of the functions of idioms in everyday discourse. And the example of idiomaticity is useful because again a prevailing view is that idioms are fixed and frozen units of meaning and that they exist in the mental lexicon in much the same way that dead metaphors do. Idioms are therefore regarded as non-creative chunks of language which are not only resistant to 'literary' use but which are immutable in form. Dictionaries of idioms and fixed expressions reinforce such notions.

Examination of real data reveals, however, that speakers and writers can exploit the very fixed nature of idiom to extend meanings in original ways

212

and to play creatively with fixed patterns. Examples in the CANCODE project data (see p.91) include the following:

1 [Two friends are discussing a third friend's stormy marriage and the fact that, as a result of continuing infidelity, relations between the couple are 'frozen' and they are barely talking]:

A: . . . he's at it again but he really wants you know just to sit down.
B: Like they just talk about how they both feel.
A: Out of the frying pan into the deep freeze this time.

2 [Here two colleagues, who are social workers, are discussing a third colleague who has a tendency to become too involved in individual cases]:

A: I don't know but she seems to have picked up all kinds of lame ducks and traumas along the way.
B: That that's her vocation.
A: Perhaps it is. She should have been a counsellor.
B: Yeah but the trouble with her is she puts all her socialist carts before the horses.

Further examples are given in Chapter 8, which contains sections specifically devoted to creative functions in casual conversation.

Goddard (1996) and Deignan (1995) are further recent studies of metaphor and imagery in relation to everyday discourse, the latter study in particular being based on COBUILD research into the most frequent and therefore culturally salient metaphors in English (of which, in relation to the conversational data in (1) above, metaphors of 'hot' and 'cold' are especially significant in structuring our perceptions and evaluations of human feelings).

2 PLEASURE AND VERBAL PLAY

The general orientation of Chapter 6 is in an ever-extending line with more recent approaches to language which underscore the literariness in 'ordinary' discourse. The notion that ordinary language users regularly and typically communicate in ways from which pleasure may be derived has gained considerable ground in recent years and correspondingly the assumption that aesthetic pleasure is the sole preserve of the highest forms of artistic encounter may need to be reinspected.

Cook (1995, 1996) focuses in particular on the idea of playing with language and argues that verbal play is characteristic of discourse in which language is used to 'fill up the spaces between necessary activity' (Cook, 1996: 198) underlining the essentially non-utilitarian nature of literary discourse. Like casual conversation, in which the motivation to talk is not necessarily determined by any specific purpose, literature is what Cook defines as a **'space-filling' discourse** (what is referred to in Chapters

6 and 8 in this section as 'non-pragmatic', as 'fictional' and as 'displaced interaction'). One consequence of this position is that more descriptive work needs to be invested in comparing and contrasting casual conversational and literary discourses (see in particular p.160). Cook also argues that literary linguistic analysis should focus more systematically on comedy, popular song, graffiti, newspaper headlines and advertisements.

In such contexts of use the relationship between subject matter and language play can be highly complex. The writers of tabloid headlines in newspapers such as the *Sun* make pervasive use of figurative language and language play, particularly puns. But the relationship of punning to the *content* of the stories for which the headlines create an introductory frame is not a simple one. There appears to be no obvious connection between the seriousness of the story and the adoption of playful linguistic games on the part of the copywriter. For example, a supermodel exposing a bare stomach is fronted by the punning headline BELLY NICE; a British judge accused of being drunk on television attracts the headline I'M IN A PICKLE BUT I WASN'T PICKLED SAYS JUDGE PICKLES; I'M BLACK AND BLUE reports an alleged attack on an black policeman by supporters of the Anti-Nazi League.

One of Cook's main conclusions is that puns and other forms of verbal play in general are *systematically* patterned into tabloid newspapers such as the *Sun*:

> the serious is succeeded by the light-hearted (from left-hand to right-hand page), often marked as such by language play. It is almost as though the arrangement of topics and the shift of emphasis from language as a transparent medium to language as something self-reflexive, combined with a greater salience of right-hand over left-hand pages, serve deliberately to elevate both trivial subject matter and language play above more serious subjects and more sober language.
>
> (Cook, 1996: 218)

Cook is not claiming that such use of language constitutes art but he is saying that it is art-*like* and that we dismiss such deployment of language or draw too sharp a distinction between 'art' and 'non-art' at our peril. Our definition of literary art and by extension literary language use is thus more likely to be better served if the descriptive net is widened to include all kinds of discourse, including the most everyday and 'ordinary'. Cook advocates *extending* the range of texts along the kind of literary/non-literary cline described in Chapter 6 for it is only by fuller examination of *less institutionalised* discourse-types such as popular verbal and written comedy, jokes and graffiti that verbal play and the pleasures derived by both sender and receiver can be more fully theorised and described. (For a discussion of the relationship between institutionalised and non-institutionalised text-types in relation to literary discourse, see also van Peer, 1991 as well as Chapter 8, below; see also McRae, 1991, for a parallel argument with particular reference to teaching texts and for a useful set of suggestions for distinguishing the terms 'referential' and 'representational' texts.)

In Cook (1995) there is, in a way which relates interestingly to work by Raymond Gibbs, described above, an attempt to explain the pleasure derived from patterning in poetry in terms of mental mechanisms which fulfil basic needs of the human species as a whole; and among the more basic of mental mechanisms are those which are renewed and refreshed as a result of the destabilising effects of literary patterning. One suggestion is that playing with words may be genetically determined and that recasting or deviating from established patterns is a natural and normal 'biological' reflex of the human mind, which cognitive linguists are in any case increasingly inclined to regard as figuratively predisposed. **Literariness in language is normal.**

3 SO JUST WHAT *IS* LITERATURE?

There are three main approaches to an answer to this question, which is in turn prompted by the question raised in Chapter 6. The first is to argue, as does Eagleton (1983: 10), that 'anything can be literature' and that it is all a matter of how we choose (or are chosen) to read a text. Because texts are extremely varied and the social and cultural positions from which readers read texts even more varied, a definition of literature can only be relative to specific contexts. In certain specific institutionalised contexts such as a department of literature in a school or university, definitions of literature will be made by the selection of texts for study, which will do no more than reflect the 'interests', predispositions and theories of those teachers or examination boards which make the prescription.

The second approach is to proceed on the basis that certain texts are simply more highly valued than others and that texts which continue to be highly valued over a period of time become part of cultural heritage, a *canon* of texts which a community or communities then teach, study, talk about and learn to live with and by as an enduring repository of insight into the conditions of being human. (For a recent review of key issues in canon formation and for the insight that canons are defined as much by what they exclude as by what they include, see Maybin, 1996, and, for an interesting view of canon formation as a form of Darwinian 'natural selection', Herrnstein-Smith, 1988.) In general, such an approach chooses not to inspect too closely the precise processes by which canon formation takes place or is institutionalised (in other words asking how and why such texts come to be valued) preferring to 'let history be the judge'. Where judgements are made explicit, the basis for such judgement will normally be one of aesthetic value.

The third main approach in this inevitably oversimplified summary is to attempt a definition of literature using in particular forms of analysis based on the assumption that literature is dependent as a textual category on the medium of language. To explore that medium, using tools of analysis and discursive procedures which have been developed for the purpose of the analysis of language and texts, can lead to fuller understanding and then yet further hypotheses concerning the nature of literature.

These three main approaches cannot of course be so easily separated out. The third approach is the one adopted by most literary linguists interested in defining the linguistic constituency of literature and is the approach adopted in this part of the book. It is also, as is argued in several places in this book, the approach which is most likely to foster the kinds of understanding and support the kinds of pedagogy which will allow a greater integration of language and literature at all levels in the classroom.

Several recent publications, as we have seen in this postscript, have continued to explore the nature of literariness; and several recent publications in the same tradition have attempted yet more directly to develop theories of literature based on the question 'What *is* Literature?' Space does not allow extensive reference and illustration but what I judge to be studies most relevant to issues raised in Part II of this book are reviewed.

Cook's *Discourse and Literature* (1993) employs key concepts which are alive in a number of approaches discussed in Part II: he stresses the interactive nature of reading, highlighting features of textual design which activate involvement and interpersonality; and, in particular, he underlines the discoursal deviance which can act as a specific trigger to what he terms **schema refreshment**. The notion of 'schema refreshment' is based on work in artificial intelligence (AI) and is what might be termed a textual-cognitive criterion, reflecting the subtitle to Cook's study 'The Interplay of Form and Mind'. Cook analyses a wide range of discourse types for their schema-disrupting properties, arguing that what is generally understood to be aesthetically valued literature, at least within certain cultural (usually Western) conceptions of the term, will be the texts which introduce schematic or cognitive refreshment. That is, an advertisement or a joke may disrupt at a textual or linguistic level of deviance but often does not offer any real challenge to cognitive renewal in terms of how the world is perceived.[1]

Discourse and Literature explores a definition of literature by linking formal linguistic analysis with mentalistic approaches; Anders Petterson's *A Theory of Literary Discourse* (1990) explores a definition of literature by locating linguistic analysis within more established domains of literary and cultural theory. Like Attridge's *Peculiar Language* (1988), the study benefits from the adoption of an historical perspective from Aristotle to the present day. Petterson demonstrates that what constitutes literary language and literariness is historically and culturally variable and that many of the issues to do with the deviancy and self-reflexivity of literary language belong more comfortably within the twentieth century and within modernist accounts of literary formations. Petterson's main conclusion is that literature (in its most central contemporary sense) in most historical and most Western cultural settings is a verbal composition which is especially marked by its **presentationality**. For Petterson literature differs from other categories he explores such as functionally informative and directive discourse because:

> to verbally understand serious literature is . . . to understand that it is presentational and to apprehend it in the intended manner is to seek to obtain emotional, cognitive or formal aesthetic satisfaction from it.

> (1990: 256)

The notion of an aesthetically pleasing discourse, presented for the benefit of a reader or listener, is, as Bennett in *Outside Literature* (1990) has shown, problematic. Aesthetic patterns have to be evaluated by readers and those readers performing the aesthetic judgement do so in a specific institutionalised environment which is socially and politically constituted. Aesthetic values may be ascribed to texts which are 'presented' for evaluation, those values may be constructed and construed as if they were universal and transcendent but the reader is caught in a double-bind of unending circularity for the aesthetics is likely to be no more than the aesthetics of a socially dominant group embedded in the values associated with a particular set of reading practices developed between teachers and students, critics and readers, or in specific forms of examination and assessment. For Bennett, literature is a set of social conditions (1990: 284–6). Texts may have political and social values and these may take precedence for readers such as Bennett, who wish to remain in their responses and evaluations 'outside' literature as a formalist prescription. Yet, as Bennett concedes, the 'inside' (formal and structural conception of literature with its text-immanent aesthetics) is powerful in explaining the differences, distinctions and continuities between texts; and the polarities between 'inside' and 'outside' literature will therefore remain until theories and descriptions advance sufficiently for the circularity to be squared.

Petterson's position does find general support in studies devoted to more universalist and cognitive preoccupations with aesthetic functions. Baumann (1977, 1986), for example, stresses the 'designed for performance' aspect of literary presentation, drawing many examples from more oral-based cultures and arguing that 'aesthetic' satisfaction may simply result from a display and appropriate evaluation of verbal skill, the evaluation being based on a judgement of the extent to which clear public rules for the performance have been adhered to. Bever (1986), however, points out that aesthetic satisfaction is produced not simply by straightforward arousal but rather by the **pleasure** which ensues when difficulty is followed by resolution, a good example being when a complex narrative is resolved by an ingenious plot outcome or when a specific moral problem is addressed and solutions proposed. Parallelism is another example in which the first part is resolved by the reinstatement of a related pattern in the second part.

In earlier studies Berlyne (1971) went even further, and with an apparent recognition of the demands of many modernist texts, arguing that a presentation of aesthetic arousal can be autonomous and that, indeed, complexity need not be resolved and may even be all the more pleasurable for remaining unresolved. Cognitive anthropologists in this tradition are, however, less concerned with specific textual functions than with the universal, non-culture-specific character of verbal art. Fabb (1997) explores this ground lucidly and within a tradition of investigation which contrasts with the more discourse-oriented, text-specific analyses found in this book.

Text-based linguists and literary stylisticians have, however, not had an exclusive concern with the intrinsic or 'inside' properties of 'aesthetic' discourse. For example, van Peer (1991), in a paper entitled 'But what *is* literature? Toward a descriptive definition of literature', attempts to account for different socially functional varieties of text-type. As in Chapters 6 and 7, the notion of a cline is also found helpful by van Peer in order to distinguish the co-occurrence of different textual properties along a continuum from highly institutionalised varieties to varieties which are discoursally more informal and which van Peer classifies as **homilectal** varieties. Different texts are defined by van Peer in terms of discoursal difference, with the meaning of discourse here being reserved for the nature of the 'situational configuration' between the sender and the receiver of a message.

For van Peer the term 'discourse' is largely reserved for linguistic messages which take place within an immediate face-to-face exchange and therefore the more displaced a text is in time and space the more features of 'textuality' (a term close to the term 'semantic density' used in Chapter 6) it will possess. The more a particular text is detached in time and space *and* carries knowledge, belief systems and values, the more **central** it will be, with its centrality being characterised both by linguistic features and by the sociocultural forces which surround it. **Peripheral** texts would therefore include telephone conversations, shopping lists, office memos, newspapers and magazines, railway timetables, casual chat between passengers on a bus and so on.

Van Peer differentiates further, however, between **homilectal** and **institutionalised** texts. Literature, according to van Peer, is text rather than discourse in so far as peripheral texts are often no more than ephemeral, time- and space-bound communications. But van Peer advances the interesting suggestion that 'texts designated as literary are basically characterised by their homilectal nature' (van Peer, 1991: 133). Accordingly, he does not discount the fact that casual conversation, which is homilectal, can exist along a textual continuum of literariness, whereas institutionalised textual forms such as an office memo, school textbook or railway timetable are unlikely to contain many literary features (although some readers may, unusually, choose to apply literary readings to them).

Homilectal texts share specific characteristics which, according to van Peer, are shared by all texts which are potentially able to be classified as literary or to be read in conventionally literary ways, that is, 'they aim at reflectivity, group cohesion and the experience of delight' (1991: 135). Such texts create pleasure for the sender and the receiver, they are powerful in the establishment of an interpersonal communality of shared feelings, values and beliefs (van Peer refers to this as a 'special bond') and they manifest, by being outside institutionally defined practical needs and purposes, a reflective stance by creating space for considering the general nature of human life and processes of living.

4 SO JUST WHAT *IS* LANGUAGE?

In addressing the question 'What is literature?', the issue of appropriate models of language and appropriate theories of language may be in danger of being overlooked, not least because a consideration in Part II of the nature of literariness entails a view of language which is socially and functionally oriented, which is located in specific contexts of real use and which cannot for such purposes be adequately analysed unless units larger than the clause and the sentence, the conventional site for much linguistic description and theorisation, are considered. The view of language which is consistently adopted is therefore one of language as discourse.

Recent research reported in section 1 of this postscript underlines the pervasively 'literary' character of ordinary language. If so much ordinary discourse involves ordinary language users in creative processes, then what is it about human involvement with language that might explain such a predisposition? An answer to this question in part demands that conventional approaches to meaning which centre on truth and reference and literalness are suspended in favour of a view of language in which its essential character is inherently figurative and in which users regularly derive an essential pleasure from their engagement and involvement with such language in use. Traditional approaches to semantics which seek referential, context-free, unambiguous and truth-conditional determinations of meaning need to be displaced by an approach which does not see poetic language as a distortion or violation, nor as a mere embellishment of objective content, but which recognises non-literalness as a basic linguistic and communicative characteristic of human languages.

Such a position is echoed in the writings of many twentieth-century literary theorists and philosophers, beginning with pre-modernist thinkers such as Nietzsche, who is quoted as follows in a wide-ranging survey of literary language entitled *What is Literary Language?* (Tambling, 1988: 55):

What then, is truth? A mobile army of metaphors, metonyms and anthropomorphisms – in short a sum of human relations, which have been enhanced, transposed, and embellished poetically and rhetorically, and which after long use seem firm, canonical and obligatory to a people: truths are illusions about which one has forgotten that this is what they are; metaphors which are worn out and without sensuous power.

('On truth and lie in an extra-moral sense', Nietzsche, 1873)

Tambling points out that for Nietzsche all language is literary language because even supposedly referential language has no original reference point and because even a referential statement is a rhetorical device, one which is designed to persuade the listener or reader to act or to think in a particular way. The position is close to that of Derrida's discussions of textuality in which for him, as Tambling argues:

'Literary language' is a pleonasm . . . .: all language is literary, because it is all mere writing (the earlier meaning of 'literary'), and it can all be read for the guileful, ambiguous and indeterminate uses of language that literature employs . . . 'what is literary language?' is not a question to be asked merely by those who study 'literature': it affects those who write history, philosophy, political science or science itself.

(Tambling, 1988: 74)

Lecercle (1990) adopts a not dissimilar line, arguing that many models of language this century have been impoverished by a failure properly to examine the more creative 'remainder' of language. The 'remainder', as he terms it, is necessarily ignored by more formalist-inspired models which idealise language systems and which, following the lead of De Saussure in particular, focus on *langue* to the exclusion of *parole*. The 'remainder' only comes to our notice when we examine real uses of conversational language or investigate it diachronically or explore everyday metaphors, puns, riddles and verbal games. Lecercle questions whether such uses of language can ever be fully formalised but he argues that linguistic systems would be all the richer for recognising their existence:

The strain in Spain

We may wonder what it is that the reader must know in order to understand the title, even before he has read the article, which deals with social unrest in Spain. A dictionary will provide the conventional meanings of the words . . . The encyclopaedia is much more helpful, for it provides the reader with a real understanding of the title: it points out the source of the allusion, a sentence (mis)pronounced by Eliza Doolittle in *Pygmalion* 'The rain in Spain falls mainly in the plain' . . . The reader has now understood the origin of the title. But has he understood the title completely? Not yet. For now comes the work of the remainder, which is contained not in any body of knowledge, but in the reader's close relationship to his own language. For the title is successful in so far as it plays on assonance (as in the original phrase), contains a word within a word ('strain'/'rain') and has added on an alliteration, 'the strain in Spain', that was not present in the original sentence . . . The title re-semanticizes this jingle, makes it relevant to the current political situation in Spain by following the paths of the remainder. All this is covered not by an encyclopaedia, because it all remains within language; not in the dictionary, which is the semantic component of *langue*; but in the remainder.

(1990: 138–9)

(See also Harris, 1987 for a similar and increasingly influential position.)

5 RELEVANCE TO EDUCATION AND PEDAGOGY

1. One of the aims of this postscript is to reinforce a main point of Part II of this book that all learners of a language and all students of literature already possess considerable powers of response to and creativity with the literariness potential, the 'remainder' which exists in all languages. Methodologies and practices should therefore continue to be devoted to exploration of the continuities between literary and non-literary language. Literature teaching should proceed from a more complete openness to assumptions concerning what students can already do with language.

2. The greater language awareness which results from discussion of ordinary language use, especially informal conversational use, can lead to greater explicitness and fuller awareness of processes of interpretation. Being more conscious of processes of interpretation, particularly in relation to 'everyday' interpretive work, is likely to lead to greater confidence and competence in interpretations of texts which are more 'semantically dense'.

3. Courses in linguistics and language study at all levels should pay greater attention to non-literal aspects of language. The fact that such features are seen to be not easily formalisable (or, in the case of Lecercle, believed to be impossible to formalise) should be the main reason for their inclusion. At many different pedagogic levels challenges can be established to describe such properties and to test the 'cognitive wager' hypothesis of Gibbs and others that language is intrinsically figurative. It is not just that poetry can learn from linguistics; linguistics can learn from poetry.

4. A more fundamental position is that articulated by Turner in *Reading Minds: The Study of English in the Age of Cognitive Science* (1991). Turner argues that language should serve as the common ground which unifies a profession of English Studies which is becoming increasingly fragmented and

specialised. The language basis for such a re-integration is the kind of work in cognitive linguistics outlined in this postscript and paralleled from a more functional and social orientation, in Chapters 9 and 10:

> Literature lives within language and language within everyday life. The study of literature must live within the study of language, and the study of language within the study of the everyday mind.
>
> (1991: 4)

Turner argues that language and literature study should be involved in a common enterprise of defining what it means to be human 'as the cultural and conceptual counterpart to the biological and social inquiries that help us understand our human possibilities' and that such goals are unlikely to be served by programmes which generate ever more refined appreciations of non-language fields and interpretations of texts within constantly changing literary and cultural theories but which either lack sophisticated understanding of language or, worse, dismiss language study as being the study of the straightforward and obvious. Turner asserts:

> These assumptions are deadly. Common language expressing common thought is anything but simple, and its workings are not obvious. Special language expressing special thought is an exploitation of the common and to be analyzed only with respect to it.
>
> (1991: 14)

> Most of the tools of poetic thought not only exist in everyday thought but are indispensable and irreducible there.
>
> (1991: 20)

Turner is similarly critical of departments of linguistics which, he believes, do not treat the study of language 'humanistically nor as an aspect of what it means to be human'. Turner calls for departments of English language and literature to return to the study of 'English' by drawing on the kinds of tools and data and procedures for analysis made available by cognitive science. In a manner parallel to Gibbs (1994), but in a more polemical, assertive and programmatic discourse, Turner appeals for much closer scrutiny in courses and in research of the figurative resources of everyday language and of the human conceptual frameworks generated in and through and beyond such language. In practical terms, Turner calls for courses in metaphor and metonymy and irony (for example), initially drawing on data produced by creative 'ordinary' language users, to be foundational and integrating in departments of English. It is, he says, 'the most likely path to restoring our profession to its natural place as a central cultural and intellectual activity'.

5.   A further more detailed review of issues in the teaching of 'English' in the context of discourse and literacy is Durant (1995). A major problem

222

in the relationship between language and literature and between product- and process-based teaching is that the teaching and study of literature is conventionally equated with the development of higher-order competencies such as an appreciation of cultural tradition, an understanding of aesthetic and symbolic orders and an exploration of social and individual moral identities. By contrast, language and literacy development are conventionally equated with instrumental lower-order skills such as reading and writing. Literature and literacy sit to some extent uncomfortably alongside each other. As Williams (1990: 153, quoted by Durant) puts it: 'there have been 600 years of English literature and only 100 years of English literacy' – confirming that the basic capacities for linguistic expression have been in serious historical deficit and, as Durant argues, allowing literature study to remain an elitist practice. The democratisation of access to literature continues to be dependent on an extension of the literacy skills necessary for its reading (and writing). Along lines similar to those advocated in Chapter 10, Durant argues for schools and universities (especially the latter) to regard English as a 'practice of discourse' which will not be affected by changes to curriculum content but which can bring the higher- and lower-order skills, the aesthetic and the utilitarian, into productive synthesis by comparative discourse studies, involving reading *and* writing, of a wide range of forms and genres, literary and non-literary:

> If you conceive of English as a knowledge-based field, it seems perfectly reasonable to add on units or modules incrementally . . . If, on the other hand, you think of English as a structured educational event or practice, then curriculum revisions are quite likely to be procedural or systemic, with implications fully across the range of different topics or subject areas: an alteration in aim or pedagogic method will affect how you approach a canonical literary work as much as how you approach a work from the New Literatures, a newspaper text, a film or a soap opera.
>
> (Durant, 1995: 54)

We have seen in preceding chapters that such 'events' have been more fully activated in work in the teaching of English as a foreign or second language and generally to speakers of other languages learning English internationally and as an international language (see also Smallwood, 1994; Kayman, 1994 for further discussion and Bourdieu, 1984 on the development of 'taste' by and for a social and cultural minority).

6 NEW ENGLISHES, NEW LITERATURES

Chapters 8, 9 and 10 have explored the role of literary texts in the language classroom and, in particular, as a resource for language development. Fundamentally, such a pedagogic move involves the teacher coming down from the pedestal or lectern and involves a classroom treatment of literature which does not view literature as a sacrosanct object for reverential, product-centred study.

Methodologically, this has at least the following implications: strategies drawn from the EFL classroom will be applied, if necessary in an adapted way, to the teaching of literary texts. This means that a whole range of standard procedures such as cloze, rewriting, prediction activities and role-playing are deployed in the literature lesson; or, to put it in another way, literary texts are treated in the language lesson in ways which may not be radically different from the ways in which any other kind of text is treated. Several recent publications have illustrated in theory and in practice the extent and possibilities of such work and of the pedagogies which accompany them. For example: Carter, 1982b; Short (1989); Carter *et al.* (1990); Lazar (1993); Maley and Duff (1990); Bredella and Delanoy (1996); McRae (1991); Carter and McRae (1996).

Current materials development, particularly in the field of English as a second or foreign language, is based on writing in English by writers who are 'Western', by virtue of being either native speakers of, for example, British, American, South African or Australian English, or who are Western by virtue of being based in or working as adopted citizens in an English-speaking country of the Western world. Several in this latter category are distinguished, prize-winning writers whose creativity in English is the creativity of the bi- or multilingual. Accordingly, several are engaged in pushing back the conventional limits of expressivity available in the language and are establishing new norms of creative expression in and through English.

The existence of a rapidly developing world literature in English has not so far been manifested in materials for the classroom, though the basis for such development exists in a wide range of recent descriptive, theoretical and pedagogically based studies (e.g. Kachru, 1986; Talib, 1992, 1996; Vethemani, 1996; James, 1996).

Further impetus is provided in a wide range of post-colonial literary and cultural theory and in an increasing number and variety of studies in colonial discourse. Studies by, for example, Spivak (1993), Bhaba (1994) and Said (1994) prepare the ground for the development of course books in the study of new literatures in English which, as a result of much theoretical refinement, have the potential for engaging more directly with non-Western experience and for activating a classroom exploration of contrasting value systems. For example, as Bhaba (1994) has illustrated, Western-originated notions of universality of meaning and a commitment to realist modes of signification are not culturally transferable in any seamless way. Pedagogically, too, such materials are likely to work more directly with different models of classroom authority and transmission of information (that is, through more teacher-centred methodologies) and to be positioned at an interface **between** product- and process-based pedagogy.

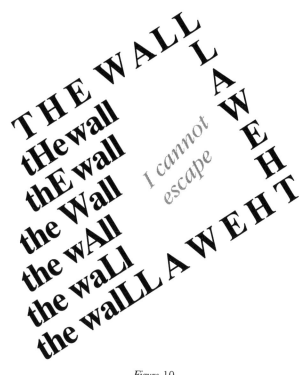

Figure 10.

A first step in introducing into classrooms worldwide what Spivak (1993) terms the 'outside' (that is, the discourses which are marginalised by Western cultural power and influence) is to set alongside each other texts which are either formally or thematically similar and to explore the nature and extent of cultural difference between them. For example, in the case of the range of texts discussed in Chapter 10, particularly Morgan's 'Off Course', 'The Wall' by the Malaysian writer Abdul Ghafar Ibrahim (Figure 10) provides a productive counterpoint.

Classroom treatment could deal with formal, typographic, thematic and representational similarities and dissimilarities between 'Off Course' and 'The Wall' employing, where appropriate, a synthesis of product- and process-based methodologies.

Such treatments are not, however, without problems. First, methodologies may not always travel easily, particularly if, as in process-based, student-oriented teaching, such methodologies have a Eurocentric character and had their origins in political challenges to authority in society and in education in the late 1960s and early 1970s. Altering as they do the relationships and roles of teacher and student, writers such as Phillipson (1991), Kramsch

(1993) and Pennycook (1994) question the extent to which students' own language use and responses to language benefit from such procedures. Both prefer to advocate a sharper classroom focus on critical language awareness and on critical language pedagogies.

A critical language pedagogy does not so much aim simply to produce competence in use of a standard language, vitally important though that is, as to enable learners to reflect on the *kind* of English they use and how far it allows them to express their own personal voice as language users. In this connection, greater use of non-native literatures in the language classroom, with local versions of English being creatively deployed, can have an instrumental role to play. An exploration of such critical pedagogy along the lines outlined by Pennycook (1994: ch. 8) could form the basis for major empirical and theoretical language in education research.

7 PROSPECTS

The following topics and issues are suggested as areas for further research. The areas continue lines of enquiry established in this part of the book but they do not by any means constitute an exhaustive list:

1. Several of the chapters and some of the material reviewed in the post-script (especially Chapters 6 and 8) include reference to clines as a method of capturing linguistic features which do not easily fall into yes/no category divisions. Analysis of clines of literariness and clines of metaphoricity could be supplemented by clines involving many aspects of figurative language use, including clines which measured different degrees of indirectness in communication. One danger is that the construction of a cline or clines can be a recipe for permanent indeterminacy; however indeterminate the features which clines attempt to capture, it is continually necessary to hypothesise and then to refine defining categories and to continue to search for more precise specification of different points along the proposed clines.

2. In Chapter 8 reference is made to the 'intersubjective accord and intimacy' which can result from a successful outcome of the *risk* taken in using figurative language such as metaphor in communicative interaction. Future studies might address the need to specify more completely the linguistic triggers of such interpersonality and at the same time take the first steps in constructing a grammar of interpersonality in which the linguistic choices (of grammar, intonation, lexis *and* figurative constructs) are described in relation to the type of interaction taking place.

The question of degrees of interpersonality and 'intersubjective accord' can also be related to the need for fuller definition of the speeech genres in which they are typically enacted. For example, is verbal play more likely to occur in informal contexts of interaction? In narrative genres rather than genres of argumentation? In casual conversation, with its varying degrees of intimacy, rather than in, say, information reports? Databases of conversational English need to be mined to discover the degrees of interpersonal embedding which occurs relative to individual speech genres. In this exploration a specification of clines of casualness in conversation will be a necessary prerequisite.

3.   The 'Overview' and other chapters in Part II address issues of *interpretation*. A central research direction would be to uncover the kinds of interpretation which take place when the discourse is mutually perceived to be marked by particular 'literary' functions. Is there any fundamental difference between such interpretations of a canonical literary text and interpretations of a non-literary text such as a timetable, a holiday brochure itinerary or a set of instructions parts of which to each of us may not 'make sense'?

4.   One area which has been generally neglected to date is the way in which deliberate indirectness in communication might be related to literariness and verbal play. Indirectness can be essential in so far as it allows a listener freedom to do interpretive work. Literary texts can also be defined by a refusal to overspecify a particular meaning and by an invitation to readers to co-construct a relevant interpretation. One starting point would be the construction of reader protocols, that is, empirical studies of readers engaging in real time processing of 'literary' and 'non-literary' text and then reporting and reflecting on the process.

5.   It is clear that the whole question of pleasure and the kinds of pleasure communicated by and in creative, literary interaction is underresearched. The topics and questions to be investigated might include: the extent to which the most prominent triggers of pleasure can be identified and the extent to which they are linguistically marked. Is pleasure more likely to be produced by the resolution of complex, problematically dense forms or by the resistance of a text to a resolution of cognitive or formal complexity? How culture-or social-group-specific is such 'aesthetic' pleasure? How far is the pleasure conveyed by literary language connected with the kinds of language which challenge conventional meanings, breaking up distinctions that have been culturally formed? To what extent is such language simply the language associated with a challenge to a dominant order? For Julia Kristeva such an order is largely male and white and middle class. Is there a practice of signification which resists unitary meaning and which creates a process of becoming, rather than being something static or fixed?

> literary practice is seen as exploration and discovery of the possibilities of language, as an activity that liberates the script from a number of linguistic, psychic and social networks, as a dynamic that breaks up the inertia of language habits and grants linguists the unique possibility of studying the *becoming* of the signification of signs.
>
> (Kristeva, 1984: 2–3)

Among the areas for stylistic exploration are: parallelism; repetition (verbatim repetition; structural repetition – of lexical and syntactic patterns); repetition with variation; and specific figures, particularly metaphor, within the range embraced in this part of the book.

6.   Finally, research in both theory and in empirical study of classroom practice might profitably investigate the extent to which discourse exists independently of language. What is the potential for 'literary' linguistic communication of new media such as fax, e-mail, the Internet, CD-ROM, computer-generated visual images and so on? All such media are becoming progressively more interpersonal and interactive and in turn promote more spoken forms of language, but to what extent does such communication go beyond language, requiring 'readers' to interpret a semiotic message which combines visual, audio, graphological and linguistic 'print' images? Among the key questions for the future of language, literacy and literature might be included the following:

1   What implications for a reader's relationship with a text are likely to be brought about by these new technologies? How can teachers best exploit the power both to create a text on screen and to change a text on screen in order to reshape it to their own purposes? How does such a facility, by making the learner more active and more in control of various versions of a text, alter previous understandings of the nature of reading and writing and previous understandings of what a text is and can be?

2   What are the implications, in particular, for the development of critical literacy if texts cannot just be decoded but *recoded* to make them mean differently? To what extent is the path to 'revision' literacy (Chapter 5) eased by the range and extent of basic word-processing programs, let alone the power to import and work with and against the wide variety of texts available on the Internet?

3   What changes in the structure of English grammar, vocabulary and discourse organisation are being generated by more interactive and inter-personal linguistic exchanges and how can they be exploited to better teach awareness of the range of choices along the continuum from spoken to written English?

4   What acts of positive discrimination can there be for those who are excluded from such possibilities by lack of access to such technologies?

NOTES

1 PROPER ENGLISH: LANGUAGE, CULTURE AND CURRICULUM

1 This is a synthesis of reports in several British newspapers of a speech given by Prince Charles.

2 Discussion here is indebted to an unpublished paper by Henry Widdowson 'Languages in the National Curriculum', Institute of Education (ESOL Department), University of London.

3 See Peter Thomas, 'Romance in Cartlandia', *Guardian*, 14 March 1992. Sections on popular fiction here owe much to the above article and to Walter Nash, *Style in Popular Fiction* (Routledge, 1990). See also Burton (1982).

4 The references are to John Smith, leader of the British Labour Party who died in 1994; and to Neil Kinnock, who was leader of the British Labour Party until his resignation in 1992.

2 THE NEW GRAMMAR TEACHING

1 See, for example, research undertaken by or reported in Macauley (1947), Harris (1960), Robinson (1960), Elley *et al.* (1975). Braddock *et al.* (1963) is representative:

> In view of the widespread agreement of research studies based upon many types of students and teachers, the conclusion can be stated in strong and unqualified terms: the teaching of formal grammar has a negligible or, because it usually displaces the same instruction and practice in actual composition, even a harmful effect on the improvement of writing.

Such conclusions do not, of course, invalidate the new grammar teaching which uses (a) different models and descriptive frameworks for grammar (b) different methodologies. See Walmsley (1984).

2 See Brian Doyle, *English and Englishness*, New Accents Series (Doyle, 1989).

3 See Milroy and Milroy (1991) for a detailed account.

4 The interview is transcribed as spoken text and hence not conventionally punctuated.

5 See, for example, the following:

Q: How do you make a Swiss roll?
A: Push him down a mountain.

('Swiss' is a modifier of the noun 'roll'; the answer (A) depends on a knowledge that 'Swiss' can also be a proper noun (designating a nationality) and that roll also operates as a verb of motion.)

GIANT WAVES DOWN QUEEN ELIZABETH'S FUNNEL

(There are several possible explanations of this headline. Most depend on GIANT being both a noun and an adjective and on WAVES being a noun and a verb of action.)

3 POLITICS AND KNOWLEDGE ABOUT LANGUAGE: THE LINC PROJECT

1 A much-quoted statement is this connection by John Rae, a headteacher, appeared in *The Observer* newspaper in 1982. It is frequently cited in support of right-wing political views:

> The overthrow of grammar coincided with the acceptance of the equivalent of creative writing in social behaviour. As nice points of grammar were mockingly dismissed as pedantic and irrelevant, so was punctiliousness in such matters as honesty, responsibility, property, gratitude, apology and so on.
>
> (7 February 1982)

2 The most detailed expositions of these positions are found in Gilbert (1989, 1990).
3 Professor Gillian Brown and Professor Henry Widdowson were members of the Kingman Committee (DES, 1988); Professor Michael Stubbs and Professor Katharine Perera were members of the Cox Committee (DES, 1989). A relevant formative document is Perera (1987).
4 A representative collection of papers articulating a set of clear positions against anticipated curricular changes is Jones and West (1988).
5 Detailed accounts of the political context of the LINC project are contained in an edition of the *English Magazine* (April 1992) devoted to LINC. An edition of *The Times Educational Supplement* (26 June 1991) contains an explanation by Minister of State, Tim Eggar, for the non-publication of LINC materials. A valuable background paper is Bourne and Cameron (1989).
6 Recent debates on the value of genre theory appeared in teachers' journals such as *English in Australia* (1988), and *English in Education* (1992).
7 See, in particular, the publications from Harcourt Brace Jovanovich in the series for schools 'Language: A Resource for Meaning' (Harcourt Brace Jovanovich, Marrickville, NSW, 1990). The authors of these materials are Frances Christie, Pam Gray, Brian Gray, Mary Macken, Jim Martin and Joan Rothery. Consultants to the project are Beverly Derewianka and Jennifer Hammond.
8 See Halliday (1996), based on the plenary address to the Inaugural Systemic Functional Language in Education Conference held at Deakin University, Geelong, Victoria in 1990.
9 Geoff Williams and Ruqaiya Hasan have pointed out to me that Labov's model copes only with a specific class of spoken narrative; it cannot be easily applied to the true dialogic narrative (Polanyi, 1985). With reference to a variety of written narrative, see Hasan (1984).
10 See Carter (1990b) and Appendix 1 to this chapter.
11 A levels are school-leaving examinations for the 16–19 age group in Great Britain.

4 STANDARD ENGLISHES: SPEECH AND WRITING

1 For information on LINC, see Chapter 3.
2 Split infinitives are regularly cited in this connection as an example of a grammatical form which should be consistently avoided in all contexts of English usage,

spoken and written, even though this particular form is convention-bound rather than rule-bound. For some users it is a social convention universally to avoid splitting infinitives but the convention is based on language use in Latin grammar and cannot be a rule codified within English grammar. It is a matter of style and is peripheral to standard grammar in a way that, for example, particular forms of subject–verb agreement are central.

3 I am grateful to Alison Jackson for permission to use this material in which the names of students have been altered to preserve a degree of confidentiality.

4 Thanks are due to Derek Fry and Ann Sanderson (for writing by Lesley, p.66) for permission to use this material from them and from their students.

5 DISCOURSE LITERACY: REWORDING TEXTS, REVISING DISCOURSE

1 The notion of the 4Rs of literacy owes much to work by Hasan (1996a, 1996b); indeed, as indicated above, the terms 'recognition' and 'reflection' literacy are adopted by Hasan in her paper 'Literacy, everyday talk and society' (Hasan, 1996b). I have sought, however, to give specifically worked examples of terms used, especially 'reflection literacy' which has in turn led me to propose both further terms and extensions to the definitions of the terms used by Hasan. The general argument advanced also follows a line developed in different ways but with a similarly envisioned end point by Wells (1987) and Gee (1990).

6 IS THERE A LITERARY LANGUAGE?

1 See also related discussion in Eagleton (1983: 1–17) and Fish (1980: ch. 14).

2 See also Fish (1980), Fowler (1981).

3 For further discussion of these issues and of the notion of a compositional and process stylistics based on rewriting by students of texts from one discourse into another, see essays in Brumfit and Carter (1986) as well as Brazil (1983).

7 METAPHOR AND CREATIVE RISKS

1 For example, in paraphrasing the sentence quoted above, most informants used the words **slums** and **city** or synonyms of them, in their paraphrase: there was no significant departure from the descriptions in isolation, in glossing these literal terms. What then of the metaphorical focus, *disease*? How creatively was this interpreted? Pulman assigns each informant's paraphrase to one of six categories, marking a cline of creativity. Use of the target word itself or a synonym in the paraphrase puts the response in category 5 (most creative). Twelve of the 13 informants supplied an interpretation of *disease* which used either a content word, or a paraphrase of a content word, that they had previously used in their description in isolation (categories 1 and 2).

2 It should be possible to run a simple informant test to get some idea of the likely relative cognitive 'processing time' of sentence triads such as the following, where (a) is literal, (b) is frozen metaphor, and (c) is more creative metaphor:

(a) Sally is unemotional.
(b) Sally is a block of ice.
(c) Sally is an emotional pygmy.

8 DISCOURSE, CONVERSATION AND CREATIVITY

1 For an interesting move in this direction see Shepherd *et al.* (1992), a textbook which contains material for intermediate learners on stories, story-telling, jokes and advertisements that illustrate various forms of creative play with language and involve learners in writing their own texts.
2 'The Left protest', *Observer 'Life' magazine*, 21 August 1994, p. 6.
3 The discussion in the paper centres more substantially on specific aspects of materials development and on related procedures for classroom assessment of literary/linguistic competence (see also Brumfit, 1991).

9 TEACHING LANGUAGE AND LITERARINESS

1 A recent paper which extends Labov's model by analysis of narrative structure is Hasan (1984). The proposed model is for 'nursery tales', but her model, which is more precise linguistically than that of Labov, can be applied to short narratives generally. Such work is appropriate for advanced students of English or linguistics. Readers may like to compare the two models with other models for narrative analysis and select that which best fits their teaching context. This in itself becomes an interesting exercise in applied linguistics, but my own preference for the Labov model is based on its usefulness for introducing a clear, simple, broad outline of narrative organisation.

10 TEACHING DISCOURSES IN DIFFERENT WAYS

1 The point here is basic to the argument of H. G. Widdowson's *Stylistics and the Teaching of Literature* (1975). Widdowson's account is more detailed and contains (ch. 6) some usefully practical teaching strategies; he also emphasises, quite rightly in my view, the extent to which literary discourse fits into a model of a context of communication. See also Leech and Short (1981).
2 A radical account of the whole question is given in Culler (1981: ch. 2, 'Beyond interpretation').
3 It would be interesting to check the relationship between stream-of-consciousness narratives and the predominance of nominal group (verbless) structures. The connection holds in the most 'famous' of such instances: Molly Bloom's soliloquy at the end of James Joyce's *Ulysses* (1922).
4 See the discussion in Widdowson (1975: ch. 6) and several chapters in Widdowson (1992).
5 For an elaboration of the argument, with a fuller consideration of its relevance for the 'politics' of English literature, see Belsey (1980: especially chs 1 and 2). A key issue here is the question of the 'subject' or what I have loosely termed the 'central consciousness' of this discourse. Another point which should also be considered here is the extent to which a text which draws attention to the arbitrariness of its own language also refuses the possibility of a conventional 'I' behind or outside the text. Such a dissolution is a function of the dissolution of meanings which are found in classic 'realist' representations in which the referentiality of language to an ordered and intelligible world is paramount. If meaning is not pre-given and is neither anterior nor exterior to the text then it is created not through a 'central consciousness' but by the system of language in and by which the 'I' is constituted. If such a conclusion is used as a basis for interpreting 'Off Course', then the position of the human subject is even more tenuous.

In general, however, De Saussure's theories of language are not wholly compatible with the position of investigating discourse which is adopted in this book. De Saussure was primarily concerned with a contextless underlying structural organisation of language (*langue*) and less concerned with its naturally occurring textual and discoursal manifestations (*parole*). In this instance the insights into the arbitrariness of the sign offered by De Saussure provide a valuable perspective on a text which is in part constituted by word-based patterns.

POSTSCRIPTS AND PROSPECTS (2)

1 One problem with Cook's overall approach is that he is forced to model psychological processes which are not directly observable; thus descriptions of schema refreshment become inevitably somewhat speculative and relative to individual reader preference. There are also problems, as argued in Chapter 6 above, with an emphasis on formal properties in terms only of deviance, for challenge can also be motivated by repetitions and by strict adherence to established patterns. Cook rightly stresses, however, that Jakobsonian approaches to literariness have been too limited to sub-sentential linguistic levels and that deviancy (with all its limitations) should be described at the super-sentential levels of discoursal pattern. Cook also performs the valuable service of directing attention to psychological factors (where in many studies social and sociolinguistic factors predominate) and in drawing valuable conclusions of a more pedagogical nature.

BIBLIOGRAPHY

Abraham, Sunita A. (1995) *Writing and the Process of Knowledge-Creation*, Topics in Language and Literature no. 3, Department of English Language and Literature, National University of Singapore.

Aitchison, J. (1991) *Language Change: Progress or Decay*, 2nd edn (Cambridge University Press, Cambridge).

Alptekin, C. and Alptekin, M. (1990) 'The questions of culture: EFL teaching in non-English speaking countries', in Rossner, R. and Bolitho, R. (eds) *Currents of Change in Language Teaching* (Oxford University Press, Oxford) pp. 21–6.

Andrews, R. (1995) *Teaching and Learning Argument* (Cassell, London).

Attridge, D. (1988) *Peculiar Language: Literature as Difference from the Renaissance to James Joyce* (Methuen, London).

Bain, R., Fitzgerald, B. and Taylor, M. (eds) (1992) *Looking into Language* (Hodder and Stoughton, Sevenoaks).

Bakhtin, M. (1981) *The Dialogic Imagination* (University of Texas, Austin).

Bally, C. (1925) *La Langue et la vie*, 3rd edn (Geneva).

Bardovi-Harlig, K. *et al.* (1991) 'Developing pragmatic awareness: closing the conversation', *ELT Journal* 45, 1, pp. 4–15.

Bauman, R. (1977) *Verbal Art as Performance* (Newbury House, Boston).

Bauman, R. (1986) *Story, Performance and Event: Contextual Studies of Oral Narrative* (Cambridge University Press, Cambridge).

Baynham, M. (1995) *Literacy Practices: Investigating Literacy in Social Contexts* (Longman, Harlow).

Belsey, C. (1980) *Critical Practice* (Methuen, London).

Bennett, T. (1983) *Formalism and Marxism* (Methuen, London).

Bennett, T. (1990) *Outside Literature* (Routledge, London).

Bereiter, C. and Scardamalia, M. (1987) *The Psychology of Written Composition* (Lawrence Erlbaum, Hillsdale, NJ).

Berlyne, D. (1971) *Aesthetics and Psychobiology* (Appleton-Century-Crofts, New York).

Bever, T.G. (1986) 'The aesthetic basis for cognitive structures', in Brand, M. and Harnish, R. (eds) *The Representation of Knowledge and Belief* (University of Arizona Press, Tucson) pp. 314–56.

Bex, A.R. (1996) *Variety in Written English: Texts in Society, Societies in Text* (Routledge, London).

Bhaba, H. (1994) *The Location of Culture* (Routledge, London).

Bialystok, E. (1982) 'On the relationship between knowing and using linguistic knowledge', *Applied Linguistics* 3, pp. 181–206.

Birch, D. (1989) *Language, Literature and Critical Practice* (Routledge, London).

Birch, D. (1996) 'Critical linguistics as cultural process', in James, J. (ed.) *The Language Culture Connection* (SEAMEO, Singapore).

Boardman, R. and McRae, J. (1984) *Reading Between the Lines* (Cambridge University Press, Cambridge).

Bourdieu, P. (1984) *Distinction: A Social Critique of the Judgement of Taste*, trans. R. Nice (Routledge, London).

Bourdieu, P. (1990) *The Logic of Practice*, trans. R. Nice (Cambridge University Press, Cambridge).

Bourne, J. and Cameron, D. (1989) 'No common ground: Kingman, grammar and the nation', *Language and Education* 2, 3, pp. 14–60.

Braddock, R. *et al.* (1963) *Research in Written Composition* (NCTE, Champaign, IL) pp. 37–8.

Brazil, D. (1983) 'Kinds of English: spoken, written, literary', in Stubbs, M. and Hillier, H. (eds) *Readings on Language, Schools and Classrooms* (Methuen, London).

Brazil, D. (1995) *A Grammar of Speech* (Oxford University Press, Oxford).

Bredella, L. and Delanoy, W. (eds) (1996) *Challenges of Literary Texts in the Foreign Language Classroom* (Gunther Narr Verlag, Tübingen).

Brindley, S. (1996) 'Issues in English teaching', in Mercer, N. and Swann, J. (eds) *Learning English: Development and Diversity* (Open University Press, Milton Keynes), pp. 205–27.

Brumfit, C.J. (ed.) (1991) *Assessment in Literature Teaching: Review of ELT, 1, 3* (Modern English Publications/The British Council/Macmillan, Basingstoke).

Brumfit, C.J. and Carter, R. (eds) (1986) *Literature and Language Teaching* (Oxford University Press, Oxford).

Burton, D. (1982) 'Through glass darkly: through dark glasses', in Carter, R. (ed.) *Language and Literature* (Allen and Unwin/Routledge, London) pp. 195–214.

Cameron, D. (1995) *Verbal Hygiene* (Routledge, London).

Carter, R. (ed.) (1982a) *Language and Literature: An Introductory Reader in Stylistics* (Allen and Unwin/Routledge, London).

Carter, R. (1982b) 'Responses to language in poetry', in Carter R. and Burton, D. (eds) *Literary Text and Language Study* (Edward Arnold, London) pp. 28–57.

Carter, R. (1985) 'A question of interpretation', in D'Haen, T. (ed.) *Linguistic Contributions to Literature* (Rodopi, Amsterdam) pp. 1–26.

Carter, R. (1987) *Vocabulary: Applied Linguistic Perspectives* (Routledge, London).

Carter, R. (1988) 'Some pawns for Kingman: language education and English teaching', in Grunwell, P. (ed.) *Applied Linguistics in Society* 3, *British Studies in Applied Linguistics* (CILT, London) pp. 51–66.

Carter, R. (1990a) *The National Curriculum for English: A Guide to the Development of a National Curriculum for English in England and Wales 1985–1990* (The British Council, London).

Carter, R. (ed.) (1990b) *Knowledge about Language and the Curriculum: The LINC Reader* (Hodder and Stoughton, Sevenoaks).

Carter, R. (1994) 'Language awareness for language teachers', in Hoey, M. (ed.) *Data, Discourse and Description: Essays in Honour of Professor John Sinclair* (Collins, London and Glasgow).

Carter, R. (1995) *Keywords in Language and Literacy* (Routledge, London).

Carter, R. and Long, M. (1987) *The Web of Words: Exploring Literature through Language* (Cambridge University Press, Cambridge).

Carter, R. and Long, M. (1990) 'Testing literature in EFL classes: tradition and innovation', *ELTJ* 44, 3, pp. 215–21.

Carter, R. and Long, M. (1991) *Teaching Literature* (Longman, Harlow).

Carter, R. and McCarthy, M. (1988) *Vocabulary and Language Teaching* (Longman, Harlow).

Carter, R. and McCarthy, M. (1995) 'Grammar and the spoken language', *Applied Linguistics*, 16, 2, pp. 141–58.

Carter, R. and McCarthy, M. (1997) *Exploring Spoken English* (Cambridge University Press, Cambridge).

Carter, R. and McRae, J. (eds) (1996) *Language, Literature and the Learner: Creative Classroom Practice* (Longman, London).

Carter, R. and McRae, J. (1997) *The Routledge History of Literature in English: Britain and Ireland* (Routledge, London).

Carter, R. and Nash, W. (1983) 'Language and literariness', *Prose Studies*, 6, 2, pp. 123–41.

Carter, R. and Nash, W. (1990) *Seeing through Language: A Guide to Styles of English Writing* (Blackwell, Oxford).

Carter, R. and Richmond, J. (1996) *The National Curriculum for English: A Guide to the Development of a National Curriculum for English in England and Wales 1989–1995* (The British Council, London).

Carter, R. and Simpson, P. (eds) (1989) *Language, Discourse and Literature: An Introductory Reader in Discourse Stylistics* (Routledge, London).

Carter, R., Walker, R. and Brumfit, C. (eds) (1990) *Literature and the Learner: Methodological Approaches* (Macmillan, Basingstoke).

Chafe, W. (1986) 'Writing in the perspective of speaking', in Cooper, C.R. and Greenbaum, S. (eds) *Studying Writing: Linguistic Approaches* (Sage Publications, Beverly Hills, CA).

Chiaro, D. (1992) *The Language of Jokes: Analyzing Verbal Play* (Routledge, London).

Christie, F. (1986) 'Writing in schools: generic structures as ways of meaning', in Couture, B. (ed.) *Functional Approaches to Writing* (Frances Pinter, London) pp. 221–39.

Christie, F. (1989) *Language Education* (Oxford University Press, Oxford).

Cohen, L.J. (1979) 'The Semantics of Metaphor', in Ortony, A. (ed.) *Metaphor and Thought* (Cambridge University Press, Cambridge).

Cook, G. (1992) *The Discourse of Advertising* (Routledge, London).

Cook, G. (1994) *Discourse and Literature: The Interplay of Form and Mind* (Oxford University Press, Oxford).

Cook, G. (1995) 'Genes, memes, rhymes: conscious poetic deviation in linguistic, psychological and evolutionary theory', *Language and Communication* 15, 4, pp. 375–91.

Cook, G. (1996) 'Language play in English', in Maybin, J. and Mercer, N. (eds) *Using English: From Conversation to Canon* (Routledge, London) pp. 198–234.

Cope, B. and Kalantzis, M. (eds) (1993) *The Powers of Literacy: A Genre Approach to Teaching Writing* (Falmer Press, London).

Crowley, T. (1989) *The Politics of Discourse: The Standard Language Question and British Cultural Debates* (Macmillan, Basingstoke).

Crowley, T. (1991) *Proper English: Readings in Language, History and Cultural Identity* (Routledge, London).

Crystal, D. (1995) *The Cambridge Encyclopaedia of the English Language* (Cambridge University Press, Cambridge).

Culler, J. (1976) *Saussure* (Fontana, London).

Culler, J. (1981) *The Pursuit of Signs* (Routledge and Kegan Paul, London).

Davies, F. (1995) *Introducing Reading* (Penguin, Harmondsworth).

De Beaugrande, R. and Dressler, W. (1981) *An Introduction to Text Linguistics* (Longman, Harlow).

Deignan, A. (1995) *Collins COBUILD English Guides 7: Metaphor* (HarperCollins, London).

DES [Department of Education and Science] (1921) *The Teaching of English in England* (The Newbolt Report) (HMSO, London).

DES (1988) *Report of the Committee of Inquiry into the Teaching of English Language* (The Kingman Report) (HMSO, London).

DES (1989) *Report of the English Working Party 5 to 16* (The Cox Report) (HMSO, London).

DES (1990) *English in the National Curriculum* (HMSO, London).

DfE/WO [Department for Education/the Welsh Office] (1995) *English in the National Curriculum* (HMSO, London).

Dixon, J. (1987) 'The question of genres', in Reid, I. (ed.) *The Place of Genre in Learning: Current Debates* (Deakin University Press, Geelong, Vic.) pp. 9–21.

Dixon, J. and Stratta, L. (1992) 'The National Curriculum in English: does genre theory have anything to offer?', *English in Education* 26, 2, pp. 16–27.

Donmall, G. (ed.) (1985) *Language Awareness* (CILT, London).

Doyle, B. (1989) *English and Englishness* (Routledge, London).

Durant, A. (1995) 'Literacy and literature: priorities in English studies towards 2000', in Korte, B. and Muller, K.P., *Anglistische Lehre Aktuell: Probleme, Perspektiven und Praxis* (Wissenschaftlicher Verlag, Trier), pp.37–59.

Durant, A. and Fabb, N. (1990) *Literary Studies in Action* (Routledge, London).

Eagleton, T. (1983), *Literary Theory: An Introduction* (Blackwell, Oxford).

Easthope, A. (1983) *Poetry as Discourse* (Routledge, London).

Elley, W.B. *et al.* (1975) 'The role of grammar in a secondary school English curriculum', *New Zealand Journal of Educational Research* 10, 1, pp. 26–42.

Ellis, G. and Sinclair, B. (1989) *Learning How to Learn English* (Cambridge University Press, Cambridge).

Ellis, R. (1989) *Instructed Second Language Acquisition* (Blackwell, Oxford).

Fabb, N. (1997) *Linguistics and Literature* (Blackwell, Oxford).

Faerch, C. (1985) 'Meta-talk in FL classroom discourse', *Studies in Second Language Acquisition* 7, 2, pp.184–99.

Fairclough, N. (1989) *Language and Power* (Harlow, Longman).

Fairclough, N. (ed.) (1992a) *Critical Language Awareness* (Longman, Harlow).

Fairclough, N. (1992b) *Discourse and Social Change* (Polity Press, Cambridge).

Fairclough, N. (1992c) 'The appropriacy of "appropriateness" ', in Fairclough, N. (ed.) *Critical Language Awareness* (Longman, Harlow) pp. 33–56.

Fairclough, N. (1996) 'A reply to Henry Widdowson's "Discourse Analysis: a critical view" ', *Language and Literature* 5, 1, pp. 49–56.

Fish, S. (1980) 'What is stylistics and why are they saying such terrible things about it?', in Chatman, S. (ed.) *Approaches to Poetics* (Columbia University Press, New York). Repr. in Fish, S., *Is There a Text in This Class? The Authority of Interpretive Communities* (Harvard University Press, Cambridge, MA, 1980).

Foucault, M. (1972) *The Archaeology of Knowledge* (Tavistock, London).

Foucault, M. (1974) *The Order of Things: An Archaeology of the Human Sciences*, trans. Alan Sheridan (Tavistock, London).

Fowler, R. (1981) *Literature as Social Discourse: The Practice of Linguistic Criticism* (Batsford, London).

Fowler, R. (1991) *Language in the News: Discourse and Ideology in the Press* (Routledge, London).

Fowler, R. *et al.* (1979) *Language and Control* (Routledge and Kegan Paul, London).

Garton, A. and Pratt, C. (1989) *Learning to be Literate* (Blackwell, Oxford).

Gee, J. (1990) *Social Linguistics and Literacies: Ideology in Discourses* (Falmer Press, London).

Gibbs, R.W. (1994) *The Poetics of Mind: Figurative Thought, Language and Understanding* (Cambridge University Press, Cambridge).

Gilbert, P. (1989) *Writing, Schooling and Disadvantage: From Voice to Text in the Classroom* (Routledge, London).

Gilbert, P. (1990) 'Authorizing disadvantage: authorship and creativity in the language classroom', in Christie, F. (ed.) *Literacy for a Changing World* (Australian Council for Educational Research, Hawthorn, Victoria), pp. 54–78.

Goddard, A. (1996) 'Tall stories: the metaphorical nature of everyday talk', *English in Education* 30, 2, pp. 4–12.

Gower, R. and Pearson, M. (1986) *Reading Literature* (Longman, Harlow).

Gramsci, A. (1985) *Selections from Cultural Writings*, ed. G. Forgacs and G. Nowell (Lawrence and Wishart, London).

Grice, H.P. (1975) 'Logic and conversation', in Cole, P. and Morgan, J.L. (eds) *Syntax and Semantics*, Vol. 3: *Speech Acts* (Academic Press, New York) pp. 51–8.

Griffiths, P. (1992) *English at the Core: Dialogue and Power in English Teaching* (Open University Press, Milton Keynes).

Halliday, M.A.K. (1978) *Language as Social Semiotic* (Edward Arnold, London).

Halliday, M.A.K. (1982) 'Linguistics in teacher education', in Carter, R. (ed.) *Linguistics and the Teacher* (Routledge, London), pp. 10–16.

Halliday, M.A.K. (1989) *Spoken and Written Language* (Oxford University Press, Oxford).

Halliday, M.A.K. (1994) *Introduction to Functional Grammar*, 2nd edn (Edward Arnold, London).

Halliday, M.A.K. (1996) 'Literacy and linguistics: a functional perspective', in Hasan, R. and Williams, G. (eds) *Literacy in Society* (Longman, London), pp. 339–75.

Hammersley, M. (1996) *On the Foundations of Critical Discourse Analysis*: Occasional Papers no. 42 (Centre for Language in Education, University of Southampton).

Hammond, J. (1990) 'Is learning to read and write the same as learning to speak?' in Christie, F. (ed.) *Literacy for a Changing World* (ACER, Hawthorn, Victoria) pp. 26–53.

Harris, J. (1994) *Introducing Writing* (Penguin, Harmonsworth).

Harris, R. (1987) *The Language Myth* (Duckworth, London).

Harris, R. J. (1960) 'An Experimental Inquiry into the Functions and Value of Formal Grammar in the Teaching of English with Special Reference to the Teaching of Correct Written English to Children aged Twelve to Fourteen'. Unpublished PhD thesis (University of London).

Hartmann, G. (1981) *Saving the Text: Literature, Derrida/Philosophy* (Johns Hopkins University Press, Baltimore, MD).

Hasan, R. (1984) 'The nursery tale as a genre', *Nottingham Linguistic Circular* 13, pp. 71–102.

Hasan, R. (1996a) 'The disempowerment game: language in literacy', in Baker, C.D., Cook Gumperz, J. and Luke, A. (eds) *Language and Power* (Blackwell, Oxford).

Hasan, R. (1996b) 'Literacy, everyday talk and society', in Hasan, R. and Williams, G. (eds) *Literacy in Society* (Longman, Harlow) pp. 377–424.

Hawkins, E. (1987) *The Awareness of Language*, rev. edn (Cambridge University Press, Cambridge).

Herman, V. (1995) *Dramatic Discourse: Dialogue as Interaction in Plays* (Routledge, London).

Herrnstein-Smith, B. (1978) *On the Margins of Discourse: The Relation of Language and Literature* (University of Chicago Press, Chicago and London).

Herrnstein-Smith, B. (1988) *Contingencies of Value: Alternative Perspectives for Critical Theory* (University of Chicago Press, Chicago).

Hodge, R. and Kress, G. (1981) *Language as Ideology* (Routledge, London).

Hodge, R. and Kress, G. (1988) *Social Semiotics* (Polity Press, Cambridge).

Holborrow, M. (1991) 'Linking language and situation: a course for advanced learners', *ELT Journal* 45, 1, pp. 24–33.

Howden, M. (1984) 'Code and creativity in word formation', *Forum Linguisticum* 8, 3, pp. 213–22.

Hughes, R. (1996) *English in Speech and Writing: Investigating Language and Literature* (Routledge, London).

Jakobson, R. (1960) 'Linguistics and poetics', in Sebeok, T. (ed.) *Style in Language* (Massachusetts Institute of Technology Press, Cambridge, MA), pp. 350–77.

James, J. (ed.) (1996) *The Language Culture Connection* (SEAMEO, Singapore).

James, C. and Garrett, P. (eds) (1992) *Language Awareness in the Classroom* (Longman, Harlow).

Johnson, K. (1983) 'Communicative writing practice and Aristotelian rhetoric', in Freedman, A., Pringle, I. and Yalden, J. (eds) *Learning to Write: First Language/Second Language* (Longman, Harlow).

Johnson, M. (1987) *The Body in the Mind: The Bodily Basis of Reason and the Imagination* (University of Chicago Press, Chicago).

Jones, M. and West, A. (eds) (1988) *Learning Me Your Language* (Mary Glasgow, London).

Kachru, B. (1986) *The Alchemy of English* (Pergamon, Oxford).

Kandiah, T. (1995) 'Foreword' to Parakrama, A., *De-Hegemonizing Language Standards* (Macmillan, London), pp. i–xv.

Kayman, M. (1994) 'ESSE or TELOS': English studies in Europe', *The European English Messenger*, 3, 1, pp. 35–54.

Kramsch, C. (1993) *Context and Culture in Language Teaching* (Oxford University Press, Oxford).

Kress, G. (1989) *Linguistic Processes in Sociocultural Practice* (Oxford University Press, Oxford).

Kress, G. (1993) *Learning to Write*, 2nd edn (Routledge, London).

Kress, G. (1995) *Writing the Future: English and the Making of a Culture of Innovation* (NATE Publications, Sheffield).

Kristeva, J. (1984) *Revolution in Poetic Language* (Columbia University Press, New York).

Kuiper, K. and Haggo, D. (1984) 'Livestock auctions, oral poetry, and ordinary language', *Language in Society* 13, pp. 205–34.

Labov, W. (1972) 'The transformation of experience in narrative syntax', in *Language in the Inner City* (University of Pennsylvania Press, Penn.) pp. 354–97.

Lakoff, G. and Johnson, M. (1980), *Metaphors We Live By* (University of Chicago Press, Chicago).

Lakoff, G. and Turner, M. (1989) *More Than Cool Reason: A Field Guide to Poetic Metaphor* (University of Chicago Press, Chicago).

Lazar, G. (1993) *Literature and Language Teaching* (Cambridge University Press, Cambridge).

Lecercle, J.J. (1990) *The Violence of Language* (Routledge, London).

Lee, D. (1992) *Competing Discourses: Perspectives and Ideology in Language* (Longman, Harlow).

Leech, G.N. (1983) 'Pragmatics discourse analysis, stylistics and "The Celebrated Letter" ', *Prose Studies* 6, 2, pp. 142–58.

Leech, G.N. and Short, M.H. (1981) *Style in Fiction* (Longman, Harlow).

Leitch, T.M. (1983) 'To what is fiction committed?' *Prose Studies* 6, 2, pp. 159–75.

Levin, S. (1977) *The Semantics of Metaphor* (Johns Hopkins University Press, Baltimore).

LINC (1992) *Language in the National Curriculum: Materials for Professional Development*: mimeo (University of Nottingham Dept of English Studies, Nottingham).

Lyons, H. (1988) 'Needing to know about language: a case study of a nine-year-old's usage', *Language and Education* 2, 3, pp. 175–88.

Lyons, H. (1989) 'What Katy knows about language', *English in Education* 23, 2, pp. 38–49.

Macauley, W.J. (1947) 'The difficulty of grammar', *British Journal of Educational Psychology* 17, pp. 153–62.

McCarthy, M. (1991) *Discourse Analysis for Language Teachers* (Cambridge University Press, Cambridge).

McCarthy, M. (1992) 'English idioms in use', *Revista Canaria de Estudios Ingleses* 25, pp. 55–65.

McCarthy, M. (1994a) 'Spoken discourse markers in written text', in Sinclair, J.M., Hoey, M. and Fox, G. (eds) *Techniques of Description* (Routledge, London) pp. 170–82.

McCarthy, M. (1994b) 'Conversation and literature: tense and aspect', in Payne, J. (ed.) *Linguistic Approaches to Literature* (English Language Research, Birmingham)

McCarthy, M. (1997) *Spoken Language and Applied Linguistics* (Cambridge University Press, Cambridge).

McCarthy, M. and Carter, R. (1994) *Language as Discourse: Perspectives for Language Teaching* (Longman, London).

McCarthy, M. and Carter, R. (1995) 'Spoken grammar: what is it and how do we teach it?' *ELT Journal*, 49, 3, pp. 207–18.

MacCabe, C. (1984) 'Towards a modern trivium – English studies today', *Critical Quarterly* 26, 1/2, pp. 69–82.

Macdonell, D. (1986) *Theories of Discourse: An Introduction* (Blackwell, Oxford)).

McIntosh, A. (1966) 'Patterns and ranges', in McIntosh, A. and Halliday, M.A.K. *Patterns of Language* (Longman, Harlow).

Mackay, R. (1996) 'Mything the point: A critique of objective stylistics', *Language and Communication* 16, 1, pp. 81–93.

McRae, J. (1991) *Literature with a Small 'l'* (Macmillan/MEP, Basingstoke).

McRae, J. and Pantaleoni, L. (1991) *Chapter and Verse* (Oxford University Press, Oxford).

Mailloux, S. (1983) *Interpretive Communities: The reader in the study of American fiction* (Cornell University Press, Ithaca, New York).

Maley, A. (1993) *Short and Sweet*, Vol 1. (Penguin, Harmondsworth).

Maley, A. and Duff, A. (1990) *Literature* (Oxford University Press, Oxford).

Mallett, M. (1988) 'From "human sense" to "metalinguistic awareness" ', *English in Education* 22, 3, pp. 40–45.

Martin, J. (1989) *Factual Writing* (Oxford University Press, Oxford).

Maybin, J. (1996) 'An English canon', in Maybin, J. and Mercer, N. (eds) *Using English: From Conversation to Canon* (Routledge, London), pp. 235–74.

Mills, S. (1995) *Feminist Stylistics* (Routledge, London).

Milroy, J. and Milroy, L. (1991) *Authority in Language*, 2nd edn (Routledge, London).

Moeran, B. (1984) 'Advertising sounds as cultural discourse', *Language and Communication* 4, 2, pp. 147–58.

Nash, W. (1986) 'The possibilities of paraphrase', in Brumfit, C. and Carter, R. (eds) *Literature and Language Teaching* (Oxford University Press, Oxford).

Nash, W. (1990) *Style in Popular Fiction* (Routledge, London).

New London Group (1995) *A Pedagogy of Multiliteracies: Designing Social Futures* (NLLIA Centre for Workplace Communication and Culture, Sydney).

Nunan, D. (1994) *An Introduction to Discourse Analysis* (Penguin, Harmondsworth).

Ohmann, R. (1971) 'Speech acts and the definition of literature', *Philosophy and Rhetoric*, IV, pp. 1–19.

Parakrama, A. (1995) *De-Hegemonizing Language Standards: Learning from (Post) Colonial Englishes about 'English'* (Macmillan, London).

Pecheux, M. (1982) *Language, Semantics and Ideology* (Macmillan, London).

Peirce, B.N. (1989) 'Towards a pedagogy of possibility in the teaching of English internationally', *TESOL Quarterly* 24, 1, pp. 105–12.

Pennycook, A. (1994) *The Cultural Politics of English as an International Language* (Longman, London).

Perera, K. (1984) *Children's Writing and Reading* (Blackwell, Oxford).

Perera, K. (1987) *Understanding Language* (NAAE/NATE Publications, Sheffield).

Perera, K. (1990) 'Grammatical differentiation between speech and writing' in Carter, R. (ed.) *Knowledge about Language and the Curriculum: The LINC Reader* (Hodder and Stoughton, Sevenoaks), pp. 216–33.

Perera, K. (1993) 'Standard English in Attainment Target 1: Speaking and listening', *Language Matters* (Centre for Language in Primary Education), 3, p. 10.

Petterson, A. (1990) *A Theory of Literary Discourse in Aesthetics* (Lund University Press, Lund).

Phillipson, R. (1991) *Linguistic Imperialism* (Oxford University Press, Oxford).

Polanyi, L. (1987) 'Conversational storytelling', in Van Dijk, T.A. (ed.) *Handbook of Discourse Analysis*, Vol. 3 (Academic Press, New York).

Pope, R. (1994) *Textual Intervention: Critical and Creative Strategies in English Studies* (Routledge, London).

Pratt, M.L. (1977) *Towards a Speech Act Theory of Literary Discourse* (Indiana University Press, Bloomington).

Pratt, M.L. (1987) 'Linguistic utopias', in Fabb, N. *et al.* (eds) *The Linguistics of Writing* (University of Manchester Press, Manchester), pp. 48–66.

Prodromou, L. (1990) 'English as cultural action', in Rossner, R. and Bolitho, R. (eds) *Currents of Change in English Language Teaching* (Oxford University Press, Oxford) pp. 27–39.

Pulman, S. (1982) 'Are metaphors creative?', *Journal of Literary Semantics* 11, pp. 78–89.

Quirk, R. *et al.* (1985) *A Comprehensive Grammar of the English Language* (Longman, Harlow).

Reddy, M. (1979) 'The conduit metaphor', in Ortony, A. (ed.) *Metaphor and Thought* (Cambridge University Press, Cambridge).

Riffaterre, M. (1973) 'Interpretation and descriptive poetry: a reading of Wordsworth's "Yew Trees" ', *New Literary History* 6, 2, pp. 229–56.

Rimmon-Kenan, S. (1983) *Narrative Fiction: Contemporary Poetics* (Methuen, London).

Robinson, N. (1960) 'The relation between knowledge of English grammar and ability in English composition', *British Journal of Educational Psychology* 30, pp. 184–6.

Rosch, E.H. *et al.* (1976) 'Basic objects in natural categories', *Cognitive Psychology*, 8, pp. 382–439.

Rosch, E. (1977) 'Human categorisation', in Warren, N. (ed.) *Advances in Cross-Cultural Psychology Vol. 1* (Academic Press, New York).

Rosen, H. (1988) 'Responding to Kingman', in Ashworth, E. and Masterman, L. *Responding to Kingman* (University of Nottingham, Faculty of Education).

Rutherford, W. (1987) *Second Language Grammar: Learning and Teaching* (Longman, Harlow).

Said, E. (1976) *Orientalism* (Penguin, Harmondsworth).

Said, E. (1993) *Culture and Imperialism* (Chatto and Windus, London).

Shepherd, J., Hopkins, A. and Potter, J. (1992) *The Sourcebook: An Alternative English Course* (Longman, London).

Short, M. (ed.) (1989) *Reading, Analyzing and Teaching Literature* (Longman, Harlow).

Short, M. and Candlin, C. (1986) 'Teaching study skills for English literature', in Brumfit, C.J. and Carter, R.A. (eds) *Literature and Language Teaching* (Oxford University Press, Oxford).

Simpson, P. (1993) *Language, Ideology and Point of View* (Routledge, London).

Sinclair, J.M. (1966) 'Taking a poem to pieces', in Fowler, R. (ed.) *Essays on Style and Language* (Routledge and Kegan Paul, London) pp. 68–81.

Sinclair, J.M. (1985) 'Language awareness in six easy lessons', in Donmall, G. (ed.) *Language Awareness* (CILT, London) pp. 33–7.

Sinclair, J.M. and Coulthard, R.M. (1975) *Towards an Analysis of Discourse: The English Used by Teachers and Pupils* (Oxford University Press, Oxford).

Smallwood, P. (1994) 'The unity of the subject: notes and speculations on language, literature and the teaching of English', *UCE Papers in Language and Literature* no. 1, University of Central England, Birmingham, pp. 1–18.

Soudek, M. and Soudek, L. (1983) 'Cloze after thirty years: new uses in language teaching', *English Language Teaching Journal* 37, 4, pp. 335–40.

Spivak, G. (1993) *Outside in the Teaching Machine* (Routledge, London).

Stainton, C. (1990) 'Genre: a review', *The Language of Business and Industry Project*: mimeo (Department of English Studies, University of Nottingham).

Stubbs, M. (1983) *Discourse Analysis: The Sociolinguistic Analysis of Natural Language* (Blackwell, Oxford).

Sweetser, E. (1990) *From Etymology to Pragmatics: The Mind–Body Metaphor in Semantic Structure and Semantic Change* (Cambridge University Press, Cambridge).

Talib, I. (1992) 'Why not teach non-native English literature?' *ELT Journal* 46, 1, pp. 51–55.

Talib, I. (1996) 'Non-native English literature and the world literature syllabus', in Carroll, M. (ed.) *No Small World: Visions and Revisions in the Theory and Pedagogy of World Literature* (National Council of Teachers of English, Urbana, IL) pp. 81–90.

Tambling, J. (1988) *What is Literary Language?* (Open University Press, Milton Keynes).

Tanaka, K (1992), 'The pun in advertising: a pragmatic approach', *Lingua* 87, 1–2, pp. 91–102.

Tannen, D. (1982) 'Oral and literate strategies in spoken and written narrative', *Language* 58, 1, pp. 1–21.

Tannen, D. (1988) *Talking Voices: Repetition, Dialogue and Imagery in Conversational Discourse* (Cambridge University Press, Cambridge).

Taylor, T. and Toolan, M. (1984) 'Recent trends in stylistics', *Journal of Literary Semantics*, 13, 1, pp. 57–79.

Thomas, G. (1991) *Linguistic Purism* (Longman, Harlow).

Threadgold, T. (1989) 'Talking about genre: ideologies and incompatible discourses', *Cultural Studies* 3, 1, pp. 101–27.

Threadgold, T. (1994) 'Grammar, genre and the ownership of literacy', *Idiom*, 2, pp. 20–28.

Todorov, T. (1981) *An Introduction to Poetics* (Harverster, Brighton).

Toolan, M. (1986) 'Poem, reader, response: making sense with *Skunk Hour*', in Nicholson, C.E. and Chatterjee, R. (eds) *Tropic Crucible* (Singapore University Press, Singapore).

Traugott, E. and Pratt, M.L. (1980) *Linguistics for Students of Literature* (Harcourt Brace Jovanovich, New York).

Turner, M. (1991) *Reading Minds: The Study of English in the Age of Cognitive Science* (Princeton University Press, Princeton, NJ).

Van Lier, L. (1995) *Introducing Language Awareness* (Penguin, Harmondsworth).

Van Peer, W. (1991) 'But what *is* literature? Toward a descriptive definition of literature', in Sell, R.D. (ed.) *Literary Pragmatics* (Routledge, London) pp. 127–41.

Verdonk, P. (1993) *Twentieth Century Poetry: From Text to Context* (Routledge, London).

Verdonk, P. and Weber, J.-J. (eds) (1995) *Twentieth Century Fiction: From Text to Context* (Routledge, London).

Vethemani, E. (1996) 'Common ground: incorporating new literatures in English in language and literature teaching', in Carter, R. and McRae, J. (eds), *Literature, Language and the Learner* (Longman, Harlow), pp. 204–16.

Vizmuller-Zocco, J. (1985) 'Linguistic creativity and word formation', *Italica* 62, 4, pp. 305–10.

Voloshinov, V. (1930) *Marxism and the Philosophy of Language*, trans. L. Matejka and I. R. Titunik (Seminar Press, London, 1973).

Wales, K. (1989) *A Dictionary of Stylistics* (Longman, Harlow).

Wales, K. (1995) 'The ethics of stylistics: towards an ethical stylistics?', *Moderne Sprak* 89, pp. 9–14.

Walmsley, J. (1984) *The Uselessness of 'Formal Grammar'*, CLIE working paper, no. 2, Committee for Linguistics in Education, London.

WAUDAG [University of Washington Discourse Analysis Group] (1990) 'The rhetorical construction of a President', *Discourse and Society*, 1, 2, pp. 189–200.

Waugh, L. (1980) 'The poetic function and the nature of language', *Poetics Today*, 21, pp. 57–82.

Wells, G. (1987) 'Apprenticeship in literacy', *Interchange* 18, 1, pp. 109–23.

Werth, P. (1976) 'Roman Jakobson's verbal analysis of poetry', *Journal of Linguistics*, 12, pp. 21–73.

Widdowson, H.G. (1975) *Stylistics and the Teaching of Literature* (Longman, Harlow).

Widdowson, H.G. (1984) *Explorations in Applied Linguistics*, 2 (Oxford University Press, Oxford).

Widdowson, H.G. (1992) *Practical Stylistics* (Oxford University Press, Oxford).

Widdowson, H.G. (1995) 'Discourse analysis: a critical view', *Language and Literature* 4, 3, pp. 157–72.

Widdowson, H.G. (1996) 'Reply to Fairclough: discourse and interpretation: conjectures and refutations', *Language and Literatures* 1, pp. 57–69.

Wilkinson, J. (1995) *Introducing Standard English* (Penguin, Harmondsworth).

Williams, R. (1977) *Marxism and Literature* (Oxford University Press, Oxford).

Williams, R. (1983) *Keywords*, 2nd edn (Fontana, London).

Williams, R. (1990) *What I Came to Say* (Hutchinson Radius, London).

Wodak, R. (ed.) (1988) *Language, Power and Ideology*: Studies in Political Discourse and Critical Theory no. 7 (John Benjamins, Amsterdam).

Woods, E. (1995) *Introducing Grammar* (Penguin, Harmondsworth).

Wyler, S. (1992) *Colour and Language: Colour Terms in English* (Gunter Narr Verlag, Tübingen).

INDEX